Glamour Ghoul: The Passions and Pain of the Real Vampira, Maila Nurmi
© 2021 Sandra Niemi
Published by Feral House, Inc.
All Rights Reserved

ISBN: 9781627311007

Cover illustration by Mark Hammermeister.
Back cover photo courtesy of the Jove de Renzy collection.

Feral House
1240 W. Sims Way Suite 124
Port Townsend, WA 98368
FERALHOUSE.COM

Glamour Ghoul

THE PASSIONS AND PAIN OF THE REAL VAMPIRA, Maila Nurmi

SANDRA NIEMI

FERAL HOUSE

This book is dedicated to my cousin, David Putter.
Found, at last.

To my family, Amy, Noelle, Liam. David and Judi.
I love you more.

Table of Contents

Bring on the empty hearses that I may people them with my enemies.

Isn't that, after all, why people commit autobiography? To aggrandize themselves and to destroy their enemies?

In any case, of course, the enemy shall be felled quite accidentally as the flailing sword of truth decapitates them. Now—all nonsense aside—you know I have no enemies. Only discarded lovers—and they have their memories.

—Maila Nurmi

Vampira. Courtesy of the Jove de Renzy Collection.

When she transformed into a butterfly, the caterpillars spoke not of her
beauty, but of her weirdness. They wanted her to change back to what she'd
always been.
   But she had wings.
   —Dean Jackson

Foreword

Dear Aunt Maila:

You grew wings. By the time you reached your 18th birthday, you'd begun to display them in splendiferous Technicolor, much to the consternation and confusion of your family. Collectively, they clung fast to their caterpillar consciousnesses, shook their heads, and made excuses. Your youthful impulsivity was only a phase, they said, which would pass with maturity, and then you'd commit to the traditional life they longed for you and expected of you. That of marriage and motherhood. But what does a caterpillar know of a butterfly?

Your innate desire for creative expression and the freedom to cultivate a lifestyle far different than their own was never taken seriously, and so you did the only thing you could to survive. You flew away.

Did you know you became a lifetime obsession of mine? From the first time I saw you in 1953, at age six, pre-Vampira, all beautiful blonde hair, red lips, and eyelashes, wearing transparent heels that looked every bit like glass slippers, you became my own private Cinderella.

During Vampira's early years, you appeared on television on *The Red Skelton Show*. I looked in vain for you throughout the show. It was only afterward I was told that the black shrouded woman, whom I thought was a witch, was you. Although it was only June, I assumed the show was called Red "Skeleton" as an early homage to Halloween.

It was another two years before I saw you again, and this time, Cinderella was in love. Crazy, silly, mindless love. Short hair, no makeup, baggy sweater, capri pants, and barefoot—you uttered barely a word to us and instead perched on your lover's lap and whispered in each other's ear, giggling like schoolgirls. At nine years old, I was entranced and secretly wondered if someday this kind of behavior was in my future.

In 1957, Grandma died, and I saw you for the third time. No longer the Cinderella or the giddy girl in love, with your grief etched in your sad, tear-stained face. Considering the wretched occasion of your mama's death, understandably, I think I loved you even more then.

To me, Vampira is Aunt Maila wearing a black dress and wig. To everyone else, she is the first, the original glamour ghoul—the epitome of goth beauty. Vampira was intended to share just a small part of your life. Instead, once the human cartoon burst forth into the world, she clung to you, her creator, like a second skin for the rest of your life. I know you never expected that, 75 years after the momentous birth of Vampira, she would still draw fans from around the world.

You were the architect of the goth phenomenon. From the moment Vampira first slithered onto the television screen, she captivated America. She was emaciated, with a waist so tiny it defied reality, but was somehow at once voluptuous and beautiful. A ghostly complexion, nails honed to dagger-like claws, and boomerang eyebrows, her visage and silhouette were simultaneously disturbing and curiously pleasant. Once she was observed, one couldn't look away.

Vampira was the first goth, and in that sense, you were a pioneer. With the character, you defined goth beauty and inspired and beguiled generations—and you continue to do so to this day.

During those decades, before computers, I searched for you. I wrote letters to magazines and newspapers, seeking information on Maila Nurmi a.k.a. Vampira, without a single response. I spent hours on the phone calling Information, using every name I knew you to employ. In 1977, you still couldn't be located, even as I enlisted the help of the Red Cross, in order to tell you that your brother, Bobbie, was dead.

At long last, in 1989, I found you through an article in the *Star* magazine. It had been 32 years. As adults, we spent a glorious week together in Hollywood. We laughed, cried, ate, put on the dog for brunch at the Beverly Hills Hotel, got drunk, and because you didn't own a bed or a bedroom, we slept on the floor with your puppy, Bogie. It was heaven. It was the culmination of my lifelong dream. We corresponded through letters for several years, and at Christmas, I sent you a box of assorted tins of fish and a bottle of wine. I never heard from you again after that. I was devastated. Had I upset you somehow?

On Monday, January 14, 2008, I read the news in the local newspaper. You were gone. My own private Cinderella caught the dream and flew away.

I was your only family, and even with my limited funds, I had to find a way to get to Los Angeles—and fast. Who else besides family are entrusted with final arrangements? I filled out the death certificate and paid for a future cremation. Through what can only be described as a miracle, I found your apartment. Several authorities had to be appeased before I was allowed to enter, because the county deemed you "a celebrity."

Like your mama before you, you died alone. Alone on the only piece of real furniture you owned, a sofa, with your feet propped on a plastic patio chair. My heart was broken.

You lived by yourself, so I can understand why your living room and bedroom were cluttered with castoffs, old clothes, memorabilia, and debris. But you still kept your kitchen and bathroom spotless.

The only thing I wanted were your writings. Even then, I knew you always wanted to tell your story to the world, and I knew that I would get them published, because I loved you and I owed it to you. It took 12 years.

I found those writings scattered about on the floor, in drawers, in pockets of your clothes, in satchels and handbags, in an envelope behind a picture frame. There were letters you'd written but never mailed. Sometimes there were pages of writings, and sometimes just a sentence or two. A memory here, a memory there. Written on hundreds of scraps of notebook paper, the margins of newspapers, a calendar, a diary, old hotel stationery. On the backs of photocopies of Vampira. This book is the result of cobbling those pieces together. Everything in *italics* is your own words, verbatim. I thought the public would want to hear directly from you.

They buried you at Hollywood Forever with your baby, Houdini—your dog whom you loved greatly. Your good friend, Dana Gould, told me it was what you would have wanted, and he graciously paid for it—thank you, Dana. I paid for your modest headstone. Someday, I hope to replace it with something more fitting for the Hollywood icon you were—and still are today.

Fly high, Aunt Maila. Beyond these earthly bonds. And fly proud for what you accomplished.

Love,

Sandra

Chapter One

At eight o'clock, on the evening of October 4, 1941, the Greyhound shuddered to a stop at the Los Angeles bus station.

The young woman checked her freshly bleached hairdo, the result of youthful impulse and a long layover in Portland. Her hair was a mess, and her clothes were wrinkled from two nights sleeping in a bus seat, next to a stranger. None of that mattered as she leaped off the bus into the embrace of the warm night air.

"Hollywood, here I come."

It had been a long battle for her to get to Los Angeles. But finally, two months shy of her 19th birthday, she was there.

Her life began on December 11, 1922, in Gloucester, Massachusetts, joining a brother, Bobbie, only 17 months older. Her father, Onni, christened her Maila Elizabeth after the Finnish author Maila Talvio. The name "Elizabeth" was a nod to his mother. When she was four, Maila's father went to work in Fitchburg, Massachusetts, as editor of the *Pohjan Tähti,* a Finnish-language newspaper. It was the beginning of Onni's 40-year career in journalism.

That Easter, in 1927, Maila made her public speaking debut at the Finnish Lutheran Church. For the occasion, Sophie, her American mother, made her a white dress decorated with ribbons and rosettes. There in the front pew, her mama and papa proudly sat with Bobbie between them, sticking his tongue out at her. A nod from Papa signaled that she should begin.

> *I recited the Bible verse Papa taught me. When I finished, I picked up the hem of my dress & put it in my mouth, exposing my bloomers to the congregation. And then I was in Papa's arms & he was whispering how proud he was of me as we settled back into the pew. At a young age, I knew I was the favorite of the King.*

In Fitchburg, Onni became involved with the political, social, and economic issues in Finland and the effects they had on his fellow immigrants. Although Finland's Civil War was over, Stalin's rise to power was concerning, and as a journalist, Onni felt obligated to ferret out the facts.

In 1926, Onni dropped a bombshell on his unsuspecting wife. He was going to Finland. Maybe for a year. He claimed it was his journalistic duty to witness the political upheaval in his homeland.

It was an outrageously selfish act. Sophie was still grieving over the loss of both parents less than a year before, and now she was expected to take on the responsibility of caring for their two young children alone, far away from her familial home. Onni offered to take Sophie along, but he knew she would never agree to leave her children. As an added insult, Onni used Sophie's inheritance from the sale of her parents' mercantile store to fund his trip.

The kicker is that, even though she was born in Massachusetts, Sophie was no longer an American citizen at this time. When she married Onni in 1918, the law of the land stated that the bride must take on the citizenship of her husband. So without ever setting foot in Finland, Sophie was now an American-born Finnish citizen living in the United States—*without* her Finnish husband, who was the whole reason she'd lost her American citizenship in the first place.

After a year, Onni returned to the U.S. The nation was in the throes of

Maila and brother Bobbie (my dad), in front of their house
at 3 Norseman Avenue, Gloucester, Massachusetts

Sophie on the right, her children Maila and Bobbie right in front of her,
with family friends. Gloucester, Massachusetts, 1925.

Prohibition at the time, and Onni was teetotal, preaching the evils of alcohol at temperance halls. His fellow Finns at the halls greeted him like a rock star upon his return, hungry for the news from abroad. His wife's welcome was far less enthusiastic.

It was almost as if Onni had returned to a stranger. When he came home, he found that Sophie had bobbed her hair and started wearing makeup and shorter skirts. But most alarming was that her agreeable nature had been replaced with something quite unfamiliar: defiance.

As the stalwart Finn preached the gospel of alcohol abstinence to ever increasing audiences, his wife was unapologetically enjoying bootlegged wine. Onni learned that during his absence, his wife had made new friends, and she'd been going out drinking with them, not bothering to hide her new habits. Onni was greatly dismayed by the change, but he assumed it would pass once they resumed their routine.

As an additional insult to Sophie, while her husband was away, he'd changed his surname, Niemi, back to Syrjäniemi, the original Finnish form he'd used before he emigrated to the U.S. Thereafter, a silent though salient wedge divided the family, as Sophie and her children remained Niemis.

The year following Onni's return, 1928, was an election year. The next president would be either the pro-Prohibition Protestant candidate, Herbert Hoover, or the "wet" Catholic, Al Smith. As Onni's reputation as a gifted orator gained widespread recognition, he expanded his repertoire to politics. There was never a doubt which candidate Onni preferred. He hated Catholics almost as much as he hated booze. His zeal for Hoover's candidacy was rewarded when he was selected as one of the Republican's election speakers to encourage the Finnish vote.

In April of 1929, the family moved to Cleveland, Ohio, where Onni took on the position of editor-in-chief of the Finnish-language newspaper *Kansan Lehti*. Six months later, Wall Street crashed. As America entered the Dirty Thirties, the economy began its free fall. To ward off financial ruin, the newspaper moved to

Ashtabula, 50 miles east of Cleveland, and once more, the Niemis were on the move and the children, aged eight and nine, were uprooted from their school and social life.

The kids gleefully discovered their new neighborhood was full of playmates. There was a diseased black walnut tree on the property, and Maila decided it was the perfect place to play Movie Star, as did her newfound pals.

Playing Movie Star was a favorite game of the girls in the neighborhood. Maila had recently been introduced to movie magazines, which carried stories and pictures of her favorite stars, like Greta Garbo, Louise Brooks, Norma Shearer, and Toby Wing. Women who had everything life could offer, who bathed in jewels, swathed themselves in fur, and rode around in fancy cars—no matter that most of the country was suffering during the Great Depression. Such was the life Maila dreamed of for herself.

> *Every day, the girls decided who they'd be & I always wanted to be Toby Wing. But the other girls insisted I be Joan Bennett instead. Well, I was not going to concede to their wishes without compensation. So, I said I would IF I got the highest spot in the old tree. It was perfect. Every day I, as Joan Bennett, received the benefit of free rent in the old tree's penthouse. And everywhere else, there was a depression going on. Oh, it was divine.*

A cat, Passenger, and a dog, Timmie, were added to the Niemi family, along with an apparent fugitive from someone's henhouse. An animal lover, Maila named the chicken Muna, the Finnish word for egg.

The Niemis lived in an upstairs apartment across the street from a grocery store. From her bedroom window, Maila and Bobbie watched the Mr. Goodbars melting in the sun. If the chocolate turned white, those bars could be bought on Sundays for three cents instead of five. Sunday also was allowance day and each kid got 25 cents. Maila and Bobbie would pool their money, grab ten white discounted candy bars and a pound of jelly beans, and with the nickel remaining, they'd buy a Sunday paper.

Bobbie read through the comics and was done, but for Maila, the comics opened a portal into a land of fantasy, allowing her to run wild through the streets of her imagination. When everyone was finished reading, Maila gathered up the comics and stacked them in a pile in her room so she could read them over again.

The Barsettis lived downstairs, and soon after moving in, Sophie and Addie Barsetti became friends. Addie's kitchen was the hub of her family life, and most days, the pungent, garlicky aroma of a simmering pot of marinara sauce competed with the clamor of kids and dogs running in and out of the house. Muna visited as frequently as an open door would allow, pecking at the crumbs between the floorboards, which Addie called "'crack food." The Barsettis, an Italian-American family of Catholics, enjoyed wine with every meal, Prohibition be damned. They made gallons of elderberry wine and insisted on sharing it with friends and neighbors.

To Sophie, her friend's kitchen was everything she'd hoped her married life to be: kids, dogs, laughter, the aroma of dinner cooking, and a husband who would be home every night to enjoy it all.

But it wasn't meant to be for Sophie.

When Onni was home, his children competed for his attention. Maila, imitating her orator father, took to reciting stories of her own creation. These she read aloud to Onni, as Bobbie interrupted with thunderous sound effects.

As an editor, Onni began his workday among the people, gathering information for his next op-ed. Keeping his finger on the pulse of public opinion was essential, though effortless, for the gregarious Finn. After work, the temperance hall beckoned, and it became his temple, its message his passion. He stood at the podium and raged against the "Devil's water," opposing even the use of sacramental wine, and blamed alcohol for everything from infidelity to insanity.

When Prohibition was repealed in 1933, one could buy either a bowl of soup or a drink for a dime. Each offered temporary relief; the decision was whether to appease the beast of hunger or the need for escape. For Sophie, the decision was an easy one. She needed the drink. How else could she cope?

Christmas of 1934, the holiday tree was up, and there was at least one present for everyone underneath, including the family pets. Two weeks later, Onni was fired.

Six months later, an offer arrived from Duluth for Onni to man the helm at another Finnish newspaper, *Päivälehti*. The family packed their worldly goods into their Marmon sedan and headed north, Maila sobbing as they left the pets behind with the Barsettis.

In part, Onni's new work contract read:

"I promise to pay you, Mr. Syrjaniemi, $25.00 per week, while you're in Ohio and upon your arrival with your family in Duluth, Minnesota, I will positively pay you $35.00 per week and possibly more, and I promise to reimburse you in part for moving expenses. I will fulfill this promise because I am too old a man to betray another. At a salary less than this agreed amount, you and your family cannot live in Duluth! — Carl H. Salminen, witnessed and dated July 9, 1935."

Duluth was hell.

The political climate was at a boiling point. Onni believed many of the immigrants there espoused an allegiance to socialism. This was in direct conflict with Onni's philosophies, and he made no secret of his hostility toward socialism, communism, and its proponents. Considering that he'd fled his homeland rather than be forced to join the Russian Army, his animosities never eased.

The newspaper's owner demanded he tone down his editorial rants. When Onni vehemently refused, he was fired once again.

Christmas that year was grim. Sophie picked up dead branches from the yards of neighbors, tied them together, and propped them into a corner, then decorated them with a paper chain she made from newspapers.

That Xmas, Ma said there would be no gifts, as we had no money.
I said I will buy my own. She's a doll in Walgreen's & her name is
Ruth. She's 97 cents. I saved the money babysitting. Days later, a
brokenhearted Mama asked me for the 97 cents. We had no food.

Maila and Bobbie were sent to the butcher shop with a glass jar and a nickel, to buy a quart of cow's blood. Sophie fried it up, melted some lard into it, and served it with flatbread. Maila couldn't bear to eat it, so she went hungry.

Duluth winters were harsh. Coal was two dollars a ton—two dollars the Niemis didn't have. Each family member was issued a gunny sack and sent out to retrieve chunks of coal that were dropped in the snow outside the neighbors' cellar doors. Maila thought she would starve to death if the cold didn't kill her first. Nights were the worst, when she was more aware of the icy wind blowing through the cracks in the walls. Electricity was a luxury the Niemis could ill afford, so when the nub of their last candle fizzled into a pool of molten wax, there was nothing but the interminable night as she lay on the floor, huddled next to her mother, wondering if she would live until morning.

If a local radio station hadn't paid Onni for his biweekly political news, they may not have survived the year. Although life was tough, Maila would not be denied one of the few pleasures that remained in her life: the Sunday paper. And she was not above begging to get it.

Sunday morning after church, Maila and Bobbie tramped through the snow to the corner market and stood outside its door. When someone emerged with a newspaper, Maila asked, "Mister, are you going to read those funny papers?" The blonde, blue-eyed street urchin never failed to melt a heart. Clutching their bounty, the siblings ran home to fight over their prize. And for Maila, what she found inside the pages of those comics was the difference between hope and despair.

The Dragon Lady came into Maila's life when it was its most bleak and stormed into her psyche like a tornado. The Dragon Lady preyed through the panels of *Terry and the Pirates*, an exotic beauty with a power rarely seen in a female character—she was as mysterious as she was tacitly evil. Her fearsome, beautiful image shone like a beacon through the damp, gray tunnel of Maila's life.

Meanwhile, there was no work in Duluth. Spirits were crushed and hope was dwindling, and then what can only be described as a miracle occurred. Onni's former employer sent him enough money to move the family back to Ashtabula. There was a job offer, but it wasn't for the newspaper.

Onni was a man with essentially two families: his biological family as well as a family of immigrants struggling to adapt to a new land. He learned that his new job was a way he could serve both families simultaneously.

With the help of other community activists, Onni founded an adult citizenship school—one that would prepare immigrants to apply for U.S. citizenship while allowing them to maintain their Finnish customs and proud heritage.

By this time, Onni was a naturalized citizen, and because the law was changed, Sophie was once again a U.S. citizen. Most Finns tended to isolate themselves from the general population, as they spoke little English, just as Bobbie and Maila spoke only Finnish until the first grade. Even after learning English in school, the children continued to speak Finnish at home. Onni established himself as an instructor to teach courses in U.S. history, literature, and religious studies, while Sophie handled the school's clerical work. During the summer, a curriculum for children was offered.

> *Oh, we moaned & groaned & rolled our eyes when we were told. Papa didn't fool us by calling it Summer Camp! We had to read books & make a list of 50 words we were unfamiliar with & then look up their definitions. Then we were tested on the definitions from our own lists---& we were required to study Lutheranism & The Kalevala (The national Finnish epic and from which Bob got his middle name, Kaleva). Bobbie rudely cut class to climb trees and play baseball. Whereas I, ever obedient, dolefully resigned myself to my studies.*
>
> *Being a good citizen wasn't all work & no play—that [was] from*

10

Papa himself. The body & spirit needed to be nourished as well as the
brain. Bobbie & I got to choose from a bushel of creative arts—band,
choir, dance, drama, theater, or sports. Bobbie naturally chose sports,
but I wanted to dance, dance, dance!

Sophie put the kibosh on her son playing sports. Too rough. Instead, she decided he would learn music; she bought him a five-dollar saxophone. Maila fared no better. Her father vetoed dance for drama, perhaps because he was preparing her to follow in his public speaking footsteps.

That summer, Maila sat in an overheated classroom while Bobbie again cut class to play baseball on the sly. When his mother found out, instead of punishing him, she bought him a used bicycle. Maila never forgot that slight and held a lifelong belief thereafter that Bobbie was her mother's favorite.

Maila took her dramatic lessons very seriously. A budding actress needed an audience to read dialogue, so she would seek out her mother in the kitchen. Much to Maila's irritation, Bobbie would seem to appear out of nowhere to join them. Then the fight was on. Armed with a cup of coffee and a box of soda crackers, Bobbie proceeded to make a big production out of crumbling the crackers into his coffee and drinking it, slurping loudly as Maila tried to recite her lines. She said her brother's concoction filled the room with the stench of wet baby diapers. The slurping and the stink would ultimately be too much and send Maila into screaming fits.

Whether they were called temper tantrums or nervous breakdowns, Maila continued to have meltdowns for the rest of her life. It was how she reacted to frustration. When words failed her, or when she couldn't think, she would scream or curse. The length to which she carried on depended upon the severity of her frustrations.

But in her youth, Maila still had the Dragon Lady, and she cherished the opportunities to escape with her into a private world. She went through entire tablets of paper drawing the enchantress in gowns of her own design.

If only she could sew.

Sophie was pleased that her daughter showed an interest in acquiring any domestic skills whatsoever and happier still that she took so quickly to the art of sewing. Once she learned the basics, Maila hounded her mother to take her to the secondhand shops—virtual treasure chests for a budding fashionista. Maila disassembled the garments, cut patterns from newspapers, and made herself outfits—modified, of course, to appease Onni's sense of modesty.

The citizenship school was successful, financial burdens were eased, and Sophie, who always held the purse strings in the household, graduated from wine to vodka.

It had been a long truce between husband and wife. Onni didn't know about the vodka, and Sophie kept her booze out of sight and didn't drink in front of him. But he knew her habit was increasing and that he couldn't take much more of it. While managing to discourage hundreds, perhaps thousands, to banish alcohol from their lives, he couldn't keep it out of his own home. Feeling like a failure was not something Onni could tolerate.

One night, it all came down.

Maila and Bobbie awoke to the sounds of shouting and broken glass. The kitchen table was upended, the chairs scattered about. Red wine splattered the wallpaper, coursing downward in rivulets, pooling onto the floor amid shards of glass. Onni, his steel-blue eyes ablaze and fixed upon his wife, spat out ugly words of condemnation. She was a disgrace as a wife and mother.

Sophie did not cower in fear, nor did she show remorse or try to counter her husband's tirade. She didn't even cry. Instead, she stood in a corner, her arms defiantly folded across her chest, a smug smile upon her face.

Two weeks later, Sophie boarded a Greyhound bus. Alone.

Chapter Two

John and Ida Peterson lived in Los Angeles with their only child, Ted, and their home was Sophie's destination on that July day in 1937. John, Sophie's only sibling, was 20 years her senior and devoutly religious. As a guest in the Peterson home, Sophie knew alcohol would not be tolerated. And that was the plan. Onni's ultimatum rang in her ears, "Don't come home until you're sober."

It was one thing to defy her husband, but that wouldn't happen with her brother. John never abandoned his family.

It ripped Sophie apart to leave her children. For how long, she didn't know. It depended upon how long it took her to decide between alcohol and a husband who would always put his career first. Maybe Onni was right—she could have been a better wife, a better mother. The question was: Could she do it sober?

The long bus ride lay ahead, and from her handbag, she pulled out a blue Milk of Magnesia bottle, the contents of which she'd replaced with the best vodka Onni's money could buy. She gave a silent toast to her husband and took a long swallow. It was what he deserved for sending her away.

Onni put his family problems aside and focused on his work. As he expanded the scope of his speeches to include politics and labor issues, his reputation as a champion of the Finnish people grew. Increasingly, he drew larger and more enthusiastic audiences. Whether at the podium or with his pen, Onni was never at a loss for words or for an audience to receive them.

There was a speaking tour to consider, and since Maila was only 14, he decided she was not old enough to stay home without adult supervision. So, father and daughter traveled together. That summer, the lecturer and his evangelist-in-training daughter trekked from town to town through parts of Illinois, Michigan, and Minnesota.

It was in Minnesota that Maila experienced a terrifying incident. A pastor she was sitting next to put his hand underneath her dress. Maila froze, but only for an instant before she bolted from the room. No one had seen what happened. She couldn't tell her father. Oh, how in that moment she needed her mother! Maila's face burned with shame, but she remained silent. She never mentioned the assault to either parent. Instead, she wrote about it in one of her journals. She wrote how the pastor's roving hands affected the rest of her life, making her more vigilant and mistrustful.

Frequently, Maila introduced her father to his audience. While on tour, she wrote long letters to her mother detailing her travels, and by summer's end, the father-daughter traveling show was back home in Duluth. A few weeks before Thanksgiving, so was Sophie, looking rested and well. Things settled down, and the daily routine commenced without drama.

Walt Disney's animated film, *Snow White*, came to town that year, and Maila and Bobbie met up with their respective friends to see the movie. Bobbie and pals, more intent on creating a disturbance than watching the show, sat in the seats directly behind Maila and friends, throwing popcorn and kicking the backs of their seats. Predictably, when the boys' collective sound effects were heard echoing off the walls, they ran afoul of the management and were summarily ejected from the theater by a flashlight-wielding usher.

It certainly wasn't Snow White, the someday-my-prince-will-come bore, who was emblazoned upon Maila's psyche, but The Evil Queen. When she burst

Sophie, Maila's mother, about 1935.

upon the big screen, Maila was electrified. The Queen commanded attention. She was beautiful and powerful; her presence could never be contained within the pages of a Sunday paper or comic book. The Evil Queen was the antithesis of everything Maila had known about womanhood. The thought of this woman cooking or cleaning or tending to hungry children or placating a husband was laughable. Instead, the Evil Queen was strong, fearless, commanding, and exquisitely beautiful. She was everything Maila wanted to be. In that indefinable moment when life and fantasy collided, Maila became the fantasy, and the Evil Queen forever became a part of who she was.

In a mid-'90s interview on Sandra Bernhard's show *Reel Wild Cinema*, Maila explained. "Along came The Evil Queen, who was imperious, in full control, cool. She was my escape, and I became The Evil Queen in my mind."

At home, Sophie's hopes for a happily-ever-after marriage were about to be tested.

A West Coast Finnish newspaper, the *Lännen Suometar*, offered Onni an editorial position. Since Bobbie was entering his senior year in high school, Onni decided it best that he go west alone to establish himself, and the rest of the family to join him after Bobbie graduated.

Alone again for a year, Sophie returned to the bottle. Once more, she felt abandoned. Onni was living the life of a single man, unburdened by a wife and children. She imagined him glad-handing the locals with his good looks and innate charisma, flashing his million-dollar smile while she took on the responsibilities of the family. Once again, her youthful dreams of home and hearth were shattered, and she sought solace in alcohol.

The city of Astoria occupies the northwestern tip of Oregon. In 1939, its population of 10,000 included a substantial enclave of Finns. A stone's throw from the Pacific, Astoria abuts the Columbia River and appears to have just escaped the river's mighty grasp to fling itself upon a hillside of stately fir trees. Ornate Victorian homes with wraparound porches, cupolas, and elaborate gingerbread detailing dot the landscape, mingling with the towering evergreens.

16

Countless fishing boats troll the waterways, their bounties supplying the community's lifeblood.

The Niemis set up house in a shared multi-family Victorian, just west of Hughes-Ransom Mortuary. They occupied the northwest corner of the top floor, and to everyone's delight, their living space incorporated one of two much-coveted turrets. The view was breathtaking. The windows looked north across a four-mile-wide expanse of water culminating in a crest of mountains on the Washington State side of the river. At the western horizon, a clear day afforded a sliver of the Pacific Ocean.

Onni brought home a stray gray-and-white tabby, whom Maila named Lucifer P. Catt. The kitty spent hours looking out the windows, giving every indication he longed to be outdoors. Thinking it was cruel to deny him, Maila brought him down to street level and set him in the grass. The cat freaked. Lucifer was terrified of grass. He preferred the rooftop, which he navigated from an open fourth-floor window. Weather permitting, it became his favorite spot.

Onni's editorials were popular among the local Finns. As a member of the Finnish Brotherhood, he continued his leadership role in promoting Finnish nationalism, so it came as no surprise that he was chosen to speak on Finnish Day at the San Francisco Exposition. There, he was knighted by his mother country and awarded its highest honor, the prestigious White Rose of Finland, an award he never disclosed to his children and which Maila only found out about decades after his death.

Unlike her brother, who was allowed to finish high school among his friends, Maila would graduate from Astoria High School as the new girl. She didn't mind. She had no intention of spending her life in the "quaint fishing village" she now called home. If anything, she enjoyed being a curiosity, "the girl with the cat who lives on the roof." A new start required a new name as well, and Maila announced that she would henceforth be called Libbie.

The fashions of the day were transforming into shorter hemlines, padded shoulders, and jackets with peplums. Maila couldn't afford to buy the latest fashions and didn't need to—her talent with a needle and thread had surpassed her mother's. She would go window-shopping, and if she found a mannequin wearing something she liked, she went home and made it.

But there was one thing she couldn't create with a Singer: silk stockings. Sheer, shiny silk seamed up the back of the leg. Maila begged for a pair. Her mother scoffed at the idea: "Silk stockings are for rich people, like movie stars," she said. Her father was dismissive as well. Silk stockings were inappropriate and indulgent.

Her parents' opinions aside, Maila was on a hunt for hose, with a squirreled-away garter belt at the ready. Finally, she found a pair discarded in the trash of the ladies' room at the library. Classmate Shirley Crane Schlossinger recalls one morning when Maila cornered her in the school's girls' bathroom.

"Libbie pulled a pair of silk hose from her handbag and waved them in the air. When she put them on, there were runs in them, and I told her it was a shame they were ruined. But she didn't care. She took something—it must have been a pencil—and poked holes in them until they were shredded. Then she said, 'Look, Leg Lace!' That was Libbie."

Apparently Maila's fashion statement failed to ignite a trend among her peers. She resorted to painting her legs with gravy browning and enlisted the help of a steady-handed friend to draw a line up the back of each of her legs with an eyebrow pencil. It worked perfectly, as long as she didn't get caught in the rain.

Unfortunately, it rains a lot in Astoria. A weather phenomenon known as the Pineapple Express carried bands of tropical moisture from Hawaii via the polar jet stream. Storms were commonplace and frequently stalled directly over Astoria. The locals were accustomed to the wet weather, which could last for weeks. Maila hated it. She recalled sitting on her bed and watching the incessant rain obliterate everything beyond the turret windows, Lucifer asleep beside her in a furry knot, conceding defeat. No roof access today.

Maila didn't want the kind of life that was expected of most young women; a husband, children, cooking, and cleaning. She wanted a life that was spontaneous, exhilarating, and full of laughter, shared with creative, imaginative people like herself. Free to be outrageous, bold, powerful, and sexy. Like the Dragon Lady and the Evil Queen.

In May of 1940, Elizabeth "Libbie" Niemi graduated from Astoria High School. According to her yearbook, she wrote for the school newspaper, was a member of the senior ball committee, and belonged to the drama club, wherein she appeared in the play *Graham Crackers*. Years later, Maila wrote an article chronicling her year at Astoria High School. As published in the September 14–20, 1964 issue of the *LA Weekly*, she refers to herself as "Maila Nerdna."

> *We were all high all the time up there back in 1939... All 500 or so of us. It was altudinous [sic]. Astoria High School was on top of a mountain in Astoria, Oregon.*
>
> *You could take some time off from making spitballs and look out of the window in study hall. Way, way down below, you'd see the Columbia River and the sun glinting off the water. Only that past summer, Glen [sic] Miller himself had come to the Seaside Ballroom to play, so you could dance "the Balboa." That was your high. "Marijuana, the weed that kills" was still in the future. Pot in these parts was a pal of a pan.*
>
> *The bell rings. A rude awakening. Suddenly, you become painfully aware, again, of who you are. You are Maila Nerdna. Now you must somehow get this hated, unsightly carcass down the crowded corridor to your next class. Scrawny, knock-kneed, pigeon-toed, and flat chested, with what looks like rancid spaghetti for hair, you are clearly no prospect for the yell-leader tryouts! Your face sports hairless eyes— no eyebrows, no lashes, and lids that fall nearly shut, a pig's snout, a mouth perpetually ajar, gasping for breath and revealing a broken picket fence of teeth. The icing on the cake, the ultimate embellishment*

the countenance wears is a hollow expression, as of a visitor from another planet.

You realize that you present a startling picture. The frighteningly mismatched, ill-fitting assortment of hand-me-down rags that give the distinct impression that you just dropped in on your way to the poorhouse. Nobody knows that you're sexy. It is your secret. You decided you'd show them! You'd grow up to be "the Dragon Lady." They'd see. They'd be sorry.

After graduation, her father demanded she go to work. In Astoria, women worked in any number of fish canneries that lined the waterfront. And that is where Maila found herself, wearing a cannery-issued white bandana, cotton smock, rubber apron, gloves, and boots.

It wasn't easy work. The job required standing in place all day while hacking up salmon steaks with a cleaver, the pieces to be fitted into an oval tin can. Maila, always clumsy with a knife, was lucky not to have severed a finger or two.

After one particularly grueling day, Maila came home and soaked in the bathtub. Onni was away, and her mother sat in the living room with a glass of liquor, listening to the radio. Maila could hear the man's voice saying something about airplane wings. Not that she cared about the topic. What intrigued her was the man's voice. His tone, his mastery of words, his delivery.

Suddenly, she leaped from the tub, forgetting her modesty, and raced into the living room, standing naked in front of her mother, dripping water on the rug.

"Mama, Mama, that man on the radio—that radio announcer is no ordinary radio announcer. Who is he? He's a genius."

Sophie, a little drunk and annoyed by the interruption, said, "Of course, he's a genius. That's Orson Welles. He's a famous genius. Everybody knows that."

"Well, someday I'm going to meet him, and we'll be friends."

Sophie was surly in her response. "He is not your friend. You are Maila Elizabeth Niemi, and you work in a fish cannery in Astoria, Oregon. And don't

Processing and canning salmon in Astoria, Oregon, 1940s.

you forget it."

Maila glared at her mother. "Don't you talk like that," her mother added. "People will say that you're crazy."

> *I thought: Here I am, stuck in a fish cannery, and so I sang when all I really wanted to do was cry. There was a whole world out there of which I was not a part. And as long as I volunteered to stay here, the hellishness would continue unabated. You know the part of the song that goes* [singing]: *'One of these mornings, you're gonna rise up singin', and you'll spread out your wings, and you'll take to the sky.'*

21

In that exact moment, I realized if I wanted to survive, I had to spread my wings and fly high and fast from everything and everyone I knew. I made a plan to leave and knew if I could tolerate another three or four months eviscerating fish, I could save enough money to buy wings to fly away. Of course, I didn't know then those wings would carry me straight into the merciless belly of the beast. I was unprepared. I didn't yet realize wings alone cannot slay dragons, although I tried. God knows I tried!

That September, Maila trotted off to college equipped with a drama scholarship and her summer cannery earnings. Pacific University, a private college boasting a lush, forested campus, nestled within the small, aptly named community of Forest Grove, Oregon. There, Maila enrolled in a liberal arts program with an emphasis on the performing arts.

Always an eager student, Maila felt college would cultivate the artist inside her and nurture that germ of creativity that would allow her to blossom into a performer. But it seemed that math and history classes took over her curriculum.

Within a month, she cut classes. Biology class was the first to go. To think that she would ever consider anything so monstrous as dissecting a precious little frog was appalling. She became physically ill when she learned the frog would still be alive, only anesthetized, so students could study the poor thing's still-beating heart. Such cruelty, even in the name of science, was unconscionable.

Other than attending drama class, Maila stayed in her dorm to plan on how best to break the news to her father: College was a bust. The only thing she would miss about Forest Grove was her independence.

But she wouldn't be returning to the lovely Victorian house in Astoria with its charming turret and sweeping view of the Columbia. Her parents' home was now the Victor Apartments, a nondescript two-floor walk-up.

Bobbie had gotten a job and moved out of the Victorian house, and with both kids gone, Onni decided a smaller place was in order. Sophie suspected

Maila's high school graduation picture from Astoria High School, class of 1940.

the move was not motivated by a need to trim their budget but to punish her for drinking. And in truth, the move *was* calculated: Onni decided to hide his alcoholic wife rather than divorce her. The east end of town, a Norwegian and Swedish stronghold, meant Sophie's booze outlet, the Recreation Tavern, was far less accessible and would end the chance of any of his Finnish cronies spotting his wife en route.

Although resigned to the fact that he had no control over his wife, Onni had to admit that during that horrible year in Duluth, it was his wife who showed the greatest strength. It was she who rallied the troops in their darkest hours. And even now, when he smelled liquor on her breath, it wasn't that she staggered about in a stupor. She kept a clean house, prepared timely meals, and could still manage an intelligent conversation. A divorce would be an embarrassment and equaled failure, neither of which could he tolerate.

The day after Christmas, Maila dropped the bomb. Her father was predictably furious. Although not a physically violent man, his arsenal of words stung more than a whipping. He issued an ultimatum. Since Maila was now 18, Onni was under no legal obligation to continue to support her unless she was in school. He told his daughter she couldn't move back home unless she enrolled in a local business class or found a job. Maila took the deal.

According to her diary, as 1941 began, placating Papa was nowhere in her plans. Instead, her New Year's resolution was "*to grow long fingernails.*" At 18, Maila was far more interested in running with friends than finding a job. Maila and best friend, Helen Kokko, shared a passion for movies, sewing, dancing, and boys, and when the jitterbug craze rocked onto the scene, the two friends were determined to be the best jitterbugs in the county.

It was everywhere. The jitterbug sensation blanketed the pages of magazines and newspapers and filled the airwaves with its music. Even Hollywood obliged the masses by committing its latest dance steps to film. Unfortunately, the jitterbug was not Papa-approved. Any dance other than Saturday night polkas and schottisches at the Finnish (*Suomi*) Hall, he deemed improper.

Regardless, the girls practiced every chance they got. Together, they choreographed entire songs with steps, swings, swivels, and swoops in preparation for the next dance.

The upper floor of the Labor Temple was *the* place for all the jitterbugs and jivers to cut a rug. Typically, Maila—or Libbie, as she still preferred to be called—and Helen showed up with identical hairdos and matching outfits, the result of many late-night sewing sessions at Helen's house. The girls' appearance, coupled with their growing reputation as the finest ducky shin-breakers in town, intimidated some of the young men, so the girls often partnered up with each other and danced their identical bobby socks off until they were overheated enough to flee out to the fire escape. The fire escape was a busy place, depending upon if one wanted to cool off, light up, or make out. The last was with Maila, who stepped onto the platform to kiss a young Coast Guardsman named Junior Duncan.

Junior is such a cute jitterbug, and I could tell by the way he looked into my eyes that he had a case on me. Ooh, he is just so dreamy.

Bobbie had a car, and Maila and her friends often talked him into giving them a ride to the beach in Seaside, a 16-mile jaunt. The plan was that he would see a movie and then pick them up. But he was known to abandon the group, and then they'd have to hitchhike home in the pouring rain.

It was a time of dreamy boys and corny boys, where being deemed a corny boy seriously impeded a young man's social life. A dance dominated by corny boys was a "corn bake." Corn bakes were Maila's greatest disappointment.

Dances were the highlight of every weekend, and even at the risk of encountering a corn bake, Maila was always eager to go. Some nights, a young man would walk her home, and the cross-town hike caused her to miss curfew.

Pa waiting for me. Dog house.

Unfortunately, when it came time for the Valentine's Ball, Maila was again doing time, tethered to Pa's doghouse.

She counted on her father being out that night. Her mother wouldn't tell on her if she went out. Her father was gone every Friday night. She didn't understand why he wasn't gone until she realized it was her parents' wedding anniversary. Just her luck. With youthful aplomb, Maila continued getting ready, styling her hair and slipping into her smashing new outfit, hot off the Singer. Her father sat reading in his chair, seemingly impervious to his daughter's preparations. He never so much as looked up from his newspaper until Maila reached for the front doorknob.

"You're not going anywhere," he said.

From Maila's diary:

I bawled all night long.

Pa's doghouse justice took an ugly turn. She would not be allowed to skip out on probation until she made good on her end of the deal: either school or work. Maila began working in the city's bookmobile until summer arrived.

In the Pacific Northwest, Memorial Day signaled the end of the long, rainy season and the beginning of strawberry season. For three glorious weeks in June, the sweetest, juiciest strawberries on the planet were harvested in northwestern Oregon.

Sixty miles southeast of Astoria, the strawberry farms in Woodland, Washington, produced the best of the best. Pickers were required to live on site and were provided with bunkhouse-style accommodations. The workday began at dawn and continued until the heat drove the pickers from the fields. It was back-breaking work; they were hunched for hours between endless rows of berries. But after 1 or 2 in the afternoon, the rest of the day was free.

When the strawberry buses pulled out of town, packed with young, energetic pickers, Maila was on board. At 25 cents a crate, a good picker could earn four dollars a day. Serious money.

Maila arrived home with fingernails stained and torn to the quick, but with enough money to splurge on a long-coveted portable radio. And there were stories to tell Helen, who'd stayed home. With girlish enthusiasm, Maila told of the swimming hole in the woods and of sunbathing in her red-and-white bathing suit, which she'd made from a kitchen tablecloth. She talked about a "real fun" barn dance with "real hay bales" and of dreamy boys with names like Eddie and McGee, but alas, she admitted, most of the dances were decidedly corn bakes.

With the strawberry harvest finished and plenty of summer left, Maila had to find a job fast. The tuna cannery was hiring, and although it was a tough call for Maila to decide between fish factory or doghouse, the scale tipped slightly in favor of the cannery due to the lure of a paycheck. That's when she decided that if she saved up enough of them, she could buy a one-way ticket out of town.

It was worse than the first time. The year before, she still believed that obedient, earnest, young women like herself went off to college in preparation for a career of their own choosing. Instead, she got asked to cut up frogs. And now here she was, walled into a two-square-foot space by more of God's hapless creatures, wielding a knife. This time it wasn't raw salmon but cooked whole tuna. The fish were stacked like cords of wood—headless, skinless, steaming hot from the ovens. Even though the cannery protruded over the Columbia River, inside, summer in the cannery was insufferably hot. After the tuna was canned, it was put into racks and cooked in giant round ovens that belched steam every time they were opened or closed. After a while, she didn't even notice the smell of hot fish anymore. Most days, she walked home stocking-footed to relieve her aching, swollen feet, her slime-covered fish boots tucked under her arm.

She wouldn't let this be her future. She wouldn't.

The day finally arrived when Maila had to tell her parents she couldn't take it anymore. She had plans. To punctuate how much she hated her life, she again told them she'd rather be dead. She announced she was moving to New York to pursue her art.

Her father forbade her to leave. Maila stood her ground, saying she was 18 and he couldn't stop her. Onni slapped his daughter so hard her nose bled. She claimed it was one of the few times he ever struck her.

In the end, Maila agreed to forgo New York for Los Angeles. Uncle John and Aunt Ida were again contacted to ask for their hospitality, and now they welcomed their niece, inviting her to stay as long as she needed to.

At 7:30 on the morning of October 2, 1941, Maila boarded the Greyhound bus and disappeared into her future.

Onni predicted that she'd be back home within six months. He couldn't have been more wrong.

Chapter Three

On the evening of October 4, 1941, when Maila arrived in Los Angeles, the Golden Age of Hollywood was in full swing. Its biggest stars ruled the world: Henry Fonda, Jimmy Stewart, Bette Davis, Myrna Loy, Claudette Colbert, Gary Cooper, Clark Gable, Katharine Hepburn. Just two years before, in 1939, Hollywood studios had released 365 films, and 50 years later, it would go down as the greatest year in Hollywood Film History. During this pre-television era, 80 million people would take in at least one film a week. That year, they had a choice of blockbusters like *The Wizard of Oz, Mr. Smith Goes to Washington, Dark Victory, Wuthering Heights,* and *Gone with the Wind.*

There was no doubt, Maila had stars in her eyes. She wasn't quite sure how she'd make a name for herself—she only knew that she would. Her intent was to use the skills she'd learned from her father and practiced in her mother's kitchen to become a monologist. She would read her own material, of course, using her voice to great effect, in the manner of Orson Welles.

It is interesting to note that in 1941, Orson Welles' iconic film, *Citizen Kane,* had just premiered, as well as Howard Hawks' *Sergeant York* and Bela Lugosi's *The Wolf Man.* On that night of October 4th, 1941, Maila couldn't have known yet how these three men would later impact her life.

Even though John and Ida were her aunt and uncle, she knew them only by photographs. She scanned the crowd at the bus station. An elderly man wearing a smile walked toward her. It was Uncle John, looking even older than the photos she'd seen. Greeting her warmly, he grabbed Maila's bags, explaining that Aunt Ida waited in the car.

The car slowed on Wilshire Boulevard. Neon lights atop the roof of the residential hotel illuminated the night sky. It was the Gaylord Hotel, her new home.

The lobby was stunning. Around the perimeter of the room, intricate cove moldings defined the space. The tray ceiling boasted an elaborate center medallion from which a majestic chandelier was suspended. Its prisms of cut crystals refracted the light to create the illusion of a thousand twinkling stars. Up-lit wall sconces created an ambiance of ease and privilege. Sumptuous draperies at the windows flowed to meet the mosaic-tiled floor. Maila had never seen such splendor.

The uniformed elevator operator took the trio up to the fourth floor to the Petersons' apartment. Although not nearly as lavish as the lobby, it was still more beautiful than anything she could have imagined.

Ida showed Maila to her room and led a quick tour, which culminated in the large kitchen. Ida paused and pulled a plate of food from the refrigerator, offering it to Maila. She couldn't help but gasp, responding not to the food but to the refrigerator, which she'd only seen in ads in *Life* and *Collier's*. At home, they had an icebox.

Los Angeles was a whole new world.

When Maila awoke, it was Sunday, the day the Petersons devoted to church. Wishing that God took rain checks, she dressed for church. Almost as soon as they left the hotel, Maila recognized the squat, dome-roofed building on the corner. The Brown Derby! She could barely contain her excitement and couldn't wait to write to Helen, to tell her she lived next door to the restaurant of the stars.

Within days, Maila was bored out of her mind. She'd scarcely left the hotel, and John and Ida's early-to-bed, early-to-rise routine was driving her mad. She was dying to experience big-city life. Inwardly, she cursed her father. He forced her into a compromise, insisting upon L.A. instead of New York so he could keep tabs on her, telling her he was 'always just a phone call away.'

A respite from the drudgery occurred when Ted and Millie invited Maila to dinner and a movie. Ted was the Petersons' only child. Just a few years older than his cousin Maila, he was an electrician's apprentice, while his wife, Millie, worked as a salesgirl.

The trio went to Clifton's Cafeteria on Broadway, joining a long line of people waiting to get in. As its name implied, Clifton's was a self-serve restaurant where patrons could fill their trays from a vast assortment of delectable salads, entrees, and desserts for a reasonable price. Live organ music lent itself to the festive atmosphere, while singing waiters poured coffee and offered free corsages to the ladies. Tall, lifelike faux redwoods sprung up from the floor and stretched into the far reaches of the open tri-level dining area, which easily seated six hundred or more. A lighted waterfall cascaded from 20 feet high, the water pooling on various ledges before spilling over and collecting at the ground level to form a meandering stream.

After dinner, the three toured Broadway, where grand, art deco-styled movie theaters, capable of seating thousands, lined the street with their brilliant neon marquees. Ted pointed out that *The Badlands of Dakota* was playing up the street, but the women opted for the double feature at the Tower, *Aloma of the South Seas*, starring Dorothy Lamour, along with Sonja Henie's *Sun Valley Serenade*. Robert Stack's debut as an Old West gunslinger lost out to the Ice Queen.

Directly across the street from the Gaylord Hotel, which Maila now called home, stood the grandest of all hotels: the Ambassador, with its adjoining nightclub, the Cocoanut Grove. It was there, less than two years before, that Vivian Leigh won her Oscar for her role as Scarlett O'Hara in *Gone with the Wind*. The 24-acre plot of land on which the Ambassador stood was a magnificent oasis in the heart of a city where the biggest stars of the day went to play. On any given night, Joan Crawford, Norma Shearer, Errol Flynn, or Clark Gable and his bride, Carole Lombard, could be seen maneuvering their fancy cars up the Ambassador's long driveway. The storied hotel would eventually serve as a tragic footnote in American history 27 years later, when Robert F. Kennedy was assassinated by Sirhan Sirhan in the Ambassador's kitchen.

All the familiar faces Maila saw and read about in *Movie Mirror* and *Silver Screen* magazines could now be seen in the flesh, going about their business. She was literally living among the stars, and yet she remained sadly sequestered in silence on the Gaylord's fourth floor.

After a few weeks into her life in Los Angeles, Maila no longer cared about the Brown Derby or the Ambassador—or even the ice-making refrigerator. None of it mattered if she didn't have the freedom to live her life as she wanted. But freedom required money, and her cannery money wouldn't last forever.

Maila soon set out to find a job, her day's itinerary mapped out and carefully tucked into her handbag. She graciously refused Ida's suggestion to come along to help her navigate the city. A radio job was what Maila wanted. A place where she could speak to her listening audience and relay in dulcet tones her personal stories.

Prominently occupying the famous corner of Sunset and Vine was NBC Radio City. Wearing a navy-and-cream suit, her matching suede heels clacking down the boulevard, Maila filled out an application and handed it back to the receptionist. When she was done, she stood at the corner and casually looked north, and there it was. Big white letters stretched across the ridge of the canyon's wall: H-O-L-L-Y-W-O-O-D-L-A-N-D.

The next morning, Maila stepped out into the California sun with a newspaper and renewed ambition. And there it was: an ad for a "good radio voice." The Hollywood address of the talent agency was located on the second floor of a dry cleaner. When she arrived, a man introduced himself as Mr. Kosloff and apologized for his secretary being away on vacation. The radio job, he explained, required on-air work for 15 minutes a day, four days a week, for which the pay was 50 dollars. Maila knew it was a perfect job to start her career.

She came prepared with pages of monologues she felt best demonstrated her vocal capabilities, but Kosloff brushed them off, insisting she read his material: passionate love scenes from the film *Stella Dallas*.

It seemed like a strange request, but she attributed it to the way of doing business in Hollywood. Most importantly, Maila was eager to impress.

Her efforts seemed to pay off when the talent agent gave her a qualified yes.

"Now, I must be honest with you," Kosloff began. "There is one other girl. She was good, though not as good as you. But just the same—and this is just a formality—I have some papers for you to sign." He reached into a drawer, pulled out a sheaf of papers, and pushed them across his desk to Maila. It was not a contract but an agreement for Maila to be photographed for print ads. It was imperative, he said, to see how well a girl looked through a camera lens. "Advertising is essential to success," he said. "Newspapers, magazines, playbills, maybe even billboards."

Maila couldn't believe her good luck. The door to her future was standing wide open, and all she had to do was sign a piece of paper.

No sooner had she affixed her signature than Kosloff flipped the lock on the front door and led Maila into a tiny annex at the back of the office. There he asked her to disrobe, "but only from the waist up, of course." He nodded to a tri-folded privacy screen. "You can change over there."

"Change? Change into what?" Maila asked. She was starting to panic. Never had she disrobed in front of a man.

Kosloff indicated some scarves draped over the top of the screen. Behind the partition, Maila removed her jacket and blouse. She grabbed the tail of a scarf and held it to her chest. It was sheer. She tried another and another, but they were all the same—nearly transparent.

Kosloff's entire demeanor changed. "C'mon, sweetheart," Kosloff intoned impatiently. "Do you want the job or not?"

Maila was in trouble. What kind of radio work required an applicant to undress? When she questioned Kosloff's motives, he told her he needed promotional shots to be used in advertising the show.

"Do I have to take off my brassiere, too?"

"No, not unless you don't mind looking ridiculous when you see yourself plastered on a billboard."

Maila was in a full panic. There was nowhere to run, and overpowering Kosloff would be impossible. If she screamed, no one would hear. She was locked in a second-story room with a madman, and she believed her only chance at survival was to do exactly what he asked.

From the other side of the screen, Kosloff was becoming annoyed.

"Look, if you don't want to do this, it's fine with me. I've got girls coming in to see me all day long. Time is money, and your time is about to run out."

So, she wasn't the only one. The other girl, the one Kosloff mentioned earlier, had already been photographed. Maybe she was just overreacting.

Maila took a few deep breaths and slipped out of her bra. She draped three of the scarves across her chest, covering herself as best she could, and stepped out from behind the screen.

Kosloff was holding a camera. He seemed not to notice her nakedness but pointed vaguely to a box on a nearby table. "There's some makeup over there and a mirror."

Maila did as she was told.

"And don't forget to rouge up your nipples." She spun around to face him. "What?" Maila was incredulous. "I changed my mind. I don't care if I'm on a billboard or anyplace else. I don't even care about having this job anymore either."

Kosloff looked up from fiddling with his camera. "It's just an illusion, baby. It's the lighting in here. I promise you, nothing will show."

Maila was silent, her eyes reflecting uncertainty. "Look," he said, trying to be patient. "I'm a professional, and I do this every day. Now, are you going to trust me or not?"

The photo shoot was humiliating. Maila was never completely exposed. But the nearness of Kosloff, the touch of his fingers, and the feel of his breath on her naked skin, arranging and rearranging the one scarf he allowed her, made Maila's stomach churn. She swallowed hard to keep from vomiting. Finally, she was allowed to dress.

"I'll have the proofs back in a few days," Kosloff said as Maila positioned herself by the front door. The moment the door was unlocked, Maila bolted from the room and flew down the stairs. She could hear him call after her, "I'll call you next week when they're ready."

He never called back. When after a week of waiting for a phone call, she went back to Kosloff's office and found it empty, it verified what she suspected: There was no radio job. Never had been. After the hellish week spent alternating between shame and rage, she was almost relieved to find Kosloff gone. At least she would never have to see him again.

After the Kosloff fiasco, Maila swore off talent agencies and decided to pursue a career in a safer, more traditional manner.

The United Artists Theatre advertised for usherettes. Maila stood in a long line to apply with other hopefuls. While she didn't get hired, she met a young woman, Gertie, who had a friend who was looking for a roommate.

Paula Solvin was indeed looking for someone to share expenses, and after meeting with Maila that afternoon, the two decided sharing an apartment was a grand idea. Maila was out of the Gaylord by dark.

She knew full well that when Papa got wind of her move, all hell would break loose, but until then, there was only today. And today, she was happy.

Papa's letter arrived sooner than expected. He demanded that she move into a church-sponsored Finnish boarding house for women. Piikatalo ("maid's house"), located in the Wilshire area, housed unmarried Finnish women who were working as domestics. If she chose not to move, he would cut her off financially, effective immediately. Papa didn't play fair. He knew Maila wasn't working and couldn't support herself, and so with much regret, she left Paula's for the boarding house she came to refer to as "the dungeon."

Living at Piikatalo was bad, but at least her father was paying the rent, so there was little need to find immediate employment. Besides, now that she had friends, there was precious little time for Maila to actually look for work, and she was okay with that. After the Mr. Kosloff incident, her radio aspirations were put on hold.

On Paula and Gertie's days off, the three young ladies would pack a change of clothes and take the Red Car to the beach. The Santa Monica Pier was a magical place—a West Coast Coney Island. Its concrete street and walkway jutted 1,600 feet out over the Pacific Ocean and was lined with arcades, restaurants, and an amusement park.

Just to the south side of the pier was Muscle Beach. The girls changed into their bathing suits and joined hundreds of other young women to watch the spectacle in the sand. There, bodybuilders flexed and formed human pyramids, much to the delight and admiration of the female audience.

At sunset, the girls moved on to the massive La Monica Ballroom, heralded as the largest dance floor in the world. After yet another wardrobe change, the girls joined thousands of other jivers to dance the night away.

On Broadway, in Los Angeles, the theater district was rife with amateur talent competitions, with cash prizes going to the winners. Maila dusted off her monologues and set out to compete in as many as she could. The Million Dollar Theater, the Hippodrome, La Tosca—even Clifton's Cafeteria hosted their own amateur show.

The phrase "Winner, winner, chicken dinner" became a reality for Maila. A reading from *Dorothy Dumb Meets a Vitamin* snagged Maila a free chicken dinner and the attention of a young man named Marvin Press. An aspiring actor, he gathered up his courage to ask Maila to dinner.

After a few dates and a canoe ride in Westlake Park, things got very serious. At least for Marvin.

On the Friday night after the bombing of Pearl Harbor, Maila and Marvin were walking through the theater district, and without preamble, Marvin got down on one knee and asked Maila to be his wife.

He (Marvin) proposed to me on 3rd and Broadway. Ugh! I'm never going to see him again. Told him so, too.

The poor guy never saw it coming.

Although Maila never gave Marvin a second thought, she did rethink her decision about talent agencies. Everyone was telling her that if she was wanted to find work, she needed an agent. Perhaps Kosloff was just a hideous fluke. And it was possible that radio wasn't the direction she should pursue. Maybe, with her public speaking talents, she was better suited for a career on stage.

Dressed smartly in a freshly pressed suit, this time a yellow corduroy one with matching hat and black peep-toe pumps, Maila entered a theatrical agency on Vermont. She didn't make an appointment. "Just show up and act like you own the joint," her friends said.

The receptionist took her name and offered a seat in the waiting area. Maybe her friends were right.

Before long, the woman ushered Maila to a room at the end of a long corridor. Upon entering, the man behind the desk rose and introduced himself as Mr. Clark. Maila told him that she was interested in theater work and looking for representation.

"Let me see your portfolio," Mr. Clark said.

That was a problem. Agents always wanted a portfolio, and Maila didn't have one. She was honest with Mr. Clark and confessed she was just starting out in show business and needed help to get started.

"I'm an actress and a dancer. And I know I will become a great stage actress if given the chance," Maila said. "As you can hear, I speak clearly and have a distinctive speaking voice, capable of projecting out into an audience."

"How old are you?"

"Nineteen."

"Training?"

"From the age of four, my father trained me to be a monologist. We toured together speaking to large audiences and were highly successful."

"What kind of experience have you had?"

"Experience?"

"Yeah, experience, like singing, dancing, acting. What have you done?"

"I had the lead role in my senior class play, and I won a prize in an amateur contest just last week, and I..."

"Take off your jacket."

"What?"

"Take off your jacket and stand up."

Maila stood and removed her jacket and draped it across the back of her chair.

"What are your measurements?"

"Thirty-six, twenty-two, thirty-six," she lied.

Mr. Clark walked around her in a circle, then doubled back and stood in front of her. "Maybe I can find you something at the Beverly Hills Playhouse. You say you can dance?"

"Oh, yes, sir."

"Can you dance like this?" Clark grabbed her around the waist and spun her around. "And kiss, too? I'll bet you can kiss."

He held her with one hand and with the other forced his mouth against hers. Maila's hat fell to the floor as she struggled against him with all her might. Mr. Clark maneuvered her to the desk where he bent her backwards until her back rested on its surface. His weight was upon her, and he began inching up her skirt with his hand, just like the pastor in Minnesota. Maila managed to get one hand free and swiftly used it to gouge his left eye.

Mr. Clark let out a furious howl of pain and backhanded Maila, sending her reeling into the wall.

"You bitch!" he screamed. But Maila was running down the hallway, past the bewildered receptionist. "You'll pay for this." She could hear his voice clear out onto the street.

It was like being struck twice by lightning. Humiliated by yet another man, she cried all the way back to The Dungeon. Once there, she ripped the suit from her body and flung it on the floor. The very suit that she carefully stitched by hand. Now, she took scissors to it and shredded it into a pathetic heap of scraps. She was done.

"No more show business for me," Maila wrote in her diary. *"Everyone concerned is FILTHY! In more ways than one!"*

If Papa insisted upon keeping her a prisoner in The Dungeon, then he could very well keep paying her rent. Why should she bother to look for a job at all? She was still a teenager who wanted to only hang out with her friends and have fun.

She took to sleeping all day and partying all night, which took a little creative storytelling to avoid being tossed out of Piikatalo for repeated curfew violations.

Upon the United States' entry into the war, young men were enlisting in droves. With their days numbered on home turf, they made their way to Broadway, which was considered the West Coast's version of Times Square.

Venues like The Diana Ballroom, the ballroom at the Hotel Figueroa, and the Zenda Ballroom Café were filled to capacity with jitterbugs and jivers. Tommy Dorsey was in town. Stan Kenton and his orchestra played the Palladium. Maila took it all in. If she had a date, that was fine, but most often, Maila and her gal pals wandered Broadway in a pack. And at least one night, she went solo and established herself as the belle of the ball.

Zenda's stag dance. Alone. Whee, I was a hit. I sat and refused eight or nine guys every dance before I danced just for fun!

Her birthday, Christmas, and New Year's Eve came and went. Maila spent the holidays with the Petersons and squandered the Christmas money from her parents and brother on fashion, food, and fun with friends. It was all so wonderful, until a letter from her mother threw water on her party.

"...your father has moved to Brooklyn, New York. He got a job as editor in chief of the New Yorkin Uutiset. I am staying in Astoria and working in the cannery until he gets settled and sends for me. I hope you are doing well. Have you found a job yet? Your father and I can't afford to send you money much longer. You need to work.

Love, Mother"

There it was. The pressure to be productive. To be responsible. To be an adult.

No matter what, she could not bear to be stuck behind a desk in an office like Paula. Or slinging hash like Gertie. Maila needed to be surrounded by beautiful things. Beautiful people creating beautiful things. Creative people, creating art.

Finally, a job with no walls or a boss breathing down her neck presented itself. She got a gig selling *Look* magazine subscriptions door to door. Girls were sent out in groups to canvass a predetermined area. Each was given a written text to memorize and told that success depended upon their appearance and powers of persuasion. They were dropped off at a specific location each morning and returned home at the end of the day.

It was a little like acting. Her instructions were to "flirt with the men, but not enough to make their wives jealous; compliment their children, pets, and gardens; dress appropriately; and smile." Maila couldn't wait to get home to practice her spiel in the mirror. Gale Bogdanovich, daughter of a wealthy San Diego family, was among Maila's group of sales associates. From day one, Maila and Gale hit it off and formed a strong friendship.

They spent the day canvassing, Maila on one side of the street, Gale on the other, competing to see who could sell the most. And like best friends, as they were becoming, they shared their innermost secrets, their hopes, and their dreams.

After a particularly disappointing day of sales in Torrance, Gale said, "Let's go to New York to live."

Her spontaneous proclamation hit Maila like a shot of adrenaline. It's where she wanted to go in the first place before her father intervened. She'd dreamed of being in New York City since she was a little girl. New York City was the home of artists, dreamers, creative minds, and freedom. Her mind raced with excitement as visions of Broadway, Times Square, and Radio City Music Hall flitted in her mind's eye.

But the reality was, she could never afford to go, let alone live there. Her pocketbook was empty.

"Oh, but we must," Gale insisted. "You have to help me with my six-month plan."

Although she'd been indulged her entire life, Gale's privilege had come at a price. Her father was determined to choose whom his daughter should marry, which, according to him, required a man "from a good, stable background with family business connections." The young men on her father's shortlist made Gale's skin crawl. She didn't want to get married. She wanted to be a movie star.

The deal was, if Gale could live independently for six months, without any financial help from her family, she would prove to her father that she was mature and capable of making her own life decisions.

For the next six months, Maila and Gale were on equal ground: young aspiring actresses with big dreams and barely a nickel between them.

For three months, Maila and Gale worked diligently and ratholed every penny, waiting for warmer weather before traveling east. In 1942 and still only 19, Maila was ahead of her time when, on a whim and little else, she dared to fly into uncharted territory. She deliberately chose not to tell her parents about her plans until the last minute. On her way to the bus depot, she dropped a letter into the mail.

The Greyhound lumbered along the rural Illinois roadway, making frequent stops to either pick someone up or let them off. The heat inside the airless bus, coupled with the thick stench of body odor, was becoming more unbearable by the minute.

A hundred miles outside of Chicago, a man got on board and took a seat across the aisle from Maila and Gale. He introduced himself. His name was Hank.

"Where are you going?" Gale asked.

"Just up the road," the man said. "I work the carnival circuit. I'm a roughie."

A roughie? The girls were intrigued. The man told them he was the equivalent of a nightclub bouncer—the guy who made sure that everything stayed on an even keel.

They told Hank they were actresses going to New York to work on Broadway, but the stinkmobile they were on made them think they'd be better off in Chicago. Anything to escape the heat and smell.

Hank had a better idea. If they didn't mind putting off New York for a week, the carnival was setting up just east of DeKalb, Illinois, and he suggested that the girls work there.

"I can tell you, girls as beautiful as you two could make ten dollars a day, maybe more. And that's money in your pocket. We feed you and give you a place to sleep."

The girls exchanged glances. It sounded too good to be true. But Maila was leery from her experiences with Kosloff and Clark and wanted to know exactly what was required of them to earn such good money.

"Wear costumes and walk around looking pretty."

Again, the girls exchanged glances to which Hank hastily added, "Don't worry, you keep your costumes on at all times. We're a respectable show."

"Ten dollars a day?" Maila wanted confirmation.

"At least," Hank assured her.

"What kind of costumes?"

"Nothing less than a bathing suit."

The promise of getting paid at the end of every night sealed the deal. At the next stop, the girls got off the bus with Hank.

In a farmer's field, the carnival was coming to life. The skeleton of the roller coaster was visible, and the Ferris wheel loomed high in the sky.

Carrying their suitcases, Maila and Gale walked with Hank up the newly rutted path to where perhaps 50 busy men were carrying boxes, hammering, and unfurling banners.

In the world of freak sideshows, this was a small carnival, not Ringling Brothers and Barnum & Bailey. Still, once the girls were set up in the "girl tent," they met the Gorilla Girl, the Tattooed Lady, the Rubber Girl, the girlie show strippers, and also the fakeroos, like Mermaid Girl.

Maila was curious about Mermaid Girl's costume and was particularly fascinated by the surprisingly heavy rubber fish tail. She wanted to know how the girl could tolerate wearing it.

"I sweat a lot, but I never have to diet anymore," she said. "I think it's the rubber."

The friendliest of the women, Mermaid Girl then gave Maila and Gale some timely advice. "Never go to the outhouse alone, always leave your suitcase open, don't ever 'screw around' with any of the men, and above all else, always carry your money in your brassiere."

She handed the girls two cloth bags, which she called grouches. "Put your dough in here," she instructed.

The girls emptied their wallets of money and traveler's checks. With their grouches in place, Maila shot Gale a quizzical look.

"You're all lumpy," she said.

Gale looked down at her chest. "It's my watch," she said. "I got it for graduation."

It was not only the watch but a strand of pearls as well. Added to her cash, it was too much for Gale's A-cup to conceal. The only solution was to divide up her loot with her treasureless pal Maila.

The mismatched girl tent sisterhood hunkered down for the night on beds of straw. It was uncomfortable and scratchy, and to make matters worse, the straw also served as the apparent sanctuary for numerous types of creepy-crawlers. Maila and Gale's loud complaints only produced laughter from the other women. And then a suggestion: They could trade sex for a real bed in one of the men's on-site trailers.

Maila and Gale suffered in silence for the remainder of the night.

On opening day, the midway was festooned with flashing lights, colorful balloons, and vividly painted banners. The stick shacks, with their games of chance and skill, were strategically positioned along both sides of the walkway, their prizes prominently displayed on shelves: pennants, posies, and pandas. The aroma of the concessionaires' greasy delights filled the air.

Maila and Gale meandered along the midway ready to put in their first full day of work as carnies. They were looking for their "office," otherwise known as the hoochie-coochie tent. It was the largest one along the back end, and there, a man named Mickey gave them the rundown on their duties.

They were the "outside girls" and worked in conjunction with the barker to get men to go inside the tent to see the strippers.

"Think of it like fishing," Mickey explained. "I'm the fisherman, and all them men outside are the fish. You girls, you're the lures. You can't catch no fish without a lure. The barker can take them guys to the fishing hole, but he can't make the fish bite. That's your job. The more wiggles, the more bites. We want this here tent full for the girlie show."

Mickey's abbreviated job description left no time before they were given aliases. No longer simply Maila and Gale, their assigned names were guaranteed to drive the fish mad.

"You," Mickey pointed at Gale, "you're Delectable Dora. And Blondie here is Luscious Lola."

"When you hear your name called, sashay your ass out there. Be as sexy as you can, but don't give nothin' away. No touching or grabbing allowed. Stand on the platform until the bally is over. By then, the poor bastards should be frothing at the mouth to get in. Once you get 'em inside the tent, you done your job until the next bally. And for chrissake, smile."

Maila and Gale tugged on their swimsuits and inserted the required bust pads, adjusting their grouches accordingly. A sequined length of felt, meant to pass for a beach towel, served as a prop. Their feet were squeezed into ill-fitting high heels to complete the look.

At the last moment, Gale whispered, "I don't think I can do this. I'm shaking so bad, I don't think my legs will hold me up."

There was no time for debate before the barker announced, "Delectable Dora!"

Maila grabbed her friend's hand and guided her a few steps out onto the platform, leaving her there. She didn't know what else to do. Gale was going to have to sink or swim on her own.

I remember standing there, & as one at a time their names were called, a girl would strut out onto the platform. Then I hear, "Luscious Lola," & I know it's my turn.

I was young & timid & very naïve. But here I was about to sashay my virginal ass out onto a catwalk wearing a flesh-colored swimsuit— meant to simulate nudity—to be ogled by frustrated farmers & drunken dilettantes. I don't even know if I smiled.

I was afraid to make eye contact with anyone in the sea of faces before me. I knew Ohio wasn't that far away, & even closer were some of the cities my father & I had toured not long before. My biggest fear was that someone I knew back in Ashtabula, or saw me on tour with Pa, would see my pathetic attempts at seduction. The Finns were a tight bunch. Perhaps some fallen angel had tumbled from his temperance nest & would recognize me & find a way to tell Papa of his daughter's shameful display.

We sashayed for hours, to and fro, feigning clumsiness at the drop of a sequined strip of felt—far into the night. I had blisters on my feet, & my bosoms were raw from Gale's gold. When Gale & I collected our pay, [it was] seven dollars each. Neither of us dared to question the amount. But we agreed that if the next night culminated in anything less than ten dollars, we would leave. It did, & we did. We fled without ever knowing where the strippers or Mermaid Girl concealed their grouches.

The Greyhound bus picked the girls up where, just two days before, they'd left with Hank and hearts full of hope.

Inside the bus, the heat was no less stifling and the odor no less foul than before. The only thing changed was the girls themselves. Their brief life as carnies left them more tolerant of life's petty annoyances. Maila and Gale hadn't bathed in a week, and the co-mingling of their own ripe body odor with that of the other passengers was no longer offensive. They were one with the masses.

An hour into the renewed ride east, the Greyhound stopped in Chicago. The carnival refugees, desperate for a bed, bath, and a decent meal, took one look at the Windy City and hightailed it off the bus. Their intended "just a night or two" stretched into a week. There, a fortune teller gladly relieved them of the remainder of their hoochie-coochie cash and then some.

Chapter Four

The Hotel Alexander at 306 West 94th Street in New York City seemed like the perfect place for two aspiring actresses to live on a budget. Sandwiched between the Hudson River and Broadway, the Theater District was easily accessible by bus.

In 1942, however, New York City was fully engaged in the war effort. Posters inundated public spaces extolling the virtues of buying war bonds. At night, the city was dark. The neon lights on Broadway and Times Square were low in observance of the "dim-out" to protect the city from any potential air or naval attack. No lights were permitted above street level. The upside was that, for the first time in decades, the moon and stars were visible from Times Square.

Six weeks in New York, and Maila and Gale were short of cash. Although one phone call to either of their fathers would erase their insolvency, both were determined not to allow a family bailout to taint their independence.

If Gale was "making a point," then so was Maila.

However, Gale's rich Uncle Herbert and his wife, who lived in a Central Park West penthouse, were not off-limits when it came to extracting a little succor in time of need. Even though Uncle Herbert was a terrible lech, Maila and Gale never passed up his invitation for a free meal. His wife, always nearby, chose to turn a blind eye to her husband's shameless attempts to grope their young dinner guests at every opportunity.

Jobs were plentiful, especially for women, since most of the young men had enrolled in the military. Women were training to become pilots and welders and shipfitters, learning to decode enemy communications or simply type reports. Maila wasn't interested in this type of work. But soon, one weekly free meal from Uncle Herbert wasn't enough to sustain the girls, so Maila went to work on the 44th floor of a high-rise owned by *McCall's* magazine. As a pantry girl, it was her job to wash and cut vegetables for salads and to transport them by elevator to the top-floor dining area.

Unfortunately, Maila was clumsy with a knife, and much like when she cleaned tuna in the cannery, she sustained numerous cuts to her hands and fingers before long. When a guest was served a plate with one of her Band-Aids splayed across a spear of asparagus, Maila was fired.

Waitress jobs were plentiful, but Maila stubbornly refused to wait tables.

> *I simply do not possess the required dexterity. The talent to balance four coffee cups while carrying six dinner plates must be cultivated while still in the womb, of which I was not so gifted.*

She did, however, consider herself capable of buttering toast and was hired on as a toaster girl. Presiding over a breakfast steam table in a hotel dining room, eggs congealed on plates waiting for her buttered masterpieces.

"Just slap a dab in the middle," the white-jacketed "egg man" said impatiently. "You're holding up the line."

Maila could not, in good conscience, leave the perimeters bare of butter.

"I will not," said Maila defiantly. "The edges get hard."

Another job lost.

With most of their money gone, Gale pawned her pearls and then her watch to pay their rent and meal tab.

In order to save their rapidly dwindling resources, the girls rationed their daily food consumption, eating only dinner.

> As money got tighter, Gale and I decided that the most sensible approach to life was to stay in bed all day to conserve calories. Certainly, the baking heat was more easily borne if we cast ourselves as twin Juliets, feigning morbidity. We were thus conserving our calories one afternoon when a knock came at the door.
>
> "The final eviction," I cried. Gale, less convinced, leapt from the bed to see who it was.
>
> "It's a man selling War Bonds," she announced.
>
> "Tell him to go away," I said. "We're paupers."
>
> Gale tried, but he wouldn't leave. "He says if we love our country, we'll find a way to earn the money. Besides, he says we can pay later."
>
> After a pause, she added, "He only needs two more signatures and then he can go home."
>
> "Tell him we are starving and want to die peacefully." I turned my face to the wall.
>
> "If we just sign our names, he says he'll buy us each a hamburger."

It was a cruel sales pitch. As Gale led the man inside, Maila pulled the covers over her head, signed her name in the dark, and then waited for the young man to bring back the goods. Devouring their food, the girls agonized over having lied to their government in its time of crisis for a lousy seven-cent White Castle burger.

Uncle Herbert was growing weary of the cat-and-mouse game. In a last-gasp effort, he invited them to dinner at the revolving restaurant atop Radio City Music Hall. Fortunately, the octogenarian was no match for Gale and Maila.

As they were enjoying their shrimp cocktails, Uncle Herbert was making yet another unfulfilled offer to buy Maila a new dress, when the entire dining room was plunged into darkness. It was only a temporary electrical malfunction, not a wartime blackout. Nevertheless, Uncle Herbert was determined to use the darkness to his advantage and make yet another desperate attempt at fondling his niece, but she retaliated by stabbing him with her oyster fork.

When the light was restored, the first thing Maila saw was the old man's hand dripping blood on the tablecloth and then a waiter hurrying over to tend to Uncle Herbert.

Later that night, the girls admitted their sole purpose of coming to New York was to hone their acting skills while waiting for Gale's independence clock to expire. But instead, they'd managed to fritter away their allotted time without so much as stepping foot inside the Theater District.

Gale confessed to a case of stage fright so severe, it rendered her mute on stage. Now Maila understood why Gale made excuses whenever she suggested they audition for roles.

"Delectable Dora did not have stage fright," Maila said.

"Dora didn't have to speak," Gale explained.

From that night on, the girls became quietly competitive in their nonexistent acting careers. Even before the genesis of the Beat Generation, Maila held the belief that material possessions contributed nothing to happiness. Rather, it was freedom she valued. The freedom to think and express oneself was, to her, the greatest joy life can offer.

> *Gale was the poor little rich girl, & I was the rich little poor girl—rich with ardent passions & dramatic expectations of magic. Rich with a boundless love of life. It didn't matter that our shoestring scavenging had prevented us from getting anywhere near Broadway or that our budget allowed little sustenance. Every breath I breathed was wondrous! Freedom was my sunshine & hope was my vitamin.*

After the stabbing incident, Uncle Herbert's gratuitous nature evaporated, and shortly thereafter, the girls were booted out of their room for unpaid rent. Gale, out of jewelry to hock, preferred to wait out her six months of independence by reading movie magazines and dreaming of food, which left Maila responsible for their income. And she did that, getting hied on at the Horn & Hardart automat in the heart of Times Square, refilling the open slots with salads, sandwiches, and desserts. Unfortunately, at the time of their eviction, Maila was between paydays, and they needed to find someplace to sleep for the next week. Would it be Central Park or the Greyhound bus station? Either way, they were doomed to share space with addicts, criminals, vagrants, and prostitutes. Since they carried their worldly possessions in suitcases, the Greyhound station seemed the logical choice.

"Too soon, it was time for Gale to go home and replenish her strand of graduated pearls," Maila said with genuine sadness. In saying their goodbyes, the girls promised to be friends forever, hugged and cried until their makeup ran down their faces.

As the bus departed, Gale waved from the open window and shouted, "Maila Niemi, I can still act circles around you!"

The last six months had been like a never-ending slumber party. But now the laughs and giggles were over, and Maila was broke and alone. She stayed in bed for the better part of a week and lost her job. She didn't care; she'd find another.

The third-floor yarn factory on Mott Street was hot and thankless work. Maila spent most days pushing around three-hundred-pound bins of yarn and wondering how she got herself in the same sort of mess that caused her to flee Astoria. But because there was now rent to pay, her situation seemed even more dire. Every bit as dire as her mother's.

For months, Sophie's letters to her daughter pleaded with her to go see her father. She desperately wanted to join her husband in Brooklyn and begged Maila to intercede on her behalf. With Bobbie now in the Army, Sophie was alone in Astoria, working in the cannery and waiting for a letter from Onni, saying it was time for her to join him. And yet in all the months Maila was in New York, she never once contacted her father.

Finally, Maila went to Brooklyn to see her father, not to plead for her mother's sake but to ask for the money for her to return to Los Angeles.

The New Yorkin Uutiset was a three-story brick building at 4418 Eighth Avenue. Maila found her father working at his typewriter. The brass nameplate on his desk read:

Onni K. Syrjäniemi
Editor-in-Chief

I hadn't seen him since I left home, & certainly not since he had so callously abandoned my mother in Astoria.

I cautiously told him of the purpose of my visit: that I wanted to return to Los Angeles. Thanks to Mama's continuous letter writing campaign, I'm sure he was well aware how long I'd been in New York, & I hoped he would at least give me credit for surviving in the wild without his financial help for as long as I did. He did not.

I think he was happy that New York hadn't worked out for me, but of course, I was subjected to his condemnations concerning my choices, and there I was, held as his captive audience for perhaps an hour.

When at last he had satisfied his own ego & had deemed himself the ultimate authority on my life, he pulled out his wallet & handed me the dough. But only after I agreed that once I arrived in Los Angeles, I would again become a prisoner at Piikatalo. He would pay my rent for three months but would send the checks directly to the management. It was apparent, he didn't trust me. But perhaps, sensing my despair, & in an unsuccessful attempt to soothe my wounded spirit, he wished for me to be safe and well & ended with his customary parting words:

"Good luck." And why wouldn't he. In the Finnish language, onni is the word for luck.

For his part, Onni was frustrated with the women in his family. His wife an alcoholic, and his daughter an unsettled dreamer. If she'd stayed in college, he'd be eager to help financially, but he could not in good conscience continue to support a lifestyle he did not understand or condone. Maila ignored the topic of her parents' unresolved separation. With cash in hand, it was time to head back to Los Angeles.

Hollywood wasn't the same. Now it was teeming with servicemen in uniform, most waiting to be shipped out overseas. Just as in New York City, the entertainment industry was galvanized in its support of the war effort. Most of the celebrities gave generously of their time, money, and talents toward entertaining the troops free of charge. Rationing put a crimp in the production of movies, and big-budget films were no longer practical. The result was that even the most in-demand stars were not working. Consequently, there were precious few opportunities for someone like Maila to break into the business.

As if the decreasing demand for new talent wasn't bad enough, Maila was confined to living at Piikatalo. She hated everything about it: the communal chores, the rules, and especially the 11 o'clock curfew. She craved freedom. But as long as her father was paying the rent, she was stuck.

And so, she tried very hard to find employment. She filled out applications for salesgirl, usherette, concessionaire, girl Friday. No luck. Then, just when her three months were about to expire, she landed a job.

The Broadway department store, located on the iconic corner of Hollywood and Vine, put out the call for temporary help to assist with the upcoming holiday season and its subsequent year-end inventory. The Broadway was upscale, geared to accommodate the celebrity pocketbook rather than that of the average working stiff. Maila didn't care that she could never afford to shop there. Paid to spend the day amid the latest fashions was its own reward.

It did not go unnoticed that Maila was blossoming into a real beauty. When she was asked to model hats for the store's print ads, she jumped at the chance. A beautiful face sells the hat, and in that regard, Maila was a milliner's dream.

As soon as Maila was able to rub two nickels together, she moved out of Piikatalo and into the Commodore Hotel. There, she befriended a young woman named Junie. Junie claimed to be Georgia-born and -raised but spoke without a trace of her Southern roots—until she was in the presence of a potential suitor. Then, Junie morphed into "Junebug," the sugar-tongued she-devil from Macon.

It was Junie's birthday, and on this night of all nights, the girl was without a date. That's how Maila came to be riding the Red Car with Junie wearing her best black taffeta dress and feathered hat.

No girl should have to be alone on her birthday.

The girls got gussied up, piled their hair atop their heads, and applied copious amounts of makeup.

Although they had but a few dollars between them, Junie assured Maila, "The way we look, money won't be a problem."

Junie wanted to look for movie stars, specifically Randolph Scott, with whom she was obsessed. A friend of hers had seen the handsome actor exit the Brown Derby on Vine Street a few days before, and that's where the birthday girl was certain she'd find him.

They couldn't get past the front door. After a less than warm reception, it was apparent that the girls were not considered important enough to gain access. And Junie was convinced that was because Randolph Scott was in attendance. Nevertheless, the Georgia peach wasn't about to give up entirely. If not Randolph Scott, she would settle for tracking down Errol Flynn, who at that very moment might well be tossing back a few at Musso & Frank.

Maila thought it seemed like a lot of trouble for dessert and a cup of coffee, which is all they could afford, but she went along because it was Junie's night to celebrate.

The front entrance of Musso & Frank opened onto Hollywood Boulevard,

Modeling hats for The Broadway department store, Christmas, 1942,
six months before she met Orson Welles.

but Junie, apparently more knowledgeable about such things, led Maila around the building to another door. A solitary soldier walked toward them, and in the blink of an eye, Junie looped her arm through that of the startled young man. In sugared tones, she spoke. "Suh, if you would be so kind as to escort two lonely girls inside, we would be evah so grateful."

I had never once been in a bar without a male escort. It simply was not done.

We two were now three, & in this particular situation, three was a crowd. I sat there listening to Junebug prattle on in her manufactured drawl & planned my escape.

My eyes having at last accustomed to the dim lighting, I heard this glorious voice. I whirled around & there, seated near the back, was my one true god, Orson Welles!

Well, I paid no mind to manners or protocol, & instead rushed over & descended upon him like a crazed peahen & sputtered idiotically, "Why you're Orson Welles..." or something equally as asinine.

His response, his exact words, were: "Why, yes, indeed I am. And who might you be, my winsome lass?"

I spewed accolades down upon him & his astonished guests until I realized that I'd rudely interrupted his conversation with his companions. Mortified by my outburst, I apologized & returned to my table to find Junie & her soldier boy were gone. I had been ditched.

Humiliated twice in such rapid succession, I considered what to do next. Remain seated like an available trollop or retreat to the sidewalk in haughty indignation. My as-yet-untouched cocktail was at the ready, and I greedily swallowed half of it in one delirious, unladylike swig. Its fire brought tears to my eyes, & momentarily stole my breath away. I couldn't walk home; it was much too far. While I decided how to get myself out of this predicament, I finished my cocktail with as much dignity as I could muster while reveling in the pleasure of sharing air with the incomparable Mr. Welles.

I no sooner set down my glass when I heard the voice again. This time, it was attached to its owner, on the right in my peripheral vision. "Excuse me, Miss, but my friends seem to have abandoned me. Would you care to join me?"

It was he! Orson Welles! Had he witnessed me swill my Manhattan like a seasoned Skid Row bum? Regardless, the Master was requesting that I join him for conversation. My feet did not come in contact with the earth as I moved to his corner booth.

Once ensconced with Mr. Welles, I complimented him in a more controlled way. I told him how I dreamed of a career in radio, which began a discussion on the subject. All the while, I sat entranced, simply mesmerized by the sound of his golden voice & at the same time being all atingle [sic] at the nearness of him. He said he was currently planning an outdoor extravaganza, a spectacular show to entertain American men & women in uniform. Admission would be free to all servicemen & was to be some sort of carnival or magic show. Magic being his "true passion," he said. Of course, at the mere mention of "carnival," I immediately revealed to him my brief experience in the strut-and-smile sideshow—which heretofore had been something I swore never to divulge to a living soul.

Welles went on to explain he wanted to provide a place where the servicemen could escape the uncertainty of their lives, if only for a few hours. And then he asked Maila if she would like to participate in the occasion. It wasn't a position for which she could expect payment, as all participants volunteered their services in support of the war effort.

Orson Welles, 1942. Associated Press file photo.

Maila must have felt as if her heart had leaped out of her chest. An invitation to be near her idol as he literally plied his magic was too good to be true.

Their conversation ended, and Maila prepared to leave when Welles offered to provide transportation by calling a cab. But Maila declined, not wanting to impose further upon his largesse. She told him she could walk home, without mentioning the fact she was wearing heels and was miles from home.

"Nonsense," he said. "I shall call you a taxi." And so I acquiesced. And then, the both of us were standing at the curb & Mr. Welles put his arm across my shoulders, turns me toward him & kissed me! Not just some little cheek peck, but on the lips—and on Hollywood Boulevard for all the world to see. I thought I was either dreaming or perhaps dead and in heaven.

Maila got into the taxi, and to her surprise, Welles followed. "You don't have a phone," he explained. "How else would I ever find you?"

At the Commodore, Welles asked the cab to wait while he escorted Maila up to her door. He did not kiss her again but thanked her for the evening and stated that he would stay in touch.

Funny how life is. It was Junie who set out to find her idol, and instead, I found mine.

Maila never expected to see or hear from Welles again. But in short order, a bouquet of flowers arrived for her at the front desk of the hotel. The attached card said a car would pick her up that night for dinner and was signed "Mr. Wilson." Maila didn't know anyone named Wilson. She dared not think they were from Welles, but indeed they were.

Our dinner conversation was nearly consumed with his chatting about this magic show he was producing. After dinner, Orson asked if I would care to see his etchings. Yes! He said just that. He was very excited about this project, and since I was to be a part of this whole process, I eagerly accepted his invitation. While there weren't etchings, there WERE drawings. Sketches of the carnival he was planning. Orson's home in West Hollywood on Hacienda was an unassuming bungalow—not the kind of place I had envisioned a celebrity of his magnitude would live.

I was a virgin. Pure as the driven snow. But this man in front of me was Orson Welles. The genius, this God in the flesh. I swooned. I nearly collapsed. I was breathless. I was in love.

The first time Orson saw me scantily clad in a boudoir, he said, "Magnificent carcass." I was in love for the very first time so that, when he advanced upon me, I resisted little. Indeed, I was yet so naïve as to believe that I was giving myself to my future husband.

Sex was nothing like I imagined. I found it was more painful than pleasurable. But here I was, being groped and penetrated by a man who nearly suffocated me in the course of his lovemaking. For a moment, I panicked when I realized I couldn't escape his weight upon me.

In retrospect, Orson was not a gentle lover & was possessed of an urgency to complete the act. But then, I thought I was in love and sex was simply a way to prove my neverending devotion.

Subsequent encounters followed. Each time it began with a simple note from "Mr. Wilson" attached to a bouquet of flowers, stating the arrival time of the car to pick her up.

Over the weeks, however, Maila's and Welles' couplings became more infrequent, and she was worried that he had already grown tired of her or, even worse, taken another lover. She'd willingly given her virginity to Orson, and now he was missing from her life. What did it mean? She couldn't eat and couldn't sleep. It was inconceivable that her beloved Orson could be such a cad. She wouldn't allow herself to think that.

When after another week there was still no word from Welles, Maila grew frantic. Impulsively, she hopped on a bus and went to the Hacienda address.

Dim lights illuminated the front window. She knocked on the door and it was opened by a man wearing a bathrobe. But it was not Orson.

Maila explained that she came to see Mr. Welles. The man denied knowing anyone by that name. "Maybe you know him by Mr. Wilson," she tried. The man assured her that no one by either name lived there and closed the door.

I knew that man in the bathrobe was lying!!! Lying! Why would
he do that?

She waited another week and when no invitations were forthcoming, Maila decided she would have to find Welles herself to get the answer. She wouldn't demean herself again by appearing unannounced at the bungalow, but she could go see about this carnival business. It was where Orson promised her work, only to later rescind his offer with "It would be maddeningly distracting for me to work so near you, my love."

On Cahuenga Boulevard, Welles' extravaganza was in full swing. It was touted in all the trade papers as a spectacular display of mystery, magic, and mayhem.

Outside the cordoned area of circus tents, the streets were filled with men in uniform. As Junie had done, Maila latched onto a passing soldier, and she and her borrowed escort were waved through the admissions gate. She vaguely scanned the posters that lined the bally and suddenly stopped short. She couldn't believe her eyes. The face of the man in the bathrobe was staring down at her.

It was the actor Joseph Cotten.

Maila was young and unsophisticated in the ways of the world, but she knew the implications of seeing that poster. The two men, Welles and Cotten, conspired to rent the Hacienda house for the sole purpose of entertaining their paramours.

According to Maila, the realization came while retching into the toilet for the third morning in a row. She was pregnant. And as she always did in times of extreme stress, she took to her bed. Only when she'd devised a course of action did she get up and dress.

She composed a note to Orson. There were no words of passion. No words of undying love. No words to betray their relationship should the note be intercepted. Her note asked only that he contact her immediately, as it was a "matter of life and death." It was signed simply "Maila."

She left the note with the manager at Musso & Frank, with his assurance it would be hand-delivered to Welles.

She waited and waited. Welles never replied. And a cold, desperate, empty feeling came over her.

I was just a girl. A nameless, faceless girl that he'd fucked. Nothing more. Nothing less. At 20, my life was over.

The news came over the radio. "This morning, Orson Welles and Rita Hayworth were married in a civil ceremony at City Hall."

Chapter Five

Out of options and in sheer desperation, Maila called her mother. "Mama, I'm pregnant!" She couldn't catch her breath for all the sobbing. It was like she was five years old again.

Of course, Sophie was stunned. She told Maila they needed to tell her father, which caused Maila to cry even more.

"No, I'd rather die than tell him. He'll never forgive me," she wailed.

Sophie finally convinced Maila that the situation demanded that they be together as a family.

As soon as he learned of Maila's predicament, Onni wired the money so that his wife and daughter could meet in Seattle, then proceed together on a train to New York. Further decisions would be made once they arrived.

It was a difficult trip made worse by the summer heat and Maila's waves of nausea. Even worse was the thought of having to face her father. She could only imagine what he must think of her.

To Sophie's credit, she did not ask Maila the obvious question. She knew better than to ask who the baby's father was. Her daughter was suffering enough. But she knew there was a man out there who was responsible for leaving Maila pregnant and alone, and it burned a hole of hatred in her heart. She only hoped that someday she might exact revenge upon the cad. Until that time, she appeased her hostile feelings in the club car.

Imagine Onni's thoughts when he met the train and caught sight of his unwed, pregnant daughter and his drunken wife teetering beside her. Whatever Onni's true feelings were, the women in his family were in crisis, and he would do what he could.

Onni's apartment was not intended to house a family. When they arrived, Onni declared that Maila's "situation" precluded her from sleeping on the sofa, and he claimed it for himself, which left Sophie and Maila to share the only bed.

To Maila's complete surprise and relief, her father issued no judgments upon her. Neither did he wave the finger of blame in her face, nor chastise her. If he was appalled by her pregnancy, he did not voice it. If he was unhappy with her, he did not show it. Instead, he recused himself from making any decisions beyond offering them a place to live. As far as he was concerned, Maila's condition was women's business.

His one request was directed at his wife: no alcohol.

The difficult decision of what to do about the baby loomed large. Sophie pointed out that Maila couldn't even take care of herself, let alone a baby. Adoption, she said, was the only choice, and Maila reluctantly agreed. The baby deserved both a mother and father who would provide a better life than she could. But still, Maila remained conflicted. When the time came, would she be able to follow through and hand her baby over to strangers?

Maila was in limbo. At 20, she felt her life was forever ruined. No man would ever want her after learning she had a baby outside of marriage. She had to hide from the world, while Welles went about his charmed life, married to Hollywood's most glamorous star. How she hated him—and Rita as well. She wouldn't allow herself to buy any of her beloved movie magazines for fear of seeing an article about the happy newlyweds.

Maila's appetite eventually returned, and she began to eat without moderation, but when Onni caught sight of his daughter standing in profile, he commented on her growing girth. "Of course she's put on weight," Sophie lashed out. "She's having a baby."

So strong was Onni's denial, he looked as if he was hearing the awful news for the first time. It was an innocent observation; nonetheless, Maila was traumatized, and she took to eating almost nothing but raw vegetables. Raw potatoes in particular.

Onni resigned himself to the fact that Sophie was too far into her disease to abstain from alcohol. He'd seen her tremble while drinking a cup of coffee, needing both hands to hold it. With a baby coming—something he wanted nothing to do with—he supposed that if his wife needed to calm her nerves in order to facilitate the birthing process, he'd have to relent just once more. To him, childbirth was a mystery best left for women to contend with. Maila needed her mother now more than ever, and so Onni allowed his wife to drink as long as she maintained an even keel and the liquor was kept out of sight.

As the baby's arrival approached, Maila was glad to be soon relieved of the pregnancy but increasingly apprehensive. She was terrified of the childbirth process. Sophie tried to calm her fears, but any discussion invariably led Maila into a state of high anxiety.

Maila was sent to a birthing home to wait out the remainder of her pregnancy. There, she would give birth, recuperate, and then return home without her baby.

On March 11, 1944, I spewed forth a son. It was an excruciatingly painful experience & one that I vowed never to repeat. I thrashed & cried out in agony, alone and afraid, save for the doctor & a cruel nurse, who kept tightening my restraints each time I made a sound. She kept telling me to be quiet and that it didn't hurt that bad. Later, I learned she had never given birth herself.

The child was born wailing, and they laid him on my stomach while they cut the cord. While he was still wet from the trauma of being thrust so unceremoniously into this world, I was allowed a brief

moment to see my son. He was bald & looked ever so much like a plump
& peeled potato—the most beautiful little potato in the world. In that
moment, my mother's heart yearned to snatch him up & run away. But
then he was gone.

Her infant son was born healthy and, according to Sophie, was adopted by a "rich Jewish couple" from New Jersey. What would he think if he knew his father was Orson Welles, the author, actor, and producer of arguably the greatest movie of all time? And that his mother, Maila Nurmi, starred as Vampira in the worst movie of all time. That's quite a birthright. So, whoever and wherever you are, if you're an adopted male born on March 11, 1944, this is your life, my cousin.

Too young to remain bitter, but too old to be content living with parents, Maila began to piece together her shattered life. And once more, her father opened his wallet and financed her move to the Lower East Side of Manhattan in the summer of 1944, where the rent was cheap. Her apartment building was located near a slaughterhouse, just south of what is now the United Nations building.

In her renewed effort to find work in show business, Maila developed a new strategy. If she was ever to succeed, she determined she must either live or work in close proximity to the rich and famous. And since slaughterhouses were not conducive to attracting society's elite, Maila set out to find work that would expose her to Broadway's movers and shakers.

On the northeast corner of Madison and 50th, a seven-hundred-room luxury hotel, The New Weston, advertised for a bellhop. Maila figured if she could give birth, she could carry a couple of suitcases. Exhibiting a newfound confidence, she applied for the position. Management balked at hiring a woman. Maila pointed out that most of the boys were gone to war, and her perseverance finally won them over.

It was busier than usual one afternoon when I was called to help a mother & her adult son check out of the hotel. Since I was barely aware of politics, I only dimly recognized the importance of their names: Eleanor Roosevelt & Franklin Roosevelt, Jr. The mother was tall & preoccupied but flashed me a warm smile. I knew that I might expect as much as a fifty cent tip from them, & happily grabbed the two-suiter from Mr. Roosevelt and started down the hall with it.

Jr. grabbed it back, protesting, "My dear, I can't possibly let you carry this."

I protested back, "Please!" I was used to carrying two that size, plus two more suitcases, & I didn't want to lose the tip. I wrested the bag away from him & hurried on. When I set it down to punch up the elevator, Mr. Roosevelt took his bag again, & smiled with patronizing triumph. I must have whined with a voice that betrayed my despair & greed, for suddenly his towering mother, who up til then had been distracted and absent, came to life.

"Franklin, let the girl take it. It's her work, dear."

I carried the bag the rest of the way & was tipped an unheard-of dollar.

Four days a week, she worked the elevator on the residential side of the hotel. But on Tuesdays, Maila was promoted to doorman, and it was then that she was most visible to the public.

The novelty of a woman schlepping bags and whistling down cabs grabbed the attention of the press, and *The New York World-Telegram and Sun* sent out a reporter and photographer to do a story on New York's first "belle hop."

Maila's photo in the newspaper captured the attention of photographer Ewing Krainin. Krainin was enjoying recognition for his recent work when his photos of model Chili Williams were published in *Life* magazine. Maila was flattered to learn that Krainin wanted to arrange a photo shoot. She was well aware of the man's credentials and assumed him to be nothing like the sleazy Kosloff.

She stood in Krainin's studio, fully clothed, the photographer's light trained upon her. He studied the contours of Maila's face and then circled around her like a panther stalking its prey. His assessment was candid.

"Ah, you are about 15 pounds over from being perfect for fashion photography. But you possess great beauty and can easily model for headshots."

> *Our sitting was poignantly horrible. He asked me to hold a sheer silk scarf in front of my naked torso. Not again! But I was too brave not to do it, and too cowardly not to cry. To make matters worse, he insisted on taking portraits of my swollen, traumatized countenance. These days I suppose he would be called kinky and exploitive. Then, I just thought he was an artist.*

At least, this time, there was no rouge.

As public interest in the girl bellhop abated, Maila's job became routine, and the bourgeois beast began to breathe down her neck. It was time for her to move on. The Park Avenue club, La Rue, was just the kind of place Maila was looking for: so snooty, its patrons were required to be listed in the Social Register. It was here that Maila hoped to connect with Broadway's elite.

Unfortunately, LaRue's strict dress code challenged the way Maila planned to attract attention to herself. The cigarette girls were required to present themselves in what can best be described as Eastern European Army vogue. She complained about slicking her hair back into a tight chignon knotted at the nape of her neck, as well as the tailored gray suit worn over a turtleneck, which she said, "pushed modesty up my throat." It was boring work, strolling leisurely among the guests, offering smokes and hoping to make enough tips to pay the rent so that the entire charade could be repeated over again.

Maila quickly grew tired of the pretense and of the clientele's seeming engrossment in their artificial world. But most of all, she hated being invisible. She needed to shake things up.

When she spied some grapefruit in the kitchen, the answer became apparent. She stuffed two of the grapefruits into her brassiere before returning to the floor with suddenly enormous bosoms. With the grace of a ballerina, she glided from table to table, pausing demurely to ask, in her best Radcliffe College girl affect, "Cigars? Cigarettes? Grapefruit?"

The spectacle was noticed only by her boss, who tried to reprimand her through fits of laughter. But Maila had made her point. "These people never see servants," she explained.

Her resolve to work among the rich eventually dissolved, and Maila grew weary of catering to the thrice-named blue bloods of the world. Days spent immersed in their pretentiousness had siphoned off her creativity, and Maila needed to reacquaint herself with the common man.

The Hobo News, or as Maila called it, "the paper of the great unwashed," was a weekly newspaper printed for anyone who was curious enough to pay a dime for it. The hobos, remnants from the Great Depression, still commanded a presence. Several of them banded together and moved into a space on East 23rd and Third Avenue.

For Maila, it was like being back in Ashtabula in Mrs. Barsetti's kitchen. Just past the business end of the enterprise, the office opened up into a large space where an endless pot of stew simmered for the hungry and provided a place to flop for anyone who needed it. The family dynamics were in constant flux as some hobos moved on and others arrived. Occasionally, a lady hobo chanced by. Maila held those women in the highest regard and marveled at their courage and fearlessness.

It was then that Maila developed a deep compassion for the homeless and disenfranchised that remained a part of her for the rest of her life. In some ways, their transient lifestyle somewhat mirrored her own life, and she felt comfortable among them.

And so began Maila's brief but satisfying sojourn into the world of journalism, as she became a columnist for *The Hobo News*. Her father could finally be proud of her.

Drawing upon her recent fly-on-the-wall observations regarding the privileged, she named her column "The Comings and Goings of the Four Hundred"—the precise number allowed on the Social Register. With a natural satirical wit, Maila took to writing her column with great enthusiasm.

Week after week, the hobos laughed themselves sick over Maila's essays. Buoyed by their reaction, she decided to try selling the newspaper as well. If she were successful, she could garner enough tips to survive. But to do that, she needed a hook, a gimmick, something to drum up interest.

Duffy's Tavern, a popular Irish pub at 156 West 48th Street, was just the sort of place where the aspiring actress in Maila could perform her shtick. No matter that her audience was almost always intoxicated; they were happy and generous drunks, unlike the stingy and suicidal alcoholics on 8th Street.

Maila set upon creating a couple of characters, crafted to persuade Duffy's patrons to part with their money in exchange for a copy of *The Hobo News*. She haunted the secondhand clothing shops to come up with costumes. "Dahling Dietrich" wore an inordinate amount of makeup and spoke in a German-accented contralto. She swept into Duffy's dressed in a long pleated reefer coat and a wide-brimmed slouch hat, which was precariously positioned to one side. On alternate weeks, "Countess Coo-Coo" arrived with a bundle of newspapers. Dressed in white from turban to fur-cuffed boots, she exuded confidence. Maila dazzled the crowd in her thrift store costume: a rhinestone-encrusted ascot, a Joan Crawford-shouldered dress, and an oversized costume ring on an index finger.

I would wait at the end of the bar with my stack of newspapers til
someone put on a selection from the jukebox. Once music was playing,
I danced and passed out all the papers & announced, "This is your
Hobo News."

At the end of her performance, the Countess would plug her column and collect the money, usually realizing a hefty 90-cent profit from each ten-cent newspaper.

Countess Coo-Coo and Dahling Dietrich were very successful characters for Maila and caught the attention of a trio of legitimate columnists: Damon Runyan, Walter Winchell, and Irving Hoffman. At one time or another, each of the three called the apartments above Duffy's Tavern their home.

In particular, Irving Hoffman, drama critic and columnist for the gossipy and influential entertainment trade newspaper *The Hollywood Reporter*, took an interest in Maila.

In Hoffman, Maila found not only a friend but a guardian—an older gentleman whom she could trust. To Hoffman, Maila was not only a talented and beautiful young woman, but she was a delightful dinner guest who laughed easily and shared his sense of humor. Especially when the humor rose from his renowned bad eyesight. One evening while dining at the Stork Club, Hoffman bent so near his tea water that he scalded the tip of his nose.

The nearsighted columnist came to play a pivotal role in Maila's life. Respected by his peers, Hoffman could and often did command the ear of his dear friend, Walter Winchell. And it was just that kind of influence which offered Maila a chance to audition for theater producer Mike Todd.

"Get to the Forrest Theatre on Seventh Avenue at 51st." It was Hoffman on the phone. "Winchell said they're holding auditions for a new Mae West show."

Maila was at work painting neckties on an assembly line when she got the call, and she left for the theater as soon as she could clean her brushes. There was no time to change out of her black slacks and oversized men's white shirt covered in paint splatters. Nor could she do anything about her yellow fingernails and blue toenails, evidence of a recent nail polish sale at Woolworth's.

Upon arriving, Maila's heart sank. At least a hundred young hopefuls awaited an audition. Just the month earlier, Billy Rose told her, "It's a damn shame you're not an inch taller." Rose and Mike Todd fought tooth and nail over the most beautiful chorus girls, and now here she was again, about to audition her heart out, this time for Todd. Out in the empty auditorium, Maila made out an audience of two: Todd and his director, Roy Hargrave.

It was down to the final selections. Every part was cast except for the ladies-in-waiting. All the aspiring actresses lined up and nervously hoped to be chosen for the last six roles.

Maila stood at attention, figuring she and the rest must be among the ugliest women in all of New York. On Broadway, it was common knowledge that Miss West demanded her directors surround her with only the most nondescript females.

One by one, someone was singled out for a role. Then, Mr. Hargrave called out the words that would change Maila's life: "The girl with the blue toenails."

"Mama, Mama, I got the part. I'm on Broadway!"

Maila could scarcely believe it. She was chosen to be handmaiden to Mae West's character, the Empress of Russia, in *Catherine Was Great*. Her Broadway debut paid 45 dollars a week and meant there'd be no more painting neckties or juggling two jobs to make ends meet.

Rehearsals began for the August premiere at the Shubert Theatre.

The ladies-in-waiting doubled as peasant wives. The opening scene called for one of the wives to receive the news that her husband had been killed. To Maila's astonishment, Hargrave, the director, chose her to be the recipient of the awful news. Instructed to scream, she was then directed to crumple into a faint. Maila was not about to let this opportunity pass without fanfare. She let loose with a piercing, prolonged wail, the same sort she would later make famous.

The scream was sensational; the faint needed work. When Maila fell on her leg, a tingle shot up her spine, but there was no time to recover before hastily transitioning to a dance number. Unfortunately, Maila's leg went numb from her collapse, and after several missteps, the exasperated director called for a break.

The rehearsals continued for several days in preparation of scrutiny by its star and playwright, Mae West. Among the theater folk, West was known as a notorious snob—demanding and petty. So when the day arrived for the grand reveal, it came as no surprise when Hargrave announced that the cast was not to joke, whisper, or move off their marks. As a final word of caution, Hargrave demanded, "No one is to speak directly to Miss West."

Not unlike a military troop awaiting inspection, this troupe waited in rigid silence for the star to appear. And when she did, she was nothing like Maila expected.

> *I saw that her movie stature was only an illusion of the camera. She was really a tiny little biscuit of a girl. She wore an Aunt Jemima scarf tied round her weary peroxided hair & walked on tall, awkward platform shoes. She wore a faded peignoir that likely began its life as pink but had since grayed with age. The garment was cut on the bias, revealing a surprisingly buoyant cleavage even as her pot belly gave away her age. She wore no make-up, save for a huge pair of black nylon eyelashes. I didn't understand why a purported legend could not afford a new bathrobe.*

For the benefit of Miss West, the peasant scene unfolded; on cue, Maila screamed and collapsed into a swoon. West watched motionless from a chair at the corner of the stage. At the completion of the scene, there was only glacial silence. The director crouched near his star so she would not have to hold her head up or raise her voice. Concerning Maila's performance, West uttered a simple question.

"Does it have to be so big?"

And with that, Maila's moment was cut.

That was not the worst of it. One of the other peasant girls missed a step, which Maila claimed caused her to stumble and fall into another dancer. A domino effect of flailing peasantry ensued. The choreographer exploded into a torrent of accusations directed at Maila. The troupe took the tirade as call for a break, as Maila fell to the floor declaring her innocence and weeping.

Old Bob, the stage manager, approached and put a hand on her shoulder.

"Maila," he said, "let me tell you something. I've been in this business for a long time. The thing you're going to have to learn is that temperament is for stars."

On August 2, 1944, Maila made her Broadway debut in Mike Todd's *Catherine Was Great*. Having altered the spelling of her first name, she was billed as Mila Niemi.

The reviews were less than kind. The August 21, 1944 issue of *Life* proclaimed, "Catherine Was Great, but Mae West makes her dull." The consensus was that West took herself and her play much too seriously. Regardless, *Catherine* continued to draw large audiences.

Midway through the show's run, Maila's castmate revealed that she was hopelessly in love with a fellow actor who ignored her. The young man, who was making his Broadway debut in *I Remember Mama*, was a real heartbreaker. After two weeks of listening to the girl's lovesick histrionics, Maila said, "I'll fix that," and set out at four in the morning to confront the scoundrel.

Armed with a name and an address, she walked up to his door and knocked sharply. When the door was opened by the half-asleep young man, Maila lit into him. It was a talent she'd honed to perfection. But on this night, what started out as a tongue-lashing changed quickly when the man invited her inside.

His name was Marlon Brando. Maila left his home when the sun was high in the sky, having given more than just a piece of her mind to the young actor. After that first encounter, her friendship with the jilted castmate ended, while her relationship with Brando endured for decades.

Although Maila was never allowed to speak directly to Miss West, she began to sense that the star disliked her. During rehearsals, through whispered conversations between West and Hargrave, Maila was singled out for a purported misstep or an ill-timed movement time after time. Some of the other ladies-in-

Marlon Brando, 1955. Michael Ochs, Michael Ochs Archives via Getty Images.

waiting even commented on it. Maila tried mightily to win West's favor, practicing at home in front of a mirror and making sure she was never late to rehearsals. She smiled sweetly at her even as silently she cursed her.

Eventually, Maila fell into complete disfavor with West, and the star dispatched her minions to fire her. Maila claimed she was dismissed because she upstaged West but didn't explain further, and she harbored a lifelong resentment toward West thereafter.

Hayride, another Mike Todd production, ran concurrently with Catherine Was Great, but Todd was convinced to bankroll even yet another play, Spook Scandals, a glorified series of skits set in a cemetery. Performances for Scandals were scheduled to begin at midnight, and because of the late show times, it wouldn't conflict with the actors' other commitments. The casts from both of Todd's other plays, including the newly released Maila, auditioned for roles.

What made Spook Scandals so appealing to performers was that it was never meant to be a serious undertaking. Loosely directed, its skit format allowed for plenty of improvisation. Maila won the part of the dancing skeleton. Still rankled over West's perceived spitefulness and convinced that her scream-and-faint act from Catherine was perfectly good, Maila decided to incorporate it into her dancing skeleton role.

Todd, not fully committed to the success of the play, made two critical errors. He allowed for open rehearsals, and he scheduled opening night just 24 hours after Billy Rose's The Seven Lively Arts opened at the Ziegfeld.

At midnight on December 8, 1944, Spook Scandals premiered at the 300-seat President Theater. Few came to watch Maila bumping, grinding, screaming, and fainting in her skeleton bodysuit. The turnout was so miserable that Todd pulled the plug after only one performance.

It didn't matter. In the audience that night was Maila's frequent dinner companion, columnist Irving Hoffman. While he panned the show, he lavished praise upon his friend's performance: "Mila Niemi is Hollywood's answer to every dream."

The column, routinely scoured by movie bigwigs, resulted in Maila being inundated with movie offers. Within weeks, there were so many, Maila needed help sorting them out—and who better than Hoffman for the job?

"You should go with Hawks," he advised. "If you do, you can't miss."

Howard Hawks' latest film, *To Have and Have Not*, paired Humphrey Bogart with newcomer Lauren Bacall, Hawks' latest discovery. Judging by the publicity surrounding the movie, Hawks' reputation for star-making was never higher.

Maila could scarcely believe it. She was invited by the big-name producer to an interview. She told her parents she was going to Hollywood to become the next Lauren Bacall.

They were both less than thrilled. Hadn't their daughter already gotten her fill of that town? Sophie especially feared for Maila's safety and suggested that Hawks was a charlatan who only wanted to take advantage of her.

Their concern was dismissed. Maila was going, and that was final. Before she left, her father gave her a few Finnish words of caution: "*Ei sitä koskaan tiedä, missä puussa piru istuu.*" You never know which tree the Devil is sitting on.

The long train ride left plenty of time for Maila to think. If everything went as she hoped, reporters would soon vie for her attention. And all that attention would surely lead to questions about her personal life, and the truth was a certain career-buster: a fanatic for a father and a drunk for a mother. What Maila needed was a new story, one that told of exotic roots, romantic aspirations, and drama.

By the time she arrived in Hollywood, she was Maila Nurmi, born in the frigid north of Finnish Lapland, the niece of the famous Olympic track star, Paavo Nurmi. That's all the public needed to know. She'd fill in the blanks later. Almost 75 years after the fact, most of the world still believes this story.

February, 1945

There's something about a train ride. The rock-a-bye motion & the constant sound of metal on metal is conducive to dreams ... or nightmares. Riding a train is like a lullaby ... or a funeral dirge. Depending upon if you want to live or die.

This time is not like the last. This time it sings me a lullaby.

The train ride is a long one. Cross country, New York to Hollywood. Not my first such trip, but my first without a companion.

So I am alone amongst strangers, free to dream whatever I choose.

They say I'm to be the next Lauren Bacall. God, I hope not. Home wrecker! Shameful—stealing another woman's husband as she did. I never want to be Lauren Bacall!

I am excited to be at the end of this trip & again in Hollywood. I am here because my performance as a sexy skeleton made an impression upon the famous Hollywood director Howard Hawks. Ironic, because my family closet is full of the unsexy variety & if I can help it, none will ever see the light of day.

So goodbye to you Mr. Welles. Coward! You are nothing like your public perceives you to be. You are the unabashed Saint of Deceit. I'd hate you if I didn't still love you, my forever closeted skeleton. But don't be afraid, you're not alone in there. No one will ever know that my family moved from town to town like a band of ragged gypsies. Or that my father was a fanatical temperance man who lectured thousands against the evils of alcohol while my mother stayed home to swill bootlegged wine.

Mama didn't practice what Papa preached.

Goodbye to you as well, Papa. We never shared a surname anyway... your choice. You've made it perfectly clear my aspirations are complete foolishness. Pity you'll never understand that the pursuit of art cannot be denied.

Now is my beginning... Maila Niemi of Gloucester, Massachusetts, is dead... and resurrected as Mila Nurmi, niece of Paavo Nurmi, the 'Flying Finn' of Olympic fame. She will say she was born in a log cabin in the far reaches of northern Finland in an area known as Petsamo. Her grandfather, a man of hope and optimism, was the town crier. During his nightly rounds, he sang & played the kantele (Finnish harp). Her father was a poet. On the ship to America & a new life, he threw his written rhymes into the sea and watched as the rudder churned them under. Quite the romantic, that one.

She was two & her brother three when they arrived in America with their parents. And they all lived happily ever after. Such a lovely story. Wouldn't you agree?

To be continued in the event of stardom.

Chapter Six

Maila arrived in Hollywood prepared to dazzle. Aided by her gossip columnist pals and the theater grapevine, she learned everything she could about Hawks.

At the time, Howard Hawks was one of the most respected directors in Hollywood. In an era dominated by the studios, Hawks refused to be tethered to one particular studio and eventually worked for all eight major studios, which he accomplished by not only directing but also producing his films. Not beholden to any particular genre, Hawks made movies that spanned the gamut across comedy, film noir, thriller, Western, and science fiction. Orson Welles is said to have opined that while John Ford's work was poetry, Hawks' was prose. Just before Maila's arrival, Hawks' work was celebrated for such films as *Bringing Up Baby*, *Only Angels Have Wings* and *His Girl Friday*. In 1941, Hawks was nominated for an Oscar for Best Director for *Sergeant York*, and Gary Cooper went on to win one for Best Actor thanks to his role in the film. This was the big chance Maila had waited for.

With Bacall on her way to stardom, Hawks was eager to know more about "Hollywood's answer to every dream," Mila Nurmi (as Maila spelled her first name without the 'a'). Trusting Hoffman's assessment, Hawks immediately dispatched his men in New York to send photos of the darling of *Spook Scandals*. Based on these photos, Hawks extended a contract to Maila, which she then accepted.

When Maila walked into Hawks' office in February of 1945, what she didn't know was that Hawks was so certain he'd found his next big star, he'd prepared a vehicle in which to debut his newest protégée. If everything panned out as he hoped, he'd cast her to play the female lead in a vampire-based saga, *Dreadful Hollow*. Written by Hawks' good friend and drinking buddy, William Faulkner, it was the story of an evil Eastern European countess who preyed upon young visitors to her Victorian mansion.

Groomed and coiffed to perfection, Maila was poised and confident at the meeting with Hawks, moving with the practiced grace of a ballerina. The introduction could not have gone better. When the small talk was over, it was time to see how Miss Nurmi played out on film.

"Let's get her into hair and makeup and run a screen test on her," Hawks told an assistant.

An impromptu screen test is like being stripped naked in front
of strangers. Visions of Kosloff and Clark ricocheted in my brain. I'd
never had a legitimate screen test before. Would I need to be naked?

Maila had always been insecure about her hair—to the point where she often covered it with wigs and hats—but as a result of her recent pregnancy, it was thick and shiny, so she knew it would film well. What alarmed her was that her meticulously applied makeup was removed, and a studio makeup artist then made a slapdash effort to reapply it. She thought the look was distorted and that it made her look older by years.

Maila was ushered into a room, fully clothed, for her big shot at stardom. Her self-confidence destroyed, she was subjected to full body shots and close-ups from every angle, then directed to give a cold reading from a prepared script.

Hawks took one look at Maila's screen test and scowled. "You need your

*Earl Carroll Theatre. Maynard L. Parker photographer,
courtesy of The Huntington Library, San Marino, CA.*

teeth fixed," he said. As an aside to an assistant, he added, "Let's send her out and
see what happens."

At 22, Maila had never seen a dentist. At home, she studied her face and
took inventory of the small gap between her front teeth, the slight overbite, the
crowded lowers, and the way her smile exposed her gums. It was the reason
she never smiled when photographed. After her brother, Bobbie, had relayed
the horrors of having his upper teeth pulled by an Army dentist without any
Novocaine, Maila was terrified of suffering the same fate.

She didn't wait around to see if Hawks would fix her teeth. After a week
of waiting with no phone call, Maila decided she needed to have a talk with Mr.
Big Shot. She walked into Hawks' office and refusing the seat she was offered,
she said, "You have someone make me up to look like an unwashed harlot, and

turn me out into the streets. I am not a commodity to be traded or sold to the highest bidder."

Hawks was dumbstruck.

Before he could respond, Maila removed her contract from her handbag and ripped it in half before tossing it on Hawks' desk. "Kindly," she said in haughty indignation, "find a place for this in one of your numerous wastebaskets." Slamming the door as she exited, she burned the last bridge to any significant film career she may have had.

Just as Mae West's "so big" comment hit a nerve, so did Hawks' observation. Maila did not handle rejection well. She had yet to develop a strong sense of self and still believed that anyone who would judge her using anything but the blinding glow of adoration was out to destroy her.

Because her father's supplemental rent income would soon disappear, Maila found herself in a familiar jam. No work, no money. She considered volunteering for a USO tour to survive. Even though entertainers received no wages, they were housed and fed. But the thought of boarding a drafty, noisy military plane to fly to God knows where sent her into a panic. Maila may have ruined her opportunities in theater and film, but she could dance a little, and her résumé included legitimate work on Broadway. And so began her brief career as a chorus girl.

The Florentine Gardens on Hollywood Boulevard catered to people from all walks of life: soldiers, the working class, as well as people in the movie industry. As part of the chorus line, Maila danced alongside Lili St. Cyr, who later became a well-known burlesque star. Singer and actor Rudy Vallee was heard to comment, "Let me just say, Maila is a real looker, and when she dances, she acts like she's on stage alone. I can't keep my eyes off the gal."

I had to devise a way to stand out from the pack. All those beautiful women. How was I to leave my mark—distinguish myself from the others? So, when I danced, I would frequently single out someone in the audience and engage in a spiritual fuck with said stranger.

It isn't any wonder that Vallee couldn't keep his eyes off Maila.

One night after the show, a man had positioned himself in front of the dressing room door so that anyone coming in or out had to maneuver around him. Deep in conversation with a gaffer, the man made no move to ease the congestion he was creating.

It was Welles.

He spoke to Maila as casually as if they'd seen each other last week, asking if she'd wait until he finished his conversation because he wanted to speak with her. Maila had waited for this opportunity for two years and had many times rehearsed exactly what she would say to him. That she became pregnant and gave birth to their son. But even now, her resolve was weakening.

When Welles returned to where Maila waited, she asked, "How did you find me?"

"Irving Hoffman," he answered.

It wasn't like it sounded. Welles did not purposely look for her. When Maila left for Hollywood, she and Hoffman continued to communicate through letters. When Hoffman heard of Maila's disastrous meeting with Howard Hawks, he took it upon himself to advocate for her with his celebrity pals, and that included Welles. Hoffman believed Maila's talents may find a home in radio, and since Welles was still the undisputed king of radio, he believed it was worth a shot.

It's doubtful that Welles let Hoffman know that he and Maila were more than strangers. And as Maila soon learned, Welles wasn't at the Florentine Gardens to open any career doors for her but rather to satisfy his needs—even though he was still married to Rita Hayworth and they had an infant daughter.

It was 1945, and the sudden death of President Roosevelt had plunged the nation into mourning. Welles considered the President a personal friend, and he was not only deeply affected by his passing but also concerned about how his death would politically impact the United States and its allies. He was leaving for San Francisco to attend an international symposium and asked Maila to accompany him.

Before she was even aware of it, she'd jumped headlong into the vortex of Welles' manic energy. She told him that her employer had died. Assured her job was secure until "after the funeral," she was free to go to San Francisco with Welles.

Years later, she explained her decision.

> *How could I not? I'd already fallen down the rabbit hole. I was*
> *Alice in Wonderland to his March Hare.*

Maila said Welles left their hotel room early each morning and didn't return until late at night. To pass the time until her lover's return, she walked around the city for hours, thinking about how to tell Welles about the baby.

Ultimately, she decided it was too late. Even if he could leave Rita and the baby to be with her, what good would it do to tell him now? And in that moment, she was glad she wasn't Rita: The star had money, fame, incomparable beauty, and a baby to love, but the one thing she didn't have was a committed husband. Meanwhile, Maila would have to be content with being Welles' mistress and nothing more.

Everlasting love runs contrary to the mind of a raging genius.
Perhaps they were meant to be solitary beings, capable only of
committing to their own intellect.

When Maila returned to work at the Florentine Gardens, it was without a promise from Welles as to when—or even if—she would see him again. As it turned out, he continued to pop in and out of her life for another year.

Maila needed a change of pace. Film, radio, and stage were out. Dancing was still okay in a pinch, but she wondered if she had a shot at professional modeling. During her brief stints doing print ads and runway work for department stores, she'd toyed with the idea, but she dismissed it to pursue her acting career.

She went directly to the best in the biz, photographer Bruno Bernard, a.k.a. "Bernard of Hollywood," the master of the pin-up.

Since the war began, cheesecake and pin-up photography was coming into its own, and every soldier had a few photos to remind him of the girls back home. Calendars and magazines with photos of scantily clad girl-next-door types flew off the newsstand shelves.

Imagine Maila's disappointment when Bernard told her she wasn't right for cheesecake. "You carry a little too much weight and not enough definition," he said. But all was not lost. She begged and pleaded for work to remain in the modeling game, in order to learn, and it paid off. She landed a job as his photography assistant.

Instead of being in front of the camera, her behind-the-scenes vantage point served her well. Just as she had in school, Maila was an ambitious student, and she took it all in: the hair, the makeup, the lighting, the costuming, the poses. All of the models were pretty young girls looking to break into show business. One of Bernard's girls, conspicuous for her little-girl voice that clashed almost comically with her voluptuous body, was named Norma Jeane Dougherty. Maila remembered her from long before she morphed into the sex symbol Marilyn Monroe.

> *I always felt a little sorry for Norma Jean* [sic]. *She was like a wounded animal......nervous & wary. She cried easily & just as quickly she seemed to recover from whatever it was that had made her unhappy. We were acquaintances, not friends. I think friendships were difficult for her because she kept a distance between herself & the other models. She was already married then but still quite shy. Her hair was a kind of mousy brown and frizzy, but I felt she knew how to pose while showing off those knockers of hers to best advantage & still maintain that little girl lost look. But she was a lovely woman. And as it came to be, tragic.*

There was a tacit rivalry between the West Coast and East Coast models. The gossip among Bernard's girls was that the New York models were largely prostitutes and strippers, while they, as decent, moral and proper young women, aspired to work for Catalina. Being chosen to model swimsuits for the respected brand immediately elevated one's status among the other girls.

Unfortunately, a photographer's assistant didn't get paid nearly as well as a dancer did. So, whether by necessity or by choice, Maila returned to work as a chorus girl.

The Mocambo, Café Trocadero, and the Earl Carroll Theatre attracted Hollywood celebrities and industry bigwigs. If a girl wanted to get noticed, Earl Carroll's was the place to be. Located at Sunset and Argyle, the outside of the building displayed a 20-foot neon portrait of the face of Carroll's girlfriend, Beryl Wallace. Inside, it boasted a massive, two-tiered, 60-foot revolving stage. Above its entrance, the famous maxim blazed in neon splendor: "Thru These Portals Pass the Most Beautiful Girls in the World." It was while working at Earl Carroll's in the fall of 1946 when who should emerge from the shadows once again but Orson Welles.

This time, he asked her to go to New York with him. Again, she followed him.

Onni and Sophie were living in Brooklyn at this time and had no idea their daughter was in town. While in New York, Maila and Welles had a terrific fight. If she finally told him about their child, it would only be speculation, because she never spoke or wrote about the cause of the clash—only its aftermath.

Maila appeared on her parents' doorstep in Brooklyn, suitcase in hand and soaked to the skin from the rain. An impromptu family summit ensued, in which Maila's blowout with Welles would seem like a mere ripple in her personal raging river of betrayal, shame, and anger.

The story was patched together from the recollections of mother and daughter. Maila wanted the money to get back to Hollywood. Her father refused until she told him how she came to be standing in his living room, soaking wet. She said she came with a boyfriend who'd abandoned her in the city. Onni wanted to know a name. Who was this boyfriend?

"His name is Orson," Maila said.

"Orson Welles?"

Maila was stunned. *He put the names together.* She'd confessed to her mother begging her never to tell her father, but it seemed clear that she had. Now Onni not only knew who fathered her child but probably knew the man was still married, which meant that he also knew Maila was Orson's mistress.

It would do no good to tell her father it was over between her and Welles. There was nothing more to say.

Her parents verbally sparred over how best to deal with their daughter. Onni fumed that Maila was like a wild horse who could not be tamed. She ignored all his advice; it was best to set her free. But Sophie was just as certain that Maila needed more, not less, parental guidance. She countered that their daughter left home too young, before she learned how to take care of herself. Now she was certain that once Maila found a worthy husband, she would settle down. Sophie wanted to coddle her into domesticity.

When the parental tug-of-war ended, Sophie decided she couldn't bear for her daughter to go alone on the long train ride home to Hollywood with no one to comfort her.

For Maila, it was a lesson learned. She should have known better than to trust a drunk with a secret, even if that drunk was one's own mother. But even so, she had no choice but to share a train ride back to Hollywood with her betrayer.

Once there, they moved into an apartment together. Maila returned to Earl Carroll's, and Sophie pampered Maila. She made sure her daughter's clothes were clean and pressed, doing the laundry in the kitchen sink. She took care of the household chores and paid the bills with the money Onni sent. Six months. That's all he'd promised. It was enough to pay the rent, buy groceries, and supply herself with liquor.

At the end of the six months, Sophie was informed that her husband filed for divorce.

With the arrival of divorce papers, Welles was twice despised by the family. Once for fathering Maila's baby, and again for indirectly ending a 30-year marriage. Sophie's booze-fueled logic stated that if Welles had only claimed his responsibilities in the beginning, Maila would never have been so traumatized that she needed her mother to come live with her in Hollywood. In Sophie's world, if there had never been an Orson Welles, she'd still be married and in New York with her husband.

Welles and Maila were truly over. Shortly after the final split, he produced *The Lady from Shanghai*, which he also directed and co-starred in, along with Rita Hayworth, his soon-to-be ex-wife. He had the star's signature red hair cut short and bleached blonde, and it seemed more than a coincidence that Rita's haircut and color was identical to her own.

Sophie went to work as a chambermaid at the Knickerbocker Hotel, a union house with guaranteed wages and paid vacations. Located at Ivar and Hollywood Boulevard, the Knickerbocker rented by the day, week, or month and teemed with celebrities, all with their special demands. Sophie was accustomed to the daily comings and goings of the hotel's famous guests. Until one guest in particular caught her attention—and not in a good way.

"That bastard had the nerve to show his face in my hotel."

It was Orson Welles, and Sophie was wild with rage. Rage that had been building up for almost four years and the object of that rage was just on the other side of the guest room door. She held the passkey tightly in her grip. Protocol demanded that she knock first.

"Maid service," she announced.

"I didn't call for maid service," the unmistakable voice said from the other side.

He was there. Sophie threw open the door.

"I'm Maila's mother, the goddamn grandmother of your son."

Welles was understandably stunned, and there was no question he knew exactly what she was talking about. Threats were exchanged. Welles ordered Sophie to leave or he would have security physically remove her and have her fired.

Sophie was liquored up enough that his threats rolled off her back. She cursed him again and threatened that Hedda Hopper was hungering for a story to put her poison pen into service. Welles blanched. He knew well the power Ms. Hopper wielded in Hollywood. Thirty-five million people read her columns. Just two years before, Hopper had exposed his best friend, Joseph Cotten, for an affair with married actress Deanna Durbin, and the repercussions were swift and ugly. The stalemate was breached when Welles took out his wallet and handed over $200.

Sophie didn't bicker with the amount. Instead, she snatched the cash out of Welles' hand and, in parting, snarled, "Genius, my ass. You're nothing but a common shit-heel."

Maila continued to live with her mother after the divorce, blissfully unaware that Sophie had essentially blackmailed her former lover and sold out her grandson for the cash to cover a couple of months of booze.

I disowned my father for the way he divorced my mother. He was such a bastard about it. Kept her hopeful of a reconciliation and then ripped out her guts with impunity.

By 1947, except for infrequent letters, there was no contact between Onni and his daughter or his former wife. Neither Maila nor Sophie ever saw Onni again.

Chapter Seven

At Earl Carroll's, Maila was no longer spiritually seducing from the stage. Reassigned to work the front of the house, she was the club's cigarette and camera girl.

The change of scenery served her well. While the nightclub hosted its share of servicemen, there were plenty of industry people in attendance too. The deep pockets of the celebrity clientele made for good tips, and after a few drinks, more than a few offered up their private phone numbers.

By way of one of those phone numbers came an opportunity for work on a movie. Maila was cast, albeit uncredited, as a guest in a casino scene for the 1947 movie *If Winter Comes*, starring Walter Pidgeon and Deborah Kerr. But Maila was hopeful it would ultimately lead to more work.

But on June 17, 1948, the good times came to a tragic end when Earl Carroll and his girlfriend, Beryl Wallace, were killed on United Airlines Flight 624. After that, the club was never the same. Maila left to perform in *Ken Murray's Blackouts*.

At Hollywood and Vine, the El Capitan Theatre was the home of Ken Murray's burlesque variety show. For most of its nine-year run, it was wildly popular. It was while performing there that Maila met Murray's close friend, Dean Riesner.

Riesner had just completed the film *Bill and Coo*, which he directed and co-wrote. The unusual film starred a cast of trained birds performing on the smallest set in history. It was a story about a town inhabited exclusively by parakeets that was invaded by an evil crow called the Black Menace. Produced by Ken Murray, the film was awarded an honorary Oscar.

Riesner had been a child actor, billed as Dinky Dean. His parents, Charles and Miriam Riesner, were vaudevillians. Dink, as family and friends called him, was surrounded by actors from birth. By age three, Dinky Dean acquired a vocabulary so extensive, he took to rhyming words at will. His father's friend, Charlie Chaplin, cast Dink in his film *The Pilgrim*, and shortly thereafter, his mother witnessed the crew prodding her child to rhyme the word "bucket." When, to her complete horror, Dink responded, "Fuck it," Mama Riesner pulled the plug on her only child's acting career.

The attraction between Maila and Dink Riesner was instantaneous and couldn't have been timelier. Dink more or less rescued Maila and her mother from each other. Sophie was greatly pleased that her daughter, at age 26, had at last found a man whom she deemed worthy of being her son-in-law. He was the first and only love interest of Maila's that she didn't want to push off a cliff.

Shortly after their first meeting, Maila began to call Dink her own private teddy bear. "Sweet, cuddly, confused, and rumpled Dink," she said. Teddy bear persona aside, Dink was also creative, funny, and very smart. As a child, the inventor of the Stanford-Binet Intelligence Scales test, Dr. Lewis Terman, measured Dink's IQ at 178.

He was far from perfect, however. Dink had started drinking at 13, and by the time he met Maila, he was a seasoned alcoholic. After his service in the military, Dink's father's name provided many opportunities for him, but one by one, lame excuse after missed deadline, he lost them all. With the exception of *Bill and Coo* and a few other projects, Dean Riesner was washed up in the film industry by age 30—which is when he met Maila.

So immediate was their attraction to each other, Maila and Dink decided within a few weeks to move in together.

> *My female genes had always yearned to be blissfully helpless & adored, free of all responsibility save that of inspiring my man— fortifying my man. Yes, I'm a woman. A woman whose fate had heretofore kept her foraging in a solitary manner like a frontier woodsman.*

Dink's father paid the rent, but five months later, hard financial times hit Charles, and he could no longer afford it. Dink volunteered to work at a gas station, but Maila wouldn't hear of it. She insisted that she work to support them, so that Dink could write full-time.

They cut out all extras. Maila wrapped up her free meal from work and brought it home to share with Dink at three in the morning. Still, Maila's paycheck was not enough to sustain them. They had to find a place with cheaper rent.

Cohabitation by unmarried couples was frowned upon by most landlords. Some even demanded to see a marriage certificate. Although they declared themselves as Mr. and Mrs., they never married and were fortunate to find a landlord who accepted their verbal assertion that they were wed. They moved into a tiny apartment above a garage in Laurel Canyon. The lower rent allowed Dink to continue to write, while Maila worked at the Savoy as a hat check girl.

> *A dream as old as life itself had burned in my soul. Now, at last, it was being loved! I, Maila Nurmi, was someone's very precious private "woman." It was heaven. All thoughts of personal ambition vanished as fast as cigarette smoke in a hurricane. I wanted success—power— money—for HIM. I secretly vowed to be the BEST WIFE that EVER LIVED. To anticipate his every wish & to fulfill it before he even knew he had it.*

Maila and Dink shared a love of animals. Before long, they adopted a cat. They named her Missy, and in short order she produced a litter of kittens. Dink submitted this ad to the local *Canyon Crier*:

FREE LOVE!
IF YOU'RE LONELY, A KITTEN WILL GIVE
YOU LOVE AND HAPPINESS. GUARANTEED:
IF YOU BRING THE KITTEN BACK, YOUR LONELINESS
WILL BE CHEERFULLY REFUNDED.

The neighbors took to calling Maila "Sister St. Francis, savior of animals." She was observed tending to all the strays in the neighborhood. She even nursed an injured owl back to health and collected snails in paper bags, relocating them to an unpopulated hilltop before they became victims of pesticide.

For the first couple of years, the couple drank heavily, and they fought often. Because of her mother, living with an alcoholic seemed normal to Maila. But their quarrels were never serious. The sober morning light diluted the aftershocks from the boozy night before.

He decided that in me he had a precious commodity. He proceeded
to worship me. People said they had never before seen a man so in love.
He bored everyone he met with incessant tales of my "incredibleness,"
illustrated with photos of me he would carry in his wallet.

Frequently, on Saturday afternoons, the couple attended a double feature matinee at the neighborhood theater. Westerns were the norm, as Dink was compelled to watch for professional survival. Maila found Westerns boring and formulaic, so to break the tedium, she often hung out in the lobby, where she said "the real action was." Particularly, she liked to single out a person and imagine what their life was like—their occupation, marital status, number of children, that kind of thing. In the theater lobby, she played a game with herself: Who would buy the popcorn, and who would choose candy instead?

One day, during intermission, the commercials included a promo for Catalina's new swimsuit line. Suddenly, there she was: Dink's ex-girlfriend from Laguna Beach, Barbara Freaking. Maila claimed that Dink suddenly "groaned her name in orgasmic ecstasy."

"Freako," he said—the nickname by which he lovingly called her. Maila looked up at her giant blonde nemesis.

> *To be a model was to be shallow and sunny, like Arlene Dahl. So pretty, and so empty. Like Limoges Hollow Ware.*
>
> *Was that the kind of woman Dink wanted ... thin & glamorous. Had I become too complacent in our relationship? Because I was un-thin and un-glamorous, had I become un-sexy as well? All that drinking & rich meals I cooked, sometimes in the middle of the night, had taken their toll. The imaginary battle lines were drawn. I would become more thin and more glamorous than Ms. Freako. I would become the model she never could be. Dink would see that he had the best. I would become his Madonna.*

In that moment, Maila declared war on her own body and vowed to use everything she knew about diet and exercise to transform herself.

Beginning the next morning, her breakfast consisted of water with lemon juice, and she exercised in front of a full-length mirror until exhaustion forced her to quit. She started walking until she could walk up to 35 miles a week. She invented new recipes to keep her calorie count down. Knox Gelatin became a staple in her kitchen. Aerated in a blender with a few seasonings, it added bulk without calories. She fried with mineral oil until it made her sick, but not a single drop of fat passed her lips.

Maila somehow persuaded Dink to join her in her regimen, but after a week of eating nothing but mousses and aspics, he felt a little crazed. When he caught himself with spoon in hand, ready to dig into Missy's cat food, Dink dumped the diet.

Undaunted, Maila soldiered on alone. In her quest for perfection, her standards became even more obsessive and strange. She had the notion that if steak tenderizer could break down dead meat cells, then maybe it would work the same on living tissue. She researched its ingredients and learned that the main component in tenderizer was papaya powder, readily accessible at the health food store. She mixed the powder with lanolin and slathered it around her waistline. The carnival's Mermaid Girl claimed her rubber costume made dieting unnecessary, and now Maila would find out. She then secured rubber strips of inner tube around her middle.

"You're not going to sleep with that shit on, are you?" Dink asked.

But of course, she did.

Within a month, Maila lost 30 pounds and several inches off her waist. She was ecstatic.

The Freako Challenge was about to enter Phase 2. She felt her body was pin-up-ready and wanted a photographer of some acclaim to recognize her potential. Maila first reached out to famed glamour photographer Peter Gowland, only to face rejection once more. But her heart was still set on becoming one of Bruno Bernard's girls. Maybe once he saw how trim she'd gotten, he would finally take her on as a model.

Unfortunately, her meeting with Bernard did not go well. When Maila threw off her coat to reveal a bikini and proceeded to prowl seductively around his studio, the photographer said, "Don't be ridiculous. I told you, Maila—you're not a pin-up model. Portrait model, yes. Pin-up, no."

Yet another blow to her ego, but again, not a fatal one. Bernard was simply wrong.

The war was over, but pin-up calendars were still big business. Illustrators drew models in various poses and then transferred their artwork onto calendars.

At the time, the premier pin-up artist in the country, Alberto Vargas, was living in Hollywood—he was a very good friend of Bernard's. Maila decided to try her luck with Mr. Vargas next.

> *I was somewhat taken aback by [Vargas'] almost clinical studio on Westwood Boulevard. It looked more like a surgical theater than an artist's den. Vargas slicked back his slightly receding hair, trimmed his mustache to a thin line, & wore his immaculate shirt starched. His career was in an inexplicable lull at that moment—probably the only time it ever was. As with Bernard, I wore a bikini under my coat, but when I removed it, he nodded approvingly & called in his wife.*

"Look at this wonderful body," he said.

Because all the Vargas calendar girls were buxom, Maila thought he was mocking her small bust until he explained.

"In art school, breasts are the first thing you learn to draw. There are only a few positions for them, and you can always draw them from memory. What you look for in a body is muscle tone, line, and form. A racehorse. That is what you look for. If there is no bosom or derrière, you can always paint them on."

Vargas was so impressed with Maila, he added her name to his famous, though transitory, list of the "ten most beautiful women in the world." It was a tremendous honor to even be considered for inclusion, no matter how briefly.

After such a glowing endorsement from his friend, Bernard finally agreed to take another look at Maila. And when he shot his film *Beauty on the Beach*, Maila Nurmi was in his stable of beauties.

> *The film had no dialogue. It was just a bunch of us posing in swimsuits. There were many of us—Lili St. Cyr, Irish McCulla, Joan Olander who later became known as Mamie Van Doren & others. It*

was Norma Jean's first movie. I was given the name Lorelei & I had on a gross conglomeration of provocatina. Provocatina? Anyway, I wore a red puckered cotton bikini, black fishnets, a pink garter & one pink satin toe shoe. Love it? Bernard, himself, was our wardrobe designer. It was hideous. He was given to trussing us up in the most ungodly accoutrements. It... was not made for general release but for the mail order trade, you know, the home masturbation market. You could say it was made for private release!

Hollywood was a mecca of billboards touting products, films, and events. Many featured the photography of Peter James Samerjian, who was relatively late to the pin-up photography game. As luck would have it, *Glamorous Models* was sponsoring a major contest called the Rave Discovery, and most of the in-demand models were expected to compete. Samerjian threw around the idea of entering the contest, but without the right girl, it seemed hopeless. That is, until a stunning blonde chanced to walk through the door of his studio. One look at Maila, and he knew he'd found his pin-up model.

Samerjian won the contest and a one-hundred-dollar prize, and Maila graced the cover of the September 1950 issue of *Glamorous Models*.

At long last, she was a cover girl. Take that, Freako.

In May of 1951, she landed another cover: *Night and Day*, "America's Picture Magazine of Entertainment."

In January of 1953 issue of *Art Photography*, Maila appeared in a seven-page spread. The photographer and author of the accompanying article was none other than Bruno Bernard.

According to him, Maila walked into his studio "to have some photographic fun and to prove a point." She ordered Bernard to "set up the shots, and I'll show you how versatile I can be." Shot after shot, Maila made good on her promise, posing as a teenager in toe shoes, a wistful leopard girl in a braided turban, a psychic, a bikini girl at the beach, and a spot-on Dietrich or Garbo.

I did some calendar work for Fritz Willis, Vargas & Earl Moran.
But not nude. Never nude. In those days you had to try to protect
your prospective future. All the pin-ups were stunned when Norma
Jean destroyed herself by posing naked!!!

When I rode the Red Car up Sunset past Gardner Junction, I
tried to keep my eyes mostly focused on the south side of the street.
Poor Norma Jean's nude picture ... so big ... & so naked, larger than
life above Tom Kelley's studio. All the other pin-ups said, "She killed
herself. Norma Jean's career is over."

Of course, as Marilyn Monroe, Norma Jeane later became the first nude model to hit the big time.

A little over a mile from Maila and Dink's Laurel Canyon apartment, Crescent Heights Boulevard connects with Sunset Boulevard. On that storied corner was Schwab's Pharmacy, drugstore to the stars. It was there that Maila passed the time drinking coffee and chatting with friends at the lunch counter.

With Maila's encouragement and support, Dink quit drinking. Although his writing was more inspired and marketable than ever before, success came at a cost. Maila felt neglected. She worked so hard to transform herself for him, and now she felt she was playing second fiddle to his typewriter.

My man was writing long into the night while I simply longed
for him IN the night. I was becoming frightfully lonely & then an idea
was birthed. If the mountain will not come to Mohammed, Mohammed
must go to the mountain ... wearing a garter belt & stilettos.

Maila publicly asserted there were fetish magazines laying around the house. *Bizarre* in particular offered up a plethora of fetish wear; bustiers, corsets, chains, whips, leather, and lace. At some point, Maila placed an order for them both.

Maila on the cover of Glamorous Models, *September 1950.*

for a photographer before, her experience as a dancer enabled her to easily and expertly assume the most graceful positions. She was not satisfied simply with pleasing me, moreover, but insisted on pleasing herself. I think her best features are her eyes and her long, shapely legs."

One of the images from the Glamorous Models *interior.*

Dink soon received a pair of black-and-white-striped pajamas that Maila called his "prison PJs." Dressed in her fetish gear, it was Maila who was in control, and she found it exhilarating. She was at once sexy, fearsome, and powerful. She was the Dragon Lady and the Evil Queen come to life.

But after a while, Dink began spending less and less time at home, and Maila assumed he'd taken a lover. Whether it was true or not, she could think of no other explanation for his loss of interest in their bedroom games.

> *The goddess-worship phase with Dink had soared to temporary heights. Soon, though, I found myself set alone on a pedestal, rather like a prized porcelain. One doesn't fuck porcelain. It might break. So the poor fellow was forced to fornicate with "other women" as I sat alone, undisturbed, on my familiar pedestal.*

Rather than endlessly stewing about the situation, Maila went for walks, which usually ended at Schwab's. It was on just such an outing that Maila ran into "the person I crossed the country to avoid." "Avoid" because even then, Maila knew that this man, who exuded sex appeal from every pore of his being, could lead to nothing good for any woman who was unfortunate enough to fall in love with him. That man was Marlon Brando.

After five years of success on Broadway, particularly from playing Stanley Kowalski in *A Streetcar Named Desire*, Marlon Brando had come to Hollywood and starred in his first motion picture, *The Men*. He'd just finished production on the film version of *Streetcar*, although it hadn't yet been released. He was verging on stardom.

He'd been in town for a while, and Maila sensed Brando was adrift, feeling uncomfortable in Hollywood because he still dressed like the New York actors: blue work shirt, jeans, and boots. With time on his hands, he amused himself by driving around town in his blue Ford convertible.

Marlon asked Maila if she'd like to go for a drive. She said she was involved

104

with Riesner. He said he was happy for her. And then the familiar lost-little-boy look came across Brando's face.

Before getting into Marlon's car, I silently vowed to keep my romantic energies in low gear.

Brando drove to the top of Mulholland Drive and stopped where it intersects with Coldwater Canyon Drive. It was barren except for a water tower. He parked on the side of the road, got out, and stalked the underbrush, pacing out measured footsteps. He stopped and scanned the sweeping view of the city below from various angles.

"One day," he predicted, "I'll have a house here."

When he dropped Maila off at home, he asked for her phone number. No stranger to Brando's history with women, she had no intention of again becoming a victim of his cruel and unpredictable moods. Being Marlon's friend was one thing; being his lover was inviting trouble. Before she would relinquish her number, she made him promise that any relationship between them remain platonic.

Dink's writing career took off. If he wasn't pitching his scripts, he was meeting with producers or other writers. His absence left a lonely Maila to spend more time with Brando.

The beach was a favorite destination. He was preparing for his role as Marc Antony in the film *Julius Caesar*, and he liked to take off his shoes and walk in the wet sand while reading Shakespeare aloud from a paperback.

It was bound to happen. On one of these outings, with little resistance from Maila, Brando had his way with her in the back seat of his convertible. Never mind that it was broad daylight. But despite her indiscretion, Maila wasn't ready to give up on her relationship with Dink. Clinging to the belief that he was unfaithful as well soothed her conscience.

Dink's career shifted into overdrive, and Maila continued to see Brando.

The two openly spent more time together at the beach, eating lunch or going to a movie. It was with Brando that she saw Gloria Swanson in *Sunset Boulevard*. Swanson's portrayal of aging movie star Norma Desmond captivated her. Though she didn't know it then, very shortly she would call on Norma Desmond to crawl inside the dead skin of a vampire and once more be "ready for her close-up."

> *One day, he took me to the Army Surplus Store to buy sweat sox, then to the Maxwell House Coffee Shop for hamburgers, then to the Vogue Theater for a movie. I had promised my mother I would stop by that afternoon & finally insisted Marlon tolerate a few minutes of her, since I had tolerated his sweat sox.*
>
> *He agreed & drove me to my mother's place on New Hampshire Street. After he parked his convertible & I freshened my makeup, I asked Marlon again if he would come in to meet my mother.*
>
> *"Sure," he said & grabbed a jock strap from the floor of his back seat and donned it gas mask-style. I was at a loss for words & at an even greater loss when my mother chose that precise moment to come out to the driveway & check her mailbox.*
>
> *It was a mixed blessing that Mama was too drunk to notice Marlon's antics. An elderly and heartfelt female impersonator, a drinking buddy, was also distracting her with his yammering & Marlon fell silent. His own mother was an alcoholic & he witnessed my awkward familial duties without comment.*

On the way home, Maila asked Marlon to stop at the Sunfax Market so she could pick up something for dinner at home. As was their custom, Brando pulled over a few blocks away from her house, and Maila gathered up her groceries and proceeded up the hill. Dink greeted her at the door and took one of the bags and helped Maila unpack the bags.

Imagine her horror when she turned to find Dink examining the block of cheddar, from which someone had taken a huge, horse-toothed bite.

"I was hungry," was her response. He never learned the truth.

Chapter Eight

Popsy Van Horne was past 70, with spindly legs and peroxided hair in a towering pompadour. Her resemblance to a cockatoo was unmistakable. In earlier years, while living in Europe, she claimed to have been wealthy, but now she barely managed to eke out a living as a film extra. The only vestige of her years abroad was her fake French accent.

Maila met Popsy at Schwab's lunch counter, where Maila learned the old gal had a passion for young actors. When John Garfield died in his lover's bedroom, Popsy was inconsolable.

She lived in a basement apartment off Hollywood Boulevard—a place Popsy aptly named the "Rat's Nest"—and Maila would occasionally stop by to visit her friend. One day, she found Popsy in an excited state.

"Aah, he has come to me. Everyone tells me he eez zee perfect man for me. This young actor from *Zee Men*."

"Marlon Brando," Maila asked. "I know him. Maybe I can bring him over."

That day arrived sooner than expected.

Brando and Maila left a matinee on Hollywood Boulevard and began to window-shop down the street. Of particular interest to Brando was the window display at Cooper's Donuts. According to Maila's friend, Sid Terror, she told him that Brando called it the "doughnut-shitting machine" and was fascinated by the parade of raw dough as it was dropped into a vat of boiling oil and then emerged as perfectly cooked pastries. But on this day, there was no time to watch frying doughnuts. Brando had to find a bathroom. Quickly. Under such pressure, they both forgot where the car was parked, and by the time they found the convertible, Brando's situation had elevated to a Code Red. Half a block away was the Rat's Nest and its cordial hostess, Popsy.

They rushed down the stairs to Popsy's flat and, without a word of introduction or direction to the facilities, Brando made a dash to the back of the place.

When he finished, Maila introduced Brando as Bobby Johnson, the pseudonym he routinely used. If Popsy was as enamored as she claimed, she would discover the ruse in short order.

She didn't seem to notice Marlon at all, but told us with a mixture of outrage & delight how her latest lover was so embarrassed by his filthy socks that he tried to flush them down the toilet. They jammed & the plumber had left only that morning. Our timing was perfect.

"I told you, I want to meet your Marlone Brandone?" she suddenly cawed. "Don't bother! I've already seen him."

"Bobby Johnson" choked down a startled look. I stared at them both in amazement. "You've already seen him?" I asked.

"Yes. In thees movie, 'Zee Men.' Oh, why did all mes amies tell me he was zee one for me?"

From the corner of my eye, Marlon betrayed no reaction.

"Non, merci!" Popsy concluded haughtily.

"What makes you say that?" I asked nervously.

"Everyzing!" she declared with authority. "That voice. So nasal. C'est terrible. So bourgeois!"

Brando was deeply wounded by Popsy's remarks. Never one to forget a slight, it wasn't long before he exacted his revenge. On his next film, who should show up among the extras but Popsy and her young lover. By now, Marlon had learned a thing or two about Hollywood and proceeded to humiliate both of them with insults loud enough for the entire crew to hear. Popsy fled in embarrassment. Shortly thereafter, she left Hollywood, unable to show her face among her family of extras.

When Maila got wind of Brando's stunt, she wrote him a letter condemning his behavior. "No matter how hurt you were by Popsy's comments, she was innocent of malice."

Never one to accept criticism, Brando disappeared from Maila's life.

No more Brando, no more Popsy. No problem. She still had Schwab's, which was simply called "the church" by its many famous patrons. Gossip columnist Sidney Skolsky kept an office upstairs with a peephole, from which to watch the "Schwabajeros" below. But mainly, he occupied a stool at the lunch counter. For the most part, Skolsky was respected and well-liked, and he counted among his best friends the former Norma Jeane Dougherty.

> *It was great to go into Schwab's when you'd just finished a picture—even if you'd just done a small bit part. A king for 2 days!! All the satellites revolving around your planet. Your name in the trades, Sydney [sic] comes downstairs to ask you what was shaking on the set, everybody picking up the tab for your coffee—invitations to lottsa parties.*

In 1949, a source of amusement sprouted up next door to Schwab's. It was born famous for being the first futuristic coffee shop in America and later for its patrons. The restaurant looked as if it were conceived on some distant planet and flung to Earth from a low-flying spaceship. Its cockeyed glass-and-steel façade supported a huge rectangular slab of roof that angled upward, with skewed vertical panel atop, upon which orange neon letters spelled out "GOOGIES." From the beginning of its existence, the omission of an apostrophe, whether intentional or accidental, summed up the majority of its patrons: They were strange.

Some Judases sneaked away from the fold to take up residence in
Googies. The # of new believers grew rapidly. The more pompous actors
stayed with Schwabs & the nonconforming types took over Googies.
There we were, Dennis Hopper, Ralph Meeker, Lawrence Tierney, Rod
Steiger, Tuesday Weld, Jimmy Dean, Maila Nurmi, and a microcosm
of bit players, poets, and hangers-on with the occasional appearance
of a bona-fide star with his/her entourage of bizarre henchmen, human
flotsam, and societal freaks.

While established, big-money actors like John Carradine, Shelley Winters, Lloyd Bridges, Lew Ayres, and Humphrey Bogart remained loyal to Schwab's, Googies became home turf of the malcontents. It became so popular that years later, when it closed for remodeling, the sign outside read, "Googies Closed. 10,000 left homeless."

Human nature being what it is, the number of new believers
grew rapidly ... Though there was never an actual rumble between
the Schwabajeros & the Googie-ites, there was a goodly amount of
distancing and much overt dissension.
The ceiling was like the inside of a mountain. On the low side sat
the agoraphobics & on the high side, the claustrophobics. The counter
ran down the middle, so mixed types could sit in relative comfort, each
facing his or her own chosen way.

Dink seldom went to Googies. He hated it because of the types who frequented the place. "Bums," he groused.

In his memoir, *Googies Coffeeshop to the Stars, vol. 1,* Steve Hayes recounts first meeting Maila during their lean years selling refrigerators door to door. Later, he became Googies' night manager, and it was there that he and Maila were reacquainted. Now an accomplished author and successful screenwriter, Hayes recounted to me how Maila and Dink interacted with each other.

"I seldom saw Dink with her. I'm an observer, as most writers are, and I was always puzzled by the body language between Maila and Riesner ... they seemed more like brother and sister than husband and wife or boyfriend and girlfriend."

Although still occasionally modeling for men's magazines, Maila was keenly aware that at 30, her days of doing cheesecake were numbered. Aging out was the inevitable curse of a pin-up model. But she still held her job at the Savoy. The tips were decent, and the celebrity clientele kept the place jumping.

I loved that club! All the nite [sic] crawlers breakfasted there, while disc jockey Larry Finley played the latest records. I had my own concession. The columnist Paul Coates was a regular, as was Joe Drown, the owner of the Bel-Air Hotel. Newscaster George Putnam used to come in (we were next door to the Mocambo) & so did Ronald Reagan with his wife, Jane Wyman. Then Ronnie didn't come in with Jane anymore. He came with a barren looking, thin one (looked to me like an out-of-work librarian) but he later married her. That was Nancy. She was quiet & I thought quite boring.

Mitch Miller gave a party there for Johnnie Ray & the release of "The Little White Cloud that Cried." John Barrymore Jr. was just 19 when he came in. So handsome, poetic, and charming. I'll never forget his beauty. And Robert Mitchum, who had the best ass in Hollywood.

For all its perks and excitement, the Savoy could not satisfy Maila's creative needs. She wanted something more than to check Lana's mink or Ava's sable. Film and stage careers were no longer possible, and she was aging out of dancing as well. But there was a new medium on the horizon, and it was driving the studios nuts. The movie theaters sat half-empty, while people were staying home to huddle around something called ... television.

Animal welfare was always Maila's greatest interest. Maybe she could become an evangelist and produce and choreograph religious musicals, then drive the profits into helping neglected, abused, and abandoned animals. She wasn't particularly religious, but she believed in God. However, her dream would require a sponsor and $20,000. Finding a benefactor willing to take a chance on such a flight of fancy was impossible. The only real option was for Maila to sponsor herself.

I wanted to find a way to get on television. I certainly had paid my dues & now all I had to do was make the leap. An entirely new industry awaited. I could do comedy. After all, my "husband" was a comedy writer. His credo was "You take an illogical situation & then carry it to its logical conclusion. After that, comedy writes itself."

There was a hugely successful show on at the time called "The Websters." It was sort of a soap opera & I personally found it to be incredibly boring. But I thought maybe I could do a parody of them, have this weird family go about doing everyday, mundane things. Then, I realized Charles Addams was already doing that in his cartoon "The Homebodies" which was published in the New Yorker magazine. So then I thought, that's what I'll do. I'll bring Charles Addams to television.

Maila and her friend Rudi Gernreich met frequently to have coffee and share their dreams. For years, Rudi was a performance dancer before settling in with his true passion, fashion design. At the time, Rudi's life was the best it had ever been. Not so for Maila. Her dream to be on television was going nowhere.

"If you want to get noticed by the big boys, the Bal Caribe is the place to be," Rudi told her. "I go every year. The costumes, such fun! There will be prizes!"

Maila was excited. She would bring her Charles Addams creation to the Bal Caribe costume ball. To her disappointment, Dink refused to be her escort, saying he wasn't interested in "a bunch of queens prancing around in full drag." But he atoned by giving Maila ten dollars to buy a costume.

She rented an Indian movie wig from Max Factor's Hollywood studio and bought a remnant of black rayon fabric. A pattern was unnecessary—Maila visualized the dress perfectly, sketching, then transferring the image onto newspaper. Then, piece by piece, she cut out her pattern with manicure scissors and hand-stitched her costume together.

According to Dink, an escort for Maila was arranged.

"There was a little old guy in a one-armed joint that we went to once in a while if we had the money for a cup of coffee. Maila found out that he had a highland drag—kilts and all. So she got the little counterman (everyone called him 'Scotty') to take her to the dress ball..."

They made quite a pair: the diminutive Scotsman and the black-shrouded zombie. Black stringy hair cascaded over deathly pallid shoulders. Her tomb-worn dress was in tatters; its long shreds hung from lifeless limbs. Her lips were oxygen-deprived blue, her skin a deathly gray, her eyes vacant and unblinking. Her feet bare.

The ball was held at the Moulin Rouge, formerly Earl Carroll's, and it was a huge affair. The attendance of the ball was estimated at 2,000. With much fanfare, the costume judges winnowed the contestants from 20 to 10, then down to five.

Finally, there were only two finalists: the ghoul girl and the naked cowboy. The ghoul appeared unfazed that her competition wore nothing but a hat, chaps, boots, and strategically placed blinking lights.

In a last bid to vie for the judge's votes, the finalists were directed to make their way once around the perimeter of the dance floor. The ghoul skulked while the cowboy pranced. A slight rumbling from the audience grew louder and louder until it erupted. The crowd chanted in unison, "Charles Addams! Charles Addams!"

The creepy Cinderella was crowned the belle of the ball, and Maila claimed her first-place prize: a portable radio.

One of the thousands in attendance that night was Hunt Stromberg, Jr. Recently promoted to program director at KABC television, Stromberg was anxious to prove his worth.

He remembered the zombie woman who, without speaking a word, inspired a near-riot at the ball. In fact, Stromberg couldn't keep his mind off her. He had to have her.

The station had a slew of third-rate movies they wanted to package up for late-night viewing but were challenged as to how to present it. Stromberg believed the cadaver girl who rocked the house at the Bal Caribe would be the perfect host to present the recycled horror flicks. So effusive were Stromberg's efforts to get the studio execs on board with his idea, they agreed to give the girl a shot—if they could find her. And that task fell to Stromberg.

Weeks, then months passed, and the girl's identity remained a mystery. Stromberg's superiors were on his tail with increasing urgency.

Stromberg was nervous. The name Stromberg was well known in town, thanks to his father, Hunt Stromberg, Sr., one of the most prolific producers in Hollywood history. At 23, Jr. had produced several plays on Broadway to a modicum of success. But now in Hollywood, even with the advantage of his pedigree, Stromberg Junior's quest proved difficult. Because the girl had been in costume, he wouldn't recognize her even if he were standing next to her on the street.

Still, Stromberg didn't give up, and finally, five months into his intensive search, he asked the right person: Rudi Gernreich.

"Do I know her? Of course I do," Gernreich said. "She's Maila Nurmi, the first woman in Southern California to wear backless shoes. She's in the phone book under Mrs. Dean Riesner."

On a blustery Ides of March in 1954, Maila rode the Red Car to meet with Stromberg at KABC on Prospect and Talmadge. Her haircut was short and blonde, and she'd dressed in black from head to toe: sweater, capris, flats, and cape.

Inside, she heard the secretaries' whispers. "That's Hunt's vampire girl."

Stromberg took a look at his girl ghoul sans makeup and was pleased. She was a beauty.

He explained that the studio was looking for a host to introduce a lineup of late-night horror films. They were interested in the Charles Addams character she'd portrayed at the Bal Caribe.

Here it was. The break Maila long worked for. Excited as she was, she was also curious as to who would portray the rest of Addams' cartoon family.

Stromberg's answer came as a shock. "We only want you." The proposed program was really just an experiment tethered to a skimpy budget.

Maila asked if Addams would receive credit.

Stromberg's answer was clear. "No need to. These are horror films, not cartoons."

"Well then, I can't possibly do it," Maila said. "I can't infringe upon Charles Addams' creation."

Stromberg wanted Maila. Badly. He asked her if she could change up the character. "You could make her a vampire instead of a zombie."

Maila asked for two weeks. Stromberg gave her four days.

The clock was ticking on her future as she rode the railway home. Ninety-six hours to come up with something so fantastical that, when the studio heads saw it, their eyeballs would pop out and roll across the floor. Nothing less would do.

I started by thinking what people said was inevitable, that being sex, death & taxes. Hunt wanted a vampire. So then I thought what about a sexy vampire. Addams' flat-chested, barefoot mute certainly wasn't that. I could be a sexy vampire pondering death in all sorts of crazy and urbane ways. The taxes? I'd leave those up to the Republicans.

The dress needed major work. Maila turned the dress backward so what had been the zippered, low-cut back of the ball costume was now the front of the vampire dress. For structure, she stitched a wire hanger into the bodice to support the plunging neckline. She shortened the sleeves and reattached them with tatters intact, then slit the skirt as far as modesty allowed. Finally, she adjusted the seams to accommodate her waist cincher, push-up bra, and bust and hip pads.

With a four-day time frame to make it all happen, Maila was relieved that she already owned a fetish wardrobe. She had only to shop her own closet to acquire the foundation pieces needed for the look.

The fingernails were a problem. Even Woolworth's didn't stock three-inch fingernails, so Maila cut pieces from a plastic food container, which required boiling to soften them up, and shaped them to fit over her own nails. Then she wrapped them around pencils and secured them with rubber bands. Finally, they were cooled in ice cube trays. The process was time-consuming and didn't end even after the nails were glued on and polished. Their length caused them to pop off at the slightest bump. Maila had to carry spares. Later, she bought pairs of mesh gloves and glued the nails to its fingertips. Maila would describe the recipe for her look as "one part Greta Garbo, two parts each of the Dragon Lady, Evil Queen and Theda Bara, three parts Norma Desmond, and four parts *Bizarre* magazine."

All the cutting, sewing, and polishing was simply the window dressing. The bigger task was how Maila would breathe life into her brand-new baby and animate her, as she was no longer the silent, one-dimensional cartoon character who attended the Bal Caribe.

Per Stromberg's request, Maila arrived at KABC in full costume. In the pocket of her black cape was a list of names that she and Dink had concocted for her vampire girl. It was the most fun they'd had together in months.

> *Just before Dink dropped me off at KABC, I asked him how I looked. He said, 'Looking at you is like drinking a shot of hundred-proof whiskey. After you recover from the shock of it going down, you want more.' I was unnerved by his response & so I said 'Oh, so you have to be drunk to find me appealing?' He said 'It sure as hell wouldn't hurt.' He laughed at my expense. I thought he was being callous but he said it was my own fault for setting up the punchline. I was often his unwitting straight man. Maybe he should go get drunk. Maybe then he would find me sexy.*

Maila walked into Stromberg's office, her black wig in sharp contrast against her pale skin. With the flourish of a magician, she threw off her cape to expose a figure that provoked a double take. Stromberg could scarcely believe his eyes. The evidence of Maila starving, exercising, and swathing her waist in meat tenderizer was still in evidence. A black patent-leather belt cinched Maila's waist down several inches smaller than the circumference of a 45rpm record. She pulled a long black cigarette holder from her cleavage and positioned it between two lacquered three-inch talons, painted a color she would later call "hemorrhage red."

"Cigarette?" she commanded in a low, sultry voice.

Although the specifics of Maila's audition remain a mystery, it can be assumed with certainty that she created a sensation, because before she left, a deal was hammered out.

Maila's original contract with KABC can be described as nothing more than a handshake agreement put to paper. It states that Maila would be compensated $75 per program and that the network wanted to own a percentage of the

KABC-TV Vampira publicity still. Dennis Stock/Magnum Photos.

character. She agreed to a 13-week contract, which, if the show were successful, would be increased to another 13 weeks. A two-week notice was required for cancellation.

It was my idea to give them forty-nine percent. I wanted to give
them as much as I possibly could without losing control because I
appreciated the fact that they had taken me out of obscurity.

KABC looked over Maila's list of potential names for the character and narrowed their choice down to Enchantrix and Vampira. The latter was the winner—one of Dink's ideas.

The push was on. With only weeks before the show aired, KABC trotted out their glamour ghoul at every opportunity. Suddenly, Vampira was cropping up at shopping centers, car dealerships, and nightclubs. They put her in a chauffeured Packard convertible to be driven up and down the Sunset Strip. Seated in the backseat, she shielded herself from the sun with a black parasol. Each red light elicited a primal scream that caused traffic to stop and pedestrians to point.

At long last, Maila felt she had succeeded and was thrilled beyond her wildest imaginations. She'd proven to herself—and most of all to her father—that her art could be successful.

KABC issued press releases to announce that Vampira was about to creep onto the television airwaves and into the homes of Southern California's viewers. The buzz was out, and columnists all wanted the story.

Sponsors were aggressively courted. An introductory brochure was mailed out with a picture of Vampira on the cover. The caption stated, "She's Dying To Meet You" and promised advertisers "a big Saturday night payoff." Inside, it read, "She's a magnificent, exotic, if somewhat macabre slice of womanhood. She's a girl who looks thrilling in a form-fitting shroud, a devil-doll who has Hollywood's werewolves panting at her door."

On April 30, 1954, the day before Vampira's television premiere, *Los*

Angeles Mirror columnist Paul Coates arrived at Ciro's on the Sunset Strip to interview KABC's sensational new horror host, the hollow-cheeked, wasp-waisted Vampira. She was seated with program director Hunt Stromberg, Jr., and Ciro's manager, Herman Hover.

According to Coates, Stromberg was positively giddy when introducing his girl. For her part, Vampira "stared across the room with studied disinterest" while fondling the sharp edge of a steak knife.

She remained silent until Coates asked her if she could talk.

Her eyes snapped back into focus. "Of course I can talk," she said indignantly.

"Then tell me about yourself," Coates prodded.

"There isn't much to tell," she replied. "I was born in Lapland. I'm married. My husband used to write for Ken Murray. I have an owl for a house pet. I have a 19-inch waist, 38-inch bust, and 36-inch hips. My earliest recollection as a child is that I always wanted to play with mice. I'm very antisocial. I simply detest people. I don't like snakes; they eat spiders, and I'm very fond of spiders."

During the interview, Stromberg alternately clapped his hands and emitted gasps of sheer ecstasy while continuing to gaze lovingly at his protégée. "Isn't she perfect?" he sighed.

"How do you feel about children? Do you like them?" Coates asked.

"Oh, yes," the ghoul exclaimed. "Delicious!"

Coates had to admit the girl was perfect.

Not to be left out of the conversation, Ciro's manager, Hover, added, "You could say she's just a girl from the Styx. Get it? S-T-Y-X."

When the interview was over, Coates remained unsettled. It was just weird. Was the ghoul girl psychic as well? She told him he was a Pisces because he had watery eyes. He was indeed a Pisces. He went away not realizing that Vampira was his friend Maila—the girl who worked at the Savoy, whom he'd spoken to often and nicknamed "the Nordic Empress."

Chapter Nine

The Eisenhower administration made good on its promise to restore peace and prosperity to the country. By 1954, the Korean War was over, and thanks to the G.I Bill, the American dream of home ownership was never more attainable. The economy was strong, and unemployment rates were low. More than half of American families owned a television, and families gathered around their sets to eat their dinner on aluminum trays and watch *Beat the Clock* and *I Love Lucy*.

The same year, at the stroke of midnight on the last day of April, KABC premiered a preview of Maila's show, from an episode titled "Dig Me Later, Vampira," and Los Angeles' insomniacs got their first glimpse at the phenomenon that would spawn an entire genre.

The next night, the first full episode of *Nightmare Attic*, the show's original working title, debuted. A bizarre-looking woman draped in black tatters entered the shot from the left side of the screen. Her waist was so tiny, it defied comprehension that she could be human. Soundless as an apparition, she seemed to float, before stopping in front of an upholstered Victorian sofa accented with skull finials along the back. The woman turned and spoke into the camera.

"Hello," she said, her voice low and deliberate. "It's time to do it again. Oh, but we haven't been introduced yet. I think introductions are so important. They kind of separate the living from the dead. Anyway, I am Vampira."

She sat down on the sofa and arranged herself to prime advantage. The slit in her skirt parted to reveal a long length of leg sheathed in fishnet hose. Her décolletage was exposed to the limits of decency. Her pale skin, her hollowed cheeks, her eyebrows arched like twin boomerangs. She was beautiful in a deranged sort of way. In the glow of candlelight, she spoke.

"Oh, I've got a wonderful offer to make to you tonight. It's a new hospitalization plan called the Yellow Cross. It's for people who unsuccessfully try to commit suicide. The plan pays all the bills 'til you're well enough to try again. If you're interested in such a plan, I'll be glad to get in touch with you. Of course, I hope you never have to use it. It's disheartening to hear of an unsuccessful suicide. And remember our slogan: If at first you don't succeed, die, die, then die again.

"It's time for our love story now. I hope you all enjoy ... *Condemned ... to Live*. It's a lovely tale of tender unique murders. Just the sort of thing we all hope for."

She went on.

"I went to a delightful funeral yesterday. We buried a friend of mine—alive. It takes a heap o' dyin' to make a house a tomb. This is Vampira, until next week, wishing you bad dreams, darlings."

Vampira succeeded in doing what Maila always wanted to do: rage at the establishment for their artificial lives. But Vampira was clever. Instead of angry admonitions and rebukes, she spun a dark web of sex and death and made it palatable with humor. Invited into Middle America's immaculate living rooms, she thanked them by blasting them where they lived—and sometimes serenading them.

Oh, ain't she sweet,

Lyin' drunk there in the street,

Now I ask you very confidentially,

Ain't she sweet?

As "A Pretty Girl Is Like a Melody" played softly in the background, Vampira appeared wearing an executioner's black hood while assuring the housewife that her "hat" is "suitable for indiscreet excursions or public hangings. And if your husband is so fortunate as to be the one being hanged, it can also double as mourning wear. That way, you can say you kept your head while everyone else around you was losing theirs."

The Vampira Show stretched the limits of innuendo. America was at the dawning of the nuclear age, when movies began to feature monsters and flying saucers, when a vampiric succubus appeared on the television, and beckoned you to join her in her creepy attic. And the Angelenos responded.

Three weeks later, Stromberg called Maila with news that surprised no one more than KABC. To accommodate the huge viewer response, the show would appear an hour earlier. And there was even better news: Saturday morning, *Life* magazine was sending a photographer.

That was a huge deal, and Maila knew exactly what it meant. National exposure.

Dennis Stock looked young enough to be in high school. Maila took an instant liking to the photographer. He told her she had the look for high fashion, to which Maila scoffed, "High fashion, indeed. I prefer to slink rather than strut."

It was a warm, sunny day when Stock set out with Vampira in the old convertible with its obligatory uniformed chauffeur. One of his photographs from that day is a favorite of author and filmmaker R.H. Greene's. In an addendum to his radio documentary *Vampira and Me*, Greene wrote about his friend, Maila, and the photo of her. "It shows Maila in full Vampira mode, leaning out of the back seat of her trademark 1932 Packard toward a mother and two daughters, who look like they just stepped out of a Norman Rockwell painting for the *Saturday Evening Post*. We can't see the girls' faces, but their body posture indicates hesitance. And no wonder. Because Maila's expression captures something simultaneously true to her character and to the woman who played her: She's utterly baffled by the pretty little tableau of normalcy before her. This affluent

KABC publicity still, courtesy of the Jove de Renzy collection.

trio of females is a foreign thing to Maila/Vampira, some horror from another world. A walking nightmare herself, Maila stares at a perfect icon of American middle-class bliss as if she's the one having the nightmare."

On the studio set, a cobweb-draped corridor was readied to coincide with Stock's arrival and would become the show's signature opening. Vampira took her mark behind a curtain at the end of a narrow, dark hallway. Stock poised with his camera, ready as the show went live.

The theme music—excerpts from Gustav Holst's *The Planets* and Béla Bartók's *Music for Strings, Percussion, and Celesta*—was cued. A figure emerges from the shadows and glides down a cobwebbed hallway framed by tall candelabra. Slowly, she advances down the corridor through a miasma of swirling

Maila at Liberace's "Come As You Were" show at the Riviera in Las Vegas, 1956.
Courtesy of the Jove de Renzy Collection.

dry ice vapors. For a few seconds, the juxtaposition of the woman's wasp-waisted silhouette against the white mist is startling.

She stops directly in front of the camera, her face impassive. Without warning, she screams the kind of scream that warns of bloody murder, yet in a nanosecond, her countenance changes from horror to bliss.

"Oooh," Vampira purrs, stretching like a cat waking up from a nap in the sun, "screaming relaxes me so."

Fade to black.

The censors never caught it. In a time when Lucy and Desi could not be filmed in the same bed together, Maila Nurmi feigned an orgasm on live television. Saturday night after Saturday night.

Soon, offers arrived. One of the first was an invitation to appear with established horror stars Peter Lorre, Bela Lugosi, and Lon Chaney, Jr., on *The Red Skelton Show*. KABC took the deal.

During rehearsals, Maila was introduced to one of Skelton's writers and sometime announcer, a young Johnny Carson. According to Maila, when a very ill Lugosi missed several cues, Carson could be heard laughing and belittling the aging actor. Maila developed a lifelong dislike for Carson and an affinity for Lugosi, whom she remembered as the consummate gentleman. Later, she wrote:

Just recalling that moment, I am permeated with serenity. Bela, my dear, if you're listening, let me tell you this. When at the end of the show, you took my arm to guide me to the footlights for a curtain call, I was suddenly ten feet tall & wore a fifty-foot aura of royalty. I was all the queens of history rolled into one. Yes, Bela. You touched me with a magic I have never known before or after.

From the appearance on Skelton's show, she was paid the AFTRA standard, five hundred dollars, and KABC would take 49 percent of that. But how the money came to her was bizarre. Checks were made payable not to Maila Nurmi but to Vampira and sent directly to KABC in care of Hunt Stromberg, Jr. CBS used the same method to make paychecks out to Clem Kadiddlehopper instead of the character's creator, Red Skelton. It was but another sign that Stromberg wanted to remain in control and that Maila was a nonentity. It was Vampira who mattered.

The June 14, 1954 issue of *Life* was hot off the press when Maila and her friend Rudi Gernreich met at Googies. Both had reason to celebrate. In a stroke of serendipity, their artistry was featured within the same issue: Maila for her

Vampira character and Gernreich for his fashion designs. More press followed. *Newsweek* and *TV Guide* ran stories on Vampira. Big-city newspapers published photos of television's creepy femme fatale, and fan clubs cropped up across Europe, Asia, and as far away as Australia. Vampira was a sensation, and quite unexpectedly, considering *Nightmare Attic* was a local late-night television show, available only within the greater Los Angeles area.

Around this time, the name of the show was changed to *The Vampira Show* to reflect the host's immense popularity. The station's mail room was deluged with letters from fans—Maila wished her father could see how popular she was now. Among the letters was one from a former classmate at Astoria High School, Betty Ponsness-Long.

Maila's response to Ponsness-Long survived either because it was a rough draft or because she forgot to mail it. But its importance lies in the fact that it's a window into Maila's life as television's newest sensation. Perhaps Maila engaged in a little puffery, but who could blame her?

> *Betty dear,*
>
> *You can't imagine how thrilled I was to hear from you! My press agent is coming to take me for a fitting (new Vampira gown) then I have a story conference and then a business meeting in which my personal manager and my agent fight over how they can outsmart my studio.*

Maila wrote of her happy marriage to Dink, referring to him formally as Dean. She told Betty about how she and her screenwriter husband shared their busy and successful lives with five cats in a canyon away from the city, among the butterflies. Maila professed "to have very little mother instinct," but she later admitted that she would love to adopt a little boy someday (here the word "boy" is scratched out), adding:

> *...why did I say boy when I meant girl? Maybe in a few years. An orphan, as I am afraid of childbirth.*

128

As a result of "getting religion" four years before, Maila maintained her ultimate goal was to become an evangelist. Her letter concludes by saying that "all celebrities are just people."

> *I personally like the neurotics among the performers—Marlon Brando, Shelley Winters, Laurence [sic] Tierney, John Carradine, Leslie Caron—the Ann Blythes bore me. I do value the friendship of the aforementioned wild hearts—but their public success is only an inconvenience to me.*

The requests for interviews and appearances for Vampira kept Maila jumping. In the summer of 1954, Vampira appeared on *The Saturday Night Revue*, hosted by Ben Blue. She appeared in parades and at conventions, universities, and grand openings—and even on a game show, *Place the Face*. Walter Winchell, the premier gossip columnist at the time wrote, "The only person more popular than Vampira is Eisenhower."

> *Here I was. Me, Maila Nurmi, someone who most people wouldn't even want to go out & have a hot dog with & as Vampira I had just been given the key to the city.*

The same summer, *The Vampira Show* was renewed for another 13 weeks, and a new contract was executed, wherein the network continued to control a percentage of Vampira.

Hollywood adored her. The nation adored her. But that adoration ended at her front door.

Dink's career was on the upswing. He didn't have the time or inclination to participate in all the hoopla surrounding Vampira. Between script conferences and frantic deadlines, his time was tight. The last thing he wanted to do was escort Maila to some ridiculous function as she wore that shroud. At first, he was stunned by her popularity. Then it became an liability.

To the two people in the world whom Maila loved the most—Dink and her mother—she was an embarrassment.

Trouble in Laurel Canyon was brewing. And the news troubled no one more than Maila's mother. While Sophie was in Oregon for the summer, Maila called her to complain about Dink. She said that he was cruel and heartless, a two-bit former drunk who, after she encouraged and supported him for years, now refused to participate in her success.

In the midst of another fight, Maila revealed to her mother that while experimenting with her Vampira makeup, Dink flew off the handle. She said she locked herself in the bathroom to get away from him, but it only provoked him all the more. She finally emerged and announced she was leaving the house until he cooled off, but Dink physically restrained her, mocking her appearance, saying she was foolish and looked like a clown.

Maila wrenched herself free, flew out the door, and ran down the hill, with Dink yelling after her, "Say hi to the stiffs at the morgue, will ya?"

Googies was her sanctuary. There, in full Vampira makeup sans wig and costume, she was home. There was something about looking at the world through the long, feathery lashes of her alter ego that compelled her to stay in character. She was invincible, without the frailties that confound the lives of the living. Being Vampira allowed her to escape from herself, if only for a short while.

In an email, author and former night manager of Googies, Steve Hayes, said: "I think Maila actually became more weird in real life after she became Vampira. I can say that because I ... worked alongside her when she was kind of shy and sweet and somewhat normal. But all that changed after Vampira. It's as if she believed she couldn't drop the image."

In Vampira's skin, her secret was safe. No one would suspect that Maila was terrified Dink would leave her.

The makeup job carries on while the animation hibernates.

Chapter Ten

In late August of 1954, Billy Wilder's *Sabrina* premiered in Hollywood. Like all big galas, regardless of the weather that night, the stars would shine brightly.

Throngs of fans waited in the bleachers across from the theater hoping to catch a glimpse of Audrey Hepburn or Humphrey Bogart. Among the fans was Maila, alone in a crowd. Dink had declined to go with her.

Maila may have been the hottest ticket in town, but without her Vampira costume, no one recognized her, and she was grateful for the anonymity—she was on a mission. She'd already met most of the big-name stars. What she wanted now was to find people who interested her. The stars were here to be seen. Maila wanted to find a misfit, someone who despised the dog and pony show and was only there because he was ordered to attend. Someone like herself. Someone she could relate to.

She'd spotted a young, small-framed nervous-acting fellow standing in the throngs of fans. She didn't know a thing about him other than he had no fashion sense, as confirmed by the hideous blue plaid jacket he wore, with sleeves that hung down past his fingertips.

Suddenly, the surrounding energy shifted. The crowd erupted into screams

Maila with Jack Simmons outside Googies, 1954. Michael Ochs Archives via Getty Images.

and cheers. Flashbulbs popped from every direction, and Maila focused upon the cavalcade of celebrities proceeding to their limos that lined the roadway. Clamoring photographers were rewarded by crimson lips flashing million-dollar smiles. Screaming fans were appeased by concessionary gestures—a wave of the hand, a blown kiss. The excitement was palpable.

I saw Martha Hyer. Certainly not her. She was awful, the current mistress of Hal Wallis. Bogart...already met him, he was a nasty oaf.

I had about given up when here comes this guy in a tux with Howard Hughes' whore on his arm. She had a loopy smile on her face, clearly enjoying the attention, but he is mad. It was obviously a studio date. He is angry to have to be there, & he certainly doesn't want to be with her. And I knew, I had to meet this guy.

The stars disappeared into their limousines to be chauffeured to their respective after-parties, and the fans began to disperse. Although there were no limos for Maila, she did have a party invitation, as well as a car and driver at her disposal.

"Did you see anyone interesting?" the man behind the wheel wanted to know.

"Yeah," Maila said, "the guy with Terry Moore and the guy in the oversized horse blanket."

"The guy who doesn't know how to dress is Jack Simmons. You'll meet him tonight at the party. I don't know who the other one is."

The next afternoon, Maila shared a booth in Googies with plaid-jacketed Jack Simmons, her newfound friend, and a man named Jonathan Haze. While they were socializing, a loud rumble came from the parking lot, and Maila looked out the window to see a couple arriving on a motorcycle.

A young man burst into the restaurant like a cyclone, a one-legged girl in his wake. The girl was Toni Lee Scott, a jazz singer who had lost her limb in a motorcycle accident. But on that day, it wasn't the one-legged girl who caught Maila's attention. Her mouth agape, she slammed both elbows on the table, banging her funny bones in the process. Her arms tingled to the tips of her fingers as she stood halfway to her feet.

"Jeeesus Christ," Maila gasped.

Even though he wore glasses in the restaurant, there was no mistaking him. It was the kid from the *Sabrina* premiere.

So extreme was her reaction, Haze thought she was having a seizure.

"Who *is* that?" Maila demanded of Haze.

He followed her steady gaze. "Oh, that's James Dean," Haze said matter-of-factly. "I just finished a movie with him. Why?"

"I *have* to meet him. In fact, he's the only man I want to meet in Hollywood."

"Fine, I'll introduce you," Haze said, getting up from the booth.

Even in mid-afternoon, the place was slammed, and Haze didn't return right away. When Simmons noticed Dean over by the cigarette machine, he went over to where Dean stood and motioned toward Maila.

Dean looked past Jack and saw Maila. Short blonde hair. No makeup. Very un-Vampira-like.

She got up and walked over to where Jimmy and Jack stood together and, without preamble, asked Dean, "Where is she?"

Dean was unfazed by Maila's lack of etiquette.

"She's sitting at the counter," he said and jerked his head in the direction of the girl he rode in with.

"No, not your girlfriend," Maila said.

"She's not my girlfriend," Dean said.

"No, not her."

"What are you talking about?"

"Your mother."

Dean's face reddened and he wrapped his hands around his head and made a sound like a hissing radiator. "Sssssss, yeah."

He began to look around, clearly uncomfortable.

"Well... where is she?" Maila persisted.

"Maa-aan, is it that obvious?"

"Yeah, it is."

Finally, Dean answered. "She cut out."

Maila claimed to be psychic. When she first met Jimmy, she knew nothing about him, let alone that he was motherless.

Dean on his bike, January 1955.
Hulton Archives / Stringer / via Getty Images

At the time, I thought Jimmy's mother had abandoned him. It was later I found out she died of cancer at only twenty-nine and left him alone in the world with a father who was distant. A man he could not relate to. A man who made dentures who was clinical and sensible and practical, not at all like Jimmy.

Maila and James Dean met on a cosmic path to stardom, at the precise moment of critical mass, when Maila was at the apex of her career and Dean was unknown, having just completed his first film, *East of Eden*. From the moment they met, they clicked. It wasn't sexual; it transcended anything physical. It was more of a recognition that they were alike.

Within the hour of their first meeting, Maila was astride Dean's motorcycle, clinging to his waist as they twisted up the curves of Sunset Plaza Drive. Dean's pad was essentially a room above a garage, which he often described as a "wastebasket with walls."

As they got to know each other, Maila and Dean discovered that they were both named by a literary parent of the opposite sex. Dean's mother named her son James Byron after the British poet Lord Byron, and Maila's father named her for Finnish writer Maila Talvio. A commonality established, Dean read Maila a Ray Bradbury poem about a young boy whose mother died, resulting in the kid hanging himself in the garage. As she listened to the words, Maila fixated on a small noose suspended from the ceiling in Dean's apartment.

After Dean finished the poem, Maila pointed to the noose and asked, "What is this preoccupation you have with hangings?"

"That's the way I'm going to die," Dean said, "with a broken neck."

We were psychic twins, Jimmy & I. Both of us were misunderstood in a world of strange beings. When at age thirty-one, I met Jimmy, he was the first entity of my own species I'd ever encountered.

When at twenty-three, Jimmy met me, he thought he'd at last

James Dean, 1955.
Frank Worth, courtesy of Capital Art/Hulton Archives/via Getty Images.

met someone from his own planet. We became instantly glued to one another—our psyches melded.

And so, for a time, there were two Deans in Maila's life. Vampira was becoming more than a distraction in Maila's relationship with Dink. Obsessed with cinching her waist smaller and smaller, she measured it obsessively and reported the results. A fraction of an inch larger or smaller would determine her disposition for the entire day. Seventeen inches, eighteen inches—what did it matter? But for Maila, nothing mattered more. Her hourglass figure is what got her noticed. It's what made her famous.

The Vampira Show's ratings soared, and it was arguably the only television show where the commercials and station breaks were more popular than the main feature.

All work and no slay makes Vampira a dull girl... I sign epitaphs, not autographs... I'm a Vampyromaniac, I like to set people afire... See you next week at 11 p.m., that's post-mortem.

The public ate it up.

One week, Vampira would bathe in a cauldron of boiling oil, arsenic, and belladonna. The next, she was singing a song she called "The Black 'n' Blues." Rollo, her pet tarantula, made frequent appearances, descending from the ceiling on a thin string of web. Like any sophisticated ghoul girl, Vampira mixed cocktails on-air from her well-stocked poison bar. On one show, she concocted a Mortician's Martini: one jigger of formaldehyde, a jigger of rattlesnake venom, and a dash of vulture blood. When at last it was poured into a champagne glass and garnished with a glass eyeball, she announced a most deadly toast.

Here's to Zombies, the living dead;
May you find one, beneath your bed;

They live on blood and you should too;

Hemoglobin is the drink for you!

Trickle, trickle, trickle.

Maila adored the show's writer, Peter Robinson. But she also loved that she was allowed to contribute to the scripts. On air Vampira dictated that the cocktail was to be sipped through a noose. The noose idea was Maila's, an obvious nod to her new friend, Jimmy, and his fixation with nooses.

After the cameras were off, Maila didn't go home. Doing so would either mean another fight or a stony silence. There was no in-between, and either option was a reminder of a love she was losing. So, she went where the orange neon lights beckoned the rebels and the rabble-rousers like moths to a flame: Googies. The nightly drama evolving out on the Strip always seemed to make its way through its front door, where Maila had a front-row seat. The distraction soothed her wounded heart.

For me, Jimmy seemed a mirror of my psyche, and Googies was the womb in which we lived as Siamese twins, the endless stream of coffee our placenta. Sure, we sometimes ventured away from there, but the environment outside the womb was hostile to fetuses.

Maila and Jack Simmons became a trio after midnight, when Jimmy would arrive and commandeer a booth. Even by Hollywood standards, they were an unlikely set of oddballs: television's vampire, the emerging movie star, and the gay bit actor. It was inevitable they'd become fodder for the gossip columnists, who initially dubbed them "Vampira and Her Spooks" and then later "the Night Watch."

At the time, Maila was the most famous of the trio and was often surrounded by hangers-on. As their notoriety grew, some of the hangers-on later claimed membership in the exclusive group. But the original Night Watch consisted of just the three: Maila, Jimmy, and Jack.

KABC was not happy with reports about the Night Watch. After all, their vampire girl was a married woman. Running around town until the wee hours with two single men posed a PR problem. To quell any rumors, they reported that Maila's husband was a screenwriter who worked at night, and because he required complete silence without distraction, she stayed away so he could write. It was imperative that KABC foster the belief that in her real life, Maila was a normal housewife. Nothing could be further from the truth.

> *We were a ménage à trois without the sex. But that didn't mean we were all celibate. When it came to romance, Jimmy wasn't biased by age or gender. At the time I knew him, he was seeing women, but he was basically bi-sexual.*
>
> *I remember when he first took up with Lili Kardell, whom Jimmy called "Fat Cat." She was a Swedish starlet he met at a party at Arthur Loew's. She looked so much like a female version of Jimmy, I told him she could have a mask of her face cast & it would fit him perfectly.*
>
> *We would sit drinking coffee, it would be two or three in the morning & in would come Jimmy. He'd sit down & say he'd just spent the last five hours banging Lili.*

Jimmy's love interests were of no concern to Maila. Their friendship transcended the physical. They were mutual misfits. A mother looking for her son; a boy in search of his mother.

Jimmy learned early on that Maila and Brando were longtime friends. And since Brando was Dean's idol, Dean was interested in everything he could learn about him. Reportedly, Jimmy had Brando's phone number and frequently called him, but Brando totally rejected him and refused his calls. According to Maila, she served as a go-between between the two actors, relaying messages.

Maila felt sorry for Jimmy and told Brando his attitude toward Dean was shameful. She believed his behavior was a result of Jimmy's star rising so fast, and that Marlon felt threatened. Nevertheless, whenever Maila relayed a message from Jimmy, Brando always prefaced his answer by saying, "Tell your little friend that..." When Jimmy asked Maila to find out who Brando thought was the world's best actor, he said, "Tell your little friend the answer to that is Paul Muni." Maila always relayed the message minus the preamble.

During her earlier years, Maila was an advocate of the dress-to-impress crowd, but she'd returned to her true bohemian nature, regardless of her newfound celebrity status. As her relationship with Dink soured, she no longer cared about her off-camera appearance. Devoid of makeup with her short hair sticking up willy-nilly, Maila favored oversized, well-worn sweaters paired with capri pants and ratty sandals. Jimmy's appearance gave her permission to be who she was without pretense.

Jimmy never combed his hair. He slept in his clothes, sometimes wearing the same ones for a week. And he often wore jeans or these white sailor pants covered with motorcycle grease. He was what you'd call a rumpled mess. We'd go out to a coffee shop & the waitresses would look at him in disgust. A few years later on, those same girls swooned over him in the darkness of a movie theater, but back then, they didn't even want to serve him.

Only Jack, their obsessive-compulsive sidekick, considered personal hygiene a virtue.

It seemed appropriate that the trio's usual mode of transportation should be Jack's old converted Cadillac hearse, which Jimmy customized by suspending his signature noose from the headliner. And so began what Maila called their "tombstone tours," a series of late-night romps through graveyards, stealing flowers from one grave to decorate another, and sometimes to sit around sharing a joint within the tranquil confines of a cemetery.

They traipsed about, trying to find grave markers with a familiar name and, once discovered, would make up gruesome stories to explain the deceased's fate. As Maila put it, "We all suffered greatly from a delayed adolescence."

When the game lost its appeal, Jimmy wanted to up the creep factor.

"Ever seen a dead guy?" he asked.

"Ever touch one?" Maila countered.

Jimmy's eyes lit up, while Jack's could only stare in panic. The gauntlet thrown, their twisted game of Truth or Dare commenced.

The search for the ideal corpse was on. They transitioned from prowling cemeteries to stalking mortuaries. Maila made the rules: No women, no children. The ideal candidate must be old and male. Preferably one who had been a friendless loner in life to avoid any chance of an awkward encounter at the mortuary with the deceased's kin.

They scoured the obits in the newspaper and adopted aliases for signing the visitors' registries at mortuaries. Jimmy chose Montgomery Brando, combining the names of the two actors he most admired. Maila settled upon Countess Cuntish, and although they usually called Jack "Pee-Wee," for the purposes of the game, Jimmy assigned him the nickname Jack Hoff. The three practiced writing their pseudonyms on Googies napkins.

They scored a dead guy on the first try. As they drove to the mortuary, Jimmy was excited, Maila was unnerved, and Jack was terrified. The three signed in at the registry and entered the room where the body lay.

With her hand, Maila transferred a kiss from her lips to the dead man's forehead. Jimmy was more curious, and after touching the corpse's face, he tried and failed to pry its mouth open. Jack stood in a dark corner, whimpering. Upon exiting the mortuary, he vomited into the shrubbery, then mewled and carried on as he drove the old Caddy away.

"Jesus, Pee-Wee," Jimmy exclaimed, "would you just shut up? How the fuck would I know the guy's mouth was wired shut?"

The mortuary meanderings continued.

Then another elderly man, recently deceased, was located, and the Night Watch was again on the prowl. A pair of dimly lit candelabra flanked the bier, illuminating the old man in eternal repose. Jimmy was fascinated by a ring that gleamed on the body's finger. Not a wedding band, though—the obits said the man was never married. It appeared to be from a fraternal organization or club. In a split second, Jimmy slid it off and placed it on his own finger.

"Put it back," Maila gasped.

"Dead men never tell," Jimmy whispered.

Clearly, Jimmy had overstepped the bounds of common decency, and once they were back in the hearse, Maila read him the riot act. He didn't respond, but they all knew the game was over. They never spoke of it again.

Baby Jane Fury was a fire-engine red homemade convertible with wooden bumpers, residing on the Warner Brothers lot. Whether she was street-legal or not was unknown.

Just before Vampira came to be, Dink decided it was time for Maila to learn to drive, and since he worked for Warner's, he thought it a good idea to let Maila tool around the lot in the car. The driving lessons didn't pan out, but subsequently, Maila always thought of Baby as her car.

It is not known how Maila and Jimmy came to be riding Baby Jane Fury down Sunset. In all probability, since Jimmy was under contract with Warner Brothers as well, he and Maila conspired to take "her" car for an unauthorized spin. With Jimmy at the wheel and Maila riding shotgun, Baby's motor caught fire. According to their friend Sid Terror, Maila screamed for Jimmy to stop the car. Even as he ignored her pleas, she continued to shriek in panic until they came upon a gas station and Jimmy pulled over next to the pump.

Maila fled from the car, screaming that the car would explode, as Jimmy calmly opened the hood to leaping flames. From a distance, she shouted for Jimmy to run, but he stood his ground, beating at the flames with his jacket until they were extinguished.

At Googies one night, Nicholas Ray's name came up in casual conversation, and Jimmy told of meeting the director while filming *East of Eden*. Maila commented that she'd heard that Ray had recently rescued a dog from a house fire. Since Ray lived just a block away at the Chateau Marmont, Jimmy insisted that the three of them—he, Maila, and Jack—go to Ray's bungalow immediately to find out if this rumor was true. That it was after midnight was of no concern.

Unannounced, the Night Watch appeared on the director's doorstep. When Ray opened the door, Jimmy somersaulted into the room until his momentum was terminated by a chair. When asked, the director confirmed the dog rescue story as true, and without another word, Jimmy somersaulted back out the door. Like ghosts in the night, the trio was gone. A rumor still circulates that says this bizarre visit convinced Ray that he need look no further than Dean to play the lead in *Rebel Without a Cause*.

At Halloween of 1954, requests for Vampira appearances doubled. She rode in a convertible in UCLA's Homecoming parade; a banner touted her as the "Bitter Sweet-Heart of Alpha Tau Omega." She handed out safe driving awards at a baker's convention and presided over the closing down of an old jail in Los Angeles and of a library in Pasadena. It came as no surprise that Vampira was the most popular costume in town. Zsa Zsa Gabor's maid called to find out how to turn her celebrity employer into the perfect vampire girl.

What a year it had been. The previous Halloween, Maila made caramel apples, popcorn balls, and cookies for the trick-or-treaters and, together with Dink, decorated the outside of their little house with jack o' lanterns and crepe paper streamers. No one came. "The next year," Maila said, "I *was* Halloween."

And Halloween meant it was again time for the annual Bal Caribe. It hardly mattered that again Dink refused to be her escort, because she already had one: Hunt Stromberg, Jr. Maila attended as the reigning queen of the ball, this time not as the cartoonish Addams Family matriarch but as Vampira. Certainly, all in attendance knew the success story of last year's costume winner, who had morphed into the dark goddess. The couple took to the dance floor in a kind of victory lap. Cameras flashed, and for that one night, they were royalty.

Vampira fixed an icy glare into Stromberg's leering face as he led her around the dance floor, like the proud owner of a prized racehorse. Behind his unctuous smile was a man whose *raison d'être* was to control. A man who never let an occasion slip by when he didn't take full credit for discovering Vampira and for her resounding success. A man who, from the first time Maila appeared in full costume, became obsessed.

On Halloween weekend, ABC allowed Vampira to perform two half-hour "horror shows" at the Orpheum Theatre in downtown Los Angeles. The set-up was that the Orpheum would provide a double feature of horror movies of a quality that was acceptable to ABC, and Vampira would put on her show between the two features.

Although ABC would not share in any of the profits generated from the weekend performances, the network agreed to promote the event on their Los Angeles affiliate station, KABC. If it sounded as if the network was exceptionally magnanimous in this arrangement, they were not, for they made it nearly impossible for Maila to make any money. She was responsible for the entire production: the writing and the staging, including paying any supporting performers. ABC claimed ownership of all the props used on *The Vampira Show*. If she wanted to borrow the sofa, poison bar, tombstone coffee table, or even a single candelabrum, she would have to pay ABC for its use. In addition, she was to pay any transportation charges of said props.

Maila pulled it off. She signed the contract with ABC and the Orpheum on October 18, just 11 days before the Friday night performance. It isn't known if she rented the props, made her own, or appeared on a bare stage. Regardless, she had to be fast, because after her Saturday evening performance, she had to be back at KABC for her live show at 11 p.m.

As fall progressed, Jimmy became preoccupied and more sullen than usual. Getting him to talk was impossible, so in an effort to distract him from whatever was on his mind, Maila suggested he come to the studio to watch her live show.

It was November 20, 1954. On deck that night, a segment of the script called for Vampira be a spooky librarian. But there was a problem. They needed another body for the skit: no dialogue, just someone to assume the role of a sleeping man. And there was Jimmy, conveniently. He was recruited for the part and dressed in a tweed jacket.

Filmed sitting at a table from behind, Jimmy's unruly cowlick, like an obscene finger, stood in defiance. His head rested on folded arms as he snored loudly; at his elbow, a sign commanded, "Quiet."

The camera panned to Vampira wearing black framed glasses and reading from a thick dictionary. She began to recite. "Macabre... madhouse... maim... malady... mangle... manslaughter... massacre... merriment..." Vampira stops reading, then looks right and left. "All right," she says, "who's the wise guy?"

Even as Vampira slammed the "Quiet" sign firmly on the table, there is no sound except the escalating snores of the patron. Having failed to awaken him, she conked him mightily over the head with the dictionary, and he fell to the floor, mortally wounded.

After the show, Maila expected Jimmy to comment on the show. He offered not a single word.

Although some claim to know that Jimmy did not sit astride his motorcycle across the street from the church on the day his former lover, Pier Angeli, married Vic Damone, Maila remembered it differently.

Only four days after Jimmy's anonymous cameo on *The Vampira Show*, Maila was sitting at Googies' counter, when Jimmy came in and sat down beside her. It was highly unusual that he should be there during the daytime.

"Been to a wedding," he said tersely.

That was Pier's wedding day. I'd forgotten about it & that would explain why Jimmy had been so quiet in the preceding weeks. I never knew Pier, as I met Jimmy perhaps only a week after the two of them broke up. But I was casually acquainted with her new husband, Vic Damone. I didn't know Jimmy when he was in love with Pier, although I'd heard about how she'd left him on short notice because of her overbearing mama.

The silence between Maila and Jimmy dragged on.

"You haven't lost much," Maila finally said.

No response.

"She was seeing Marlon, you know."

"No," Dean said.

"Yes," Maila insisted.

More silence. Then, "How do you know?"

"I saw her there, just leaving his place. I saw the stuffed animal she left for him with the note still attached."

Jimmy stared silently into his coffee until, without warning, he smashed his cup upside-down into the saucer and left.

Maila swore she would never forgive Pier for breaking Jimmy's heart.

The perfect opportunity soon arrived to lift Jimmy out of his doldrums, and it all came to pass at Googies. Maila and Jack sat at the agoraphobic side of the counter. A young man came in carrying a bowling bag and sat down to Jack's left. He set the bag down on the floor between them.

Without much hesitation, the man leaned over to Jack and whispered, "You wanna buy an Oscar?"

Jack looked down at the bowling bag and up again into the face of the stranger. He knew a thing or two about thieves; the Oscar was hot.

Jack leaned into Maila. "You wanna buy an Oscar? It was Sinatra's. Twenty bucks."

Maila, in sotto voce, replied, "Leave the bag where it is, and take the guy over to the cigarette machine on some pretext."

From there, it was easy. Maila called over the waitress. "Tell the cook they'll be a bowling bag at the end of the counter in a few minutes. Tell him to pick it up and put it back in the kitchen. I'll be there to pick it up."

Maila scooted over to Jack's vacant stool and pulled the bag with her feet back to her original seat, and so began a game of Pass-It-On. One by one, each patron scooted the bag along with his or her feet until it reached the end. With the bag safely stashed in the kitchen, Maila approached Jack to say she'd be waiting in the car. After picking up the goods from the kitchen, she and Jack took off.

The story was that the original thief was an usher at the 25th anniversary of the Academy Awards. All former Oscar winners were asked to bring in their awards to dress the stage. After the show, the statues were lined up awaiting workmen to load them onto trucks, so they could be returned to their rightful owners. Backstage, the usher scanned the gleaming display of statuettes and homed in on David O. Selznick's prize for *Gone with the Wind*. It was only after he got home that he realized that, in his nervousness, he'd missed Selznick's and had snatched its neighbor, Sinatra's award for 1946's *The House I Live In*.

Maila had the plaque engraved "Best Performance in Googies," intending to present it to Jimmy. But Jack stole her thunder. He picked up the Oscar from the engraver after she'd brought it there and, without Maila, presented it to Jimmy. Maila was furious and had to settle for a secondhand account of how Jimmy howled with laughter. The statue was prominently displayed on top of Jimmy's television set. It would be his only Oscar.

It wasn't that Jack was uninitiated in the art of thievery. The out-of-work actor largely supported himself by shoplifting. In the days before surveillance, clothing, records, jewelry, even small appliances made their way inside his oversized jacket, only to be returned later for a refund. Some opportunities fell right into his lap. When a delivery man deposited a box of new GE toasters just inside Googies' back door, Jack swiftly loaded them into the back of his hearse. He had a business relationship with every fence in town.

Even then, Jack often found himself short on his ten-dollar weekly rent on North Olive Drive. Inevitably, it was Maila who bailed him out. The problem was, her 75-dollar-a-week salary didn't allow for such generosity.

Jimmy had more money than Maila, but he was stingy. When it came time to pay their nightly tab, he threw down the exact amount of his share and walked off, leaving Maila to pay for Jack and herself plus the tax on the entire bill. Complaining to Jimmy was useless.

Maila decided to use a different tack. She told him, "You've got to find work for Jack. I can't do it. I'm on a cheap, one-woman show on a local television program."

Jack was Jimmy's and my court jester. He was spontaneous & capricious like we were. But get him in front of a camera & he had the charisma of a toad unless he was artificially bolstered by alcohol. So Jimmy tried to find a way to alleviate his stage fright.

By December, although not yet publicly announced, Jimmy was cast in the starring role, Jim Stark, in *Rebel Without A Cause*. Most of the cast was confirmed as well, the exception being the part of Plato, the effeminate teen boy. Although Jimmy campaigned heavily for Jack to be cast, he got nowhere with Nicholas Ray and screenwriter Stewart Stern. However, until a proper Plato could be found, Jack read Plato's part at rehearsals.

Undaunted, Jimmy continued to believe he could successfully train Jack for the role if he could relieve him of his stage fright. And he thought the best way to do that would be to expose him to a live audience.

The Garden of Allah was directly across the street from Googies. The 2.5-acre property consisted of a hotel, 25 surrounding bungalows, a bar, and a pool. In its heyday, the Garden was considered Hollywood's playground, an oasis in the middle of town where the rich and famous came to let down their hair in most hedonistic fashion. Booze and drugs flowed at parties there, which raged from dusk until dawn. Add to the mix plenty of clandestine sexual trysts, and it was no wonder that by the mid-'50s, the Garden of Allah's sordid reputation had caused it to fall into disrepair and financial distress. Even though Jimmy had done so several times, the idea to have Jack strip naked and skinny-dip in the Garden of Allah's pool was quickly rejected. Public nudity was still almost a nightly event at the Garden. Another plan would have to be hatched.

At Sunset and Doheny, Jimmy had once pissed on a Fiat that had stopped at a red light. While Jack marveled at Jimmy's total lack of inhibitions, he remained paralyzed by fear. For Pee-Wee, it was a no-go.

Maila tried to convince Jimmy that he had it all wrong. The role of Plato was that of a shy young boy, not an exhibitionist. What Jack needed, she said, was to perform artistically, as if on stage.

A building on the north side of Sunset exposed the skeleton of a billboard on its roof. Maila, Jack, and Jimmy gained access to the roof of the two-story by scaling the shaky remnants of a fire escape ladder.

The trio of trespassers climbed until they stood on the billboard's scaffolding, where they staged an impromptu performance. Maila, the appointed damsel in distress, sashayed onto the catwalk. The floodlight splashed her shadow ten feet high across the billboard backdrop. Over Maila's shrieks, Jimmy and Jack duked it out over her honor. Below, the traffic on Sunset was at a standstill. People stood outside their cars or gathered on the sidewalk and pointed up at the drama unfolding above. There was no time for a curtain call. Luckily, the three eluded the law and were safely back at Googies before the first responders could arrive.

Chapter Eleven

Even though Jimmy was unsuccessful in landing the role of Plato for Jack, he did manage to get his pal a paying gig. Maila was thrilled. When Jimmy was hired for an episode of *General Electric Theater*, he got Jack cast as well. Their co-star would be future President of the United States Ronald Reagan. The show was titled *The Dark Hours*.

It was only through Jimmy's efforts that Jack was saved from the throes of his stage fright. At Jimmy's behest, Jack performed drunk while wearing Jimmy's prescription eyeglasses. Fortunately, the viewing audience was none the wiser, as Jack's role as a delirious, mortally wounded criminal accommodated his blind drunkenness.

During the shoot, Maila was invited to lunch with Jimmy and Jack at the CBS commissary. There, they were joined by Reagan. Her impression of the future President hadn't changed from the times he and his first wife, Jane—and later he and Nancy—were guests at the Savoy.

In 1954, I lunched with Ronald Reagan. It was an accident. I was ashamed. He was quiet and acted as if it was beneath him to share a meal with the likes of us underlings. I thought he was a bore and should have been selling insurance.

In December, the network hired Gloria Pall to host a series of romantic movies employing the same formula used for *The Vampira Show*: a sexy host who introduced movies and performed vignettes during commercial breaks. In doing so, they were betting that lightning could strike twice.

Pall, a buxom, six-foot blonde, called her character Voluptua. While Vampira screamed in her attic, Voluptua purred in her boudoir.

KABC set the publicity wheels into motion and promoted the two movie hosts as the Chill and Charm Girls.

Voluptua premiered on December 15, 1954. It isn't known if program director Stromberg was responsible for its disastrous time slot: Wednesday nights at 9:30. With most families undoubtedly still awake, watching the negligee-clad, busty bombshell coo, "I'm breathless because I've been waiting for you," did not sit well with housewives and especially with conservatives.

Maila wasn't happy when KABC launched their Chill and Charm Girls promotion. Although she didn't resent Pall personally, she must have felt that the public impact of her Vampira character was diluted by the network's marketing strategy. On December 21, 1954, Maila signed a new one-year contract with Artists' Management Corporation. Perhaps she felt she needed a more powerful agent to protect her best interests.

From that point on, Maila and KABC were at war. Maila felt the studio wanted to own her character, along with the Vampira name, then syndicate the show and market it countrywide, hiring other Vampiras to host them. It wasn't long before station manager Selig J. Seligman ordered her to come to his office, after Maila had purposely ditched an appearance in protest after Gloria Pall was hired.

According to Maila, she found Selig in a surly mood. When she arrived, he kicked the bottom drawer of a file cabinet and said, "It's locked, and only I have a key. And you know what's in there? Six thousand dollars' worth of paid Vampira bookings, and that's just for January. I'll refuse them all, and you can't know who they're from."

The message was clear: Her behavior would not be tolerated by the station.

When *The Vampira Show* went on a two-week hiatus over the Christmas holidays, Maila was primed for a getaway. She went to New York and stayed at the Hotel Capitol, a few blocks off Broadway. A Christmas card to Jack from Maila survives, postmarked from New York on December 21, 1954: "Xmas won't be Xmas without you. But your career must come first, me next."

Jack's response said he'd tried to call her at the hotel four times without success. He was anxious to know if she'd spoken to anyone who'd seen his recently aired performance on the *General Electric Theater* with Jimmy and Ronald Reagan. For the time being, he was making himself available for *Rebel* interviews, but he'd run out of money and had to sell his hearse. As a footnote, he asked if she'd seen Jimmy, who was in New York as well.

So, who was Maila's traveling partner, then?

Even as his relationship with Maila teetered on the brink of collapse, Dink's career was escalating. He was working on a proposed treatment for NBC, *So This is Hollywood*, a comedy starring former child actor and Broadway star Mitzi Green. Considering the status of his and Maila's relationship and the expense involved, it is improbable that the two were together at Christmas.

And so that left Brando.

They still were close friends and sometime lovers whose friendship had already spanned a decade by the mid-'50s. In the only known photo of Maila and Brando together, he appears to be wearing a costume from the film *Desirée*, in which he played the role of Napoleon Bonaparte. Maila's dressed for an evening out. *Desiree* premiered the week before Thanksgiving of 1954. So, his Christmas schedule was free, perhaps.

> *Marlon found himself engaged to a woman he didn't love. For him, it was all a sham. She was a French fisherman's daughter, only just twenty, little more than a girl. He wanted to be rid of her, but she kept hanging around. So he purposely started seeing lots of other women.*

At the time, Brando preferred New York to Los Angeles, and most of his friends still lived there. It seems likely that Brando was Maila's companion for Christmas in New York.

On New Year's Eve, *The Vampira Show* resumed and aired live. Vampira interviewed Old Man 1954, who tried to convince her that he'd created enough disasters and bedlam throughout the past year to cash in on the benefits of her Black Cross retirement plan. Before he could finish his litany of calamities, Vampira interrupted to introduce that evening's feature film.

The show was on a tight budget. There weren't that many horror films available for the measly one hundred dollars the network was willing to pay. Often, they had to substitute third-run murder mysteries and, as Maila claimed, "pretend they were horror."

That night, *Apology for Murder* was on tap. Per Maila's script:

> *"Apology for Murder seems like a rather ambiguous title to me. Why anyone would apologize for murder is more than I can figure out. Perhaps they're apologizing because they only committed one instead of two. The young lady in this evening's film is quite the charmer. She's money-hungry, perfidious, homicidal, and alcoholic. That's the sort of girl any man would like to take home to mother."*

The rest of the script reads like a time capsule. The Indochina War, the McCarthy hearings, and the pop song "Sh-Boom" are mentioned. The distinction for the year's most spectacular catastrophes was split between the attempted assassination of five U.S. Representatives and a trio of deadly hurricanes: Carol, Edna, and Hazel. Vampira quickly rejected Old Man 1954's attempts to credit himself for these disasters, chiding him because all of the congressmen recovered. And she certainly could not forgive him for what she considered one of his greatest faux pas.

Voluptua! You were going along quite nicely for 11 months, and then in the closing weeks of your tenure, you spoiled everything with her! In a few short weeks, she's built up everything I've spent years tearing down! A program like hers could bring back radio! Police radio!

But now back to the movie. Let's see if the young couple can do away with the girl's husband. Murdering him is the best way, it seems to me. After all, divorce can be such an unpleasant thing.

This last paragraph would be insignificant, except for a notation Maila made in the margin of her personal script. After the last sentence about divorce, she wrote, "Not yet."

Just as an 18-year-old Maila resolved to grow her fingernails, now Vampira announced her New Year's resolution on live TV. And it was a clear nod to her friends James Dean and Jack Simmons and their mortuary shenanigans.

Resolved: To make better use of my spare time in 1955. No more wasting time hanging around graveyards. This year, I'll go out and recruit corpses myself!

Ultimately, Old Man 1954's proffered attempts at destruction and devastation proved inadequate, and Vampira banished him from her attic without Black Cross benefits.

Three weeks later, Maila Nurmi made an announcement to the *Los Angeles Herald Examiner's* gossip columnist, Harrison Carroll, who broke the news. On January 23, 1955, sandwiched between items on Merle Oberon and Gregory Peck, he wrote:

"Maila Nurmi, vampire of the TV screens, confirms to me that she probably will seek a divorce from her husband, Dean Riesner. Maila says, 'My husband and I have been married for six years and we are not compatible. He has social inhibitions and I am a social extrovert.'"

This was an interesting comment, in that Maila was not a social extrovert. It was only when costumed as Vampira that she could overcome that shyness.

Although Maila and Dink's common-law marriage would not require a legal divorce, dissolving their relationship would be no less difficult. Both agreed that the Laurel Canyon apartment held too many memories for either of them to stay. Because Maila didn't drive, her new address needed to be within walking distance of most essentials and near public transportation for longer errands. An apartment in West Hollywood on Larrabee Street, just south of the Sunset Strip, fit the bill.

Moving day was understandably difficult, especially for Maila. When she locked herself into the bathroom and refused to come out, Dink called Sophie, who wasn't surprised. She predicted that when Maila comprehended the finality of the breakup, she would crumble. Maila was very angry and accused Dink and her mother of conspiring to have her thrown out into the street. When Sophie arrived on Kirkwood, she found Maila barricaded in the bedroom.

Sophie told the family, "Maila didn't want anything but her clothes, the bed, and the cats."

When the movers arrived, Maila was still locked in the bedroom. Only when Dink's and Sophie's pleas became threats to remove the door's hinges did she open it. Throwing herself back onto the bed, Maila clung to it like a life raft.

"This is a bed of sanctity," she said, "where youthful naïveté once flourished and blossomed into love, and I will not abandon it to be violated by anonymous and sundry whores."

So, the bed went with her. When it was finally lifted into the moving truck, Maila made her final exit without a backward glance, barefoot and swaddled in a trailing bed sheet. There were no tears. She left with as much grace as she could muster.

Maila would never forgive Dink for turning his back on Vampira. Years later, he admitted that by refusing to become involved with her following her success, "I threw a million bucks down the toilet."

For six years, the gypsy slept while the brain was honed. Then, here I was, a bachelorette again.

I used to watch Hollywood's lovelorn come into Schwab's to pick up their bags of pills. Mayo Methot, Bogart's ex, came in wearing her full-length mink. Even her sunglasses couldn't hide her suffering. That was right after her husband left her for Lauren Bacall. Then there was Robert Montgomery's ex-wife, Elizabeth. She too, hoping for a better life through pharmaceuticals. They were always women. The men drank themselves to death. The women used pills.

It was a fate most cruel that at the peak of her success, Maila endured the pain of lost love. After the show, a starving Maila stopped only long enough to peel off her dress and wig before heading to Googies; there, she indulged in a plate of scrambled eggs and a slice of banana cream pie. She was a sight to behold with short, messy hair and a full face of Vampira makeup. Those who came in hopes of catching a glimpse of a celebrity would gawk at her and whisper.

The absurdity of the situation inspired a couple of Jimmy's napkin drawings, two of which survive. One shows a picture of Maila looking like a man in drag with arched eyebrows and a plunging neckline. The caption reads: "Why are people staring at me?" Another depicts the horror hostess with sagging breasts. Dean labeled it "Vampira, 1965." In the margin, Maila wrote an addendum, "without foundation garments."

One night it was just the three of us & Jimmy was doodling on napkins. Jack had been in love from afar for years with Steve Reeves, the body builder. So Jimmy draws this stick figure of a man hanging clothes out on the line. Except it wasn't clothes; it was a long line of male genitalia. They were all different sizes & shapes. But the last one was enormous & Jimmy wrote next to that one, "Steve Reeves." Jack was such a size queen.

February arrived. In lieu of a Valentine for their Charm Girl, Voluptua, KABC gave her show the ax. The station's gamble didn't pay off. The churchgoing public labeled her Corruptua and flooded the station's mail room with demands that she be canceled, and KABC was left no choice but to comply.

So, on February 2, she kissed the camera goodnight for the last time. With Voluptua gone, the clock was ticking on Vampira.

A photo shoot was scheduled at Woodlawn Cemetery in Santa Monica. The crew scouted out locations. Maila, still angry with Onni for his treatment of her mother in the divorce and no word from him since, insisted she be photographed kneeling in front of a headstone bearing a single word: FATHER. It resulted in the rare image of a laughing Vampira.

The most significant photograph from that day shows Vampira seated demurely in the middle of a row of empty chairs, hands folded in her lap, before a freshly dug grave. The folding chairs line the perimeter of the hole. The photo was intended to portray the undead temptress alone, at her own funeral. Later, it would hold a much more sinister meaning, resulting in near-tragic consequences.

At almost the exact time that Maila was photographed thumbing her nose at death in a Santa Monica cemetery, James Dean was photographed at a funeral parlor in his Indiana hometown, posing in a casket and hamming it up for the camera.

In March, Maila returned to the place where it all began: the Moulin Rouge Nightclub, to attend the 7th Primetime Emmy Awards. Instead of wearing the tattered gown of Charles Addams' matriarch, she wore an ice-blue evening gown, her hair dyed to match, and a rented fur stole draped around her shoulders. Her escort, Jack Simmons, lent his arm in a rented tux. And for one night, they were a part of the Hollywood elite.

Maila hadn't seen Jimmy in a while. Jack, who was with him daily at rehearsals, offered up one flimsy excuse after another: Jimmy was out of town, tied up in rehearsals, or didn't know Maila's new address and phone number.

James Dean's performance in *East of Eden* was the talk of the town even before it premiered. Because the industry elite were privy to a private screening and called his performance Oscar-worthy, the trade papers touted Dean as Hollywood's next biggest star. Warner Brothers knew they'd struck gold with the quirky, unpredictable kid from Indiana and immediately set out to prepare Jimmy for the big time.

They were well aware of the friendship between their star and television's Vampira—Jimmy had already interrupted a rehearsal at Nick Ray's bungalow in order to watch *The Vampira Show*. The fan magazines were full of their late-night prowls, alleged romance, and worse yet, purported involvement into the occult.

Vampira was deemed a blight on the image of their brightest star. It is probable that Warner Brothers demanded that Dean conduct himself with more decorum in public and that he was to be more selective about the people he was seen with. It seems his buddy Maila didn't make the cut.

At the same time in Los Angeles, the supercilious and widely feared gossip columnist Hedda Hopper was wielding her poison pen with unparalleled callousness. She was particularly contemptuous of young, unproven Hollywood talent. So, it was highly unusual that, after she attended the screening of *East of Eden*, she requested a private meeting with Jimmy at her home. James Dean had captivated the icy columnist.

During Hopper's interview with Jimmy, she asked him about his relationship with the "thin-cheeked actress who calls herself Vampira." Dean's alleged response reportedly appeared in Hopper's syndicated column: "I don't date witches, and I dig cartoons even less. Vampira was merely a subject about which I wanted to learn, and after engaging the girl in conversation, I found out that she knew absolutely nothing and is only obsessed with her Vampira makeup."

However, in Hopper's 1962 biography, *The Whole Truth and Nothing But*, she seems to have altered Jimmy's words: "I had studied the Golden Bough and the Marquis de Sade, and I was interested in finding out if this girl was obsessed by a satanic force. She knew absolutely nothing. I found her void of any true interest except her Vampira makeup. She has no absolute."

While both essentially convey the same message, Maila probably only read Hopper's column and never her later biography. The first quote is decidedly more hurtful. If either of them is accurate, Jimmy allowed his ambition to trump friendship and thereby revealed an opportunistic side of himself.

Maila was devastated. She considered Jimmy her best friend. She had finally found someone on Earth who was like herself. They had bonded to each other over that realization and it was like, according to Maila, they'd recognized each other. Now, both of her Deans, the two men she loved most, had abandoned her.

Big trouble was brewing in other aspects of Maila's life. She was invited to perform on NBC's *The George Gobel Show*. In Maila's estimation, being on Gobel's show was the pinnacle of success. Former guests included stars like Jimmy Stewart, Kirk Douglas, and Tennessee Ernie Ford. The problem was that Gobel's show aired live on Saturday night from 10 to 11, so Maila wouldn't be able to make it back to KABC for her own show, which began at 11. The station forbade Maila to appear on Gobel's show.

She accepted anyway.

Gobel was the new kid on the block. The show first aired in October of 1954, but six months later, its ratings were through the roof. The comedian boasted a crew cut and shy demeanor. He proclaimed himself Lonesome George, married to a woman he called Spooky Old Alice. He began his shows with a monologue delivered in a disjointed, wandering way that had his audience in stitches before he ever got to the punchline.

Although almost no footage of The Vampira Show still exists today, a kinescope of Vampira's appearance on Gobel's show recently surfaced. It was a stroke of unbelievable luck that it was made available just when her friend, the documentarian Ray Greene, was creating his film *Vampira and Me* in 2012. It became an integral part of Greene's documentary. For the first time in 57 years, Vampira's tiny waist, cadaverous countenance, and comedic talent were on display for modern audiences. It was easy to see why she caused such a sensation.

That night, April 9, 1955, Vampira stood next to Gobel in full costume and makeup. She was required to wear a lace modesty panel over her cleavage, but the rest of her outfit was authentically Vampira. Gobel asks her, "Is that really your waist, or do you come in two sections?"

Vampira answers, "Two sections. I'm sort of a do-it-myself kit."

Later, in a comedy sketch, Vampira plays Gobel's new neighbor, Mrs. Jones. Gobel comes over to introduce himself, and she invites him inside. The Victorian decor is similar to the future set of the television show *The Addams Family*. Ensuing small talk reveals Mrs. Jones as unconventional and bizarre. She asks Gobel if he minds if she smokes. Gobel agrees, and Mrs. Jones lies on her sofa. There isn't a cigarette in sight, but smoke begins billowing from underneath her body in ever-increasing amounts. A frightened Gobel scurries off the set.

The show was viewed by millions across the country. It was the pinnacle of her career. Fourteen years since she first stepped off that bus in Los Angeles, after endless struggle and countless rejections, she'd performed on the highest-rated show on television.

But then the clock struck midnight, and the creepy Cinderella couldn't make it back to her attic in time. In the precise moment of her greatest glory, she was done.

The network was furious. In January, they'd warned her not to disobey the network's orders, but they knew their star was headstrong. She also owned Vampira, leasing only a minority share to the network. The more they'd tried to wrest control out of her hands, the more she fought back. At the risk of becoming hamstrung, they decided it was all or nothing.

The man who owned the station called me on a Tuesday morning. He was obnoxious & making unreasonable demands & tried to manipulate me into signing my life away for nothing. I told him that he didn't know it, but there was a God & he's listening to you & watching you. And then I hung up. Then I learned that I offended one big, ugly ego who was super powerful, and he decided to fix me.

161

That man was producer Selig J. Seligman, with whom Maila had tangled before. Seligman was an attorney, having graduated first in his class at Harvard Law School, and went on to serve as an attorney with the U.S. Army. Nine years earlier, he'd served as counsel at the Nuremberg trials. But Maila was never impressed by the man's talents or intellect. She despised the round-faced man and in private referred to him as "that son of a bitch."

Seligman offered Maila a proposal that he thought she'd accept, at least if she were smart. The network wanted to buy the character of Vampira and syndicate the show. Their offer was nothing new, though, and her answer was the same. Her rights were not for sale at any price.

And with that, Seligman drove a stake through the heart of his vampire. On April 16th, a week after Vampira's appearance on *The George Gobel Show*, KABC officially pulled the plug on *The Vampira Show*. Contractually, Maila could not appear as Vampira for six months. It was long enough for people to forget about her.

Chapter Twelve

Sophie received a phone call from one of Maila's friends reporting that her daughter was in terrible shape. She rushed to Maila's apartment and found her in the bathtub, screaming and clutching a pair of scissors, which she'd used to chop off most of her hair. Every mirror in the house was shattered. The only thing Sophie could think of to do was fill a pan with water and dump it over Maila's head. She was given a sleeping pill and put to bed.

Two days later, Maila called Marlon Brando. He became alarmed by how she sounded and came over to her house. He let himself in as he always did, through her perennially unlocked living room window. Spying Maila's bald head, he said, "Oh, Maila, this is not good. You need help." A strong proponent of psychoanalysis, Marlon told Maila to go see a shrink.

Maila worried because she knew Hollywood's memory was notoriously short, and in order to save her career, she needed to get back in the public eye as soon as possible. She'd called Marlon in the hopes that she'd be comforted as she cried on his shoulder, and maybe in some capacity, he could push the door of opportunity open for her.

The timing couldn't have been worse. Albert Einstein had just died and left Marlon deeply saddened. Maila scarcely had a chance to speak before the actor launched into a dissertation on Einstein's philosophies and the worldwide impact his death would have on future generations. And it didn't end there. He felt the dead physicist was already sending him messages from beyond the grave.

"Like what?" Maila asked.

"He said to me, 'You young people, you must move quickly, time is running out. Get out there and move, change the world before it's too late.'"

As long as Marlon was insistent upon spouting esoteric nonsense from a dead man, he would be of no use to her career or otherwise. Maila would have to soldier on alone.

Googies, ground zero for gossip, was rife with the news of Maila's dismissal. The bye-bye-Vampira rumors lit up the corner like a firecracker. The rumor mill had churned out stories on how Maila was committed to an insane asylum, how she'd been caught blackmailing Seligman for some imagined indiscretion, and even how she'd attempted suicide during a live broadcast. By the time Maila sauntered casually into Googies—her shaved head hidden beneath a sombrero secured by a red ribbon tied under her chin—she was the star attraction. Everyone wanted to know the details of her recent denouement, and she held court for the curious.

If in baring her soul she hoped to gain support, she would've been sorely disappointed. Those who gathered around were only momentarily entertained before they sneaked back to their cups of coffee.

An interview with UPI's syndicated Hollywood columnist, Aline Mosby, came next. Over a bowl of tomato soup at the Brown Derby on North Vine Street, Maila described to the reporter her next incarnation: Tinkle Bell.

The headline in Mosby's syndicated column dated April 28, 1955, read: "Vampira to Thrill Fans with Jekyll-Hyde Shows." Maila claimed she'd appear on an ABC-TV live horror series. Concurrent to that, she hoped to star in another television program as a kind of benevolent storytelling fairy godmother. Apparently unconvinced, Mosby responded, "I spy some evidence to the contrary. Today, Vampira's face was nearly hidden under a huge hat and scarf, because currently, she's bald."

Maila, photo by Jack Simmons. Courtesy of the Jove de Renzy Collection.

A photo of Maila as Tinkle Bell indicates a woman trying to transition her gruesome public persona to one of benevolence. But Maila is obviously conflicted. The ghoulish makeup is gone, and the tattered dress is replaced by a modest, light blouse. Over her bald head, she holds an unmistakably Vampira-esque parasol—with a concessionary spider dangling from a gossamer thread.

Since the release of *East of Eden* earlier in April, the moviegoing public had been nuts over James Dean. While his career was soaring like a rocket, Maila's was sinking like a rock. As if to confirm his new status, he all but abandoned Googies. His new hangout was the upscale Villa Capri, home of the A-listers. Where once his presence evoked scorn, Jimmy was welcomed into the ranks of Hollywood royalty—specifically the Holmby Hills Rat Pack. This group of hard-drinking night owls included Humphrey Bogart, Lauren Bacall, Judy Garland, Sid Luft, and Frank Sinatra.

But Jimmy still found time for Googies, and that's where he found Maila and Jack one night. "Come on," he said to Maila. "Let's blow this joint."

"Where are we going?" Maila wanted to know.

"On a date," he said as he reached for the napkin dispenser and stuffed a wad in his back pocket.

"But I'm not dressed," she sputtered. "I'll have to change."

"There's no dress code where we're going. C'mon, let's go."

He grabbed Maila's hand and said to Jack, "Not tonight, Amigo. It's just me and Maila. We'll bring you a doggie bag."

On the way out the door, Jimmy grabbed squeeze bottles of ketchup and mustard. His Triumph motorcycle was parked defiantly on the sidewalk, with a red Hills Brothers coffee can hanging from a wire on the handlebars. He must have read her mind.

"Hobo stove," he said, "Don't ask. It's a surprise."

Jimmy threw a leg over the seat and gestured with his head for Maila to get on the back. She straddled the rear of the bike, her arms around Jimmy's waist. The bike rumbled to life and took off east on Sunset.

He pulled up in front of the grocery store on Beachwood Drive. Before entering, he divested his pockets of the condiments and set them on the curb. Once inside, Jimmy ordered two frankfurters from the butcher. When he next came to the bread rolls, he stopped. Selecting two, he turned to Maila and, with a sly smile, lifted up her sweater and placed them on her breasts.

"Jesus Christ, Jimmy," Maila whispered, "what the hell are you thinking?"

"Just stay cool," he intoned and headed for the door. Maila shadowed him, her hands cupping the rolls under her sweater.

On the way out, he grabbed two RC Colas.

Back at the Triumph, Jimmy reached down and returned the squeeze bottles to his pockets. He'd stolen the frankfurters, too, and he removed them from where he'd stuffed them—down his pants. The look on Maila's face only fueled Jimmy's fits of laughter.

Next stop, a stately house on Los Feliz. The front lawn was impeccably manicured and bounded by a short retaining wall, which was no obstacle for someone as lithe as Jimmy. Stealthy as a cat burglar, he darted up on the lawn and lopped off a couple of twigs from someone's ornamental cherry tree. With the sticks clenched between his teeth and the blade of his pocketknife glinting in the streetlight, he leaped from the wall like a ninja.

The thieves stole off into the night. It was good to be young.

Just up the street, Jimmy turned in to Griffith Park. They bumped along the service road, and finally onto a trail no wider than a foot path. Through the brambles they rode, until they reached a clearing on the hillside.

Maila divested herself of the buns, and the filched franks followed suit. As Jimmy fussed over dinner preparations, Maila gazed out from their covert spot at the panoramic view. Hollywood stretched below. Neon lights perched above tall hotels. Further out, Los Angeles bathed the night in a spangled glow. Beyond, the black abyss of the vast Pacific Ocean defined the end of their world.

Jimmy lit the waxed cardboard inside the can. After impaling each stick with a frank, he handed one to Maila.

The meat sizzled and popped on their skewers, dripping grease into the hobo stove. They took the sausages off of the sticks and placed them into the rolls, slathering their hot dogs with Googies' complimentary condiments, and ate in silence watching the lights below.

It was Maila who spoke first. She wanted to know what Jimmy meant when he spoke those hurtful words about her to Hedda Hopper.

"She's a harpy, Maila, and makes a living writing bullshit. Don't believe everything you read."

As if that comment sparked another thought, he went on to tell of a time from when he was a boy and lived in Santa Monica with his folks. He was afraid of the dark and wanted the blinds of his bedroom window open, so he could see the lights outside, but his father wouldn't allow it. So, his mother would sleep on the floor beside his bed until he fell asleep. Every morning when he woke up, the blinds would be open. His mother made sure of that.

It was the only time Jimmy ever spoke of his childhood to Maila, and she was deeply touched.

As the last bites of hot dog were consumed, the tenor changed. "Ever wonder what wieners are made from?" Jimmy asked.

Before Maila could respond, he informed her. "Hog balls."

"What?" Maila was aghast.

"Hog balls," he repeated. "And ears and guts, a couple of eyeballs."

"You're not serious!" Maila was horrified. Jimmy was an Indiana boy whose family had farmed pigs!

"Well, maybe not eyeballs," he conceded.

"I don't want to hear about this anymore." Was he teasing her?

"Speaking of eyeballs," Jimmy continued, "how about some dessert?" From his shirt pocket, he produced a package of marshmallows.

"You mean you… when we got the other stuff?"

Jimmy nodded and smiled.

"Your sleight of hand is impressive," Maila concluded.

Side by side roasting marshmallows, Vampira and the Rebel sat alone on the hillside above the city, enjoying the night air, the view, their conversation. It was a night Maila treasured for a lifetime. Her favorite picture of Jimmy was always one of him standing beside a giant hog on his Indiana farm. Now we know why.

Like Maila herself, her home was a paradigm of contradictions. The mauve living room of her apartment on Larrabee was serene, pleasant, and uncluttered—almost stark. One long wall was empty save for an enormous bronze picture frame, having once bordered a life-sized portrait of a former boyfriend, James "Troy" Darren. When he left, he took the photo but not the frame. A single light bulb glowed upon the conversation area, which consisted of floor cushions placed around a marble-topped coffee table. Upon the table were candles and a vase holding 13 vulture feathers, a gift from a friend, actress Francesca De Scaffa.

The bathroom, however, was an explosion of red-and-black madness. Blood-red walls were interrupted by a black tattered curtain at the window. Suspended from the dark ceiling was a family of rubber bats, while a nest of spiders hung from cobwebbed corners.

In the pre-dawn hours of June 11, 1955, Maila was walking alone on Sunset, just outside of Googies, when a man accosted her. The man, later identified as 34-year-old studio worker John G. Fenwick, grabbed her arm and said, "Come on, baby, we're going to Las Vegas." When Maila tried to free herself but couldn't, the man threw his other arm around her waist. Maila's screams brought people out from inside Googies to help her. One of her rescuers was Jack Simmons, who ran after the perpetrator.

While the man was being chased down, Maila called the police. She filed a citizen's arrest, and the man was taken into custody.

The story was picked up by the press. A few days later, Maila appeared in court, comforted by a sympathetic Jack. She was stylishly groomed in a tweed coat and gloves, her haircut somewhere between a crew cut and a pixie. Fenwick was charged with battery and disturbing the peace and fined 25 dollars.

That spring, Disneyland's ubiquitous grand opening posters had wallpapered all of Southern California, advertising for a July 17th opening. The excitement was electrifying. An invitation-only dedication ceremony was scheduled the day before opening day. Before she was fired, Maila was given two tickets to the once-in-a-lifetime celebration, one of which she gave to Jack—who himself was also feeling abandoned by Jimmy, as he filmed the Western drama *Giant* in Marfa, Texas.

Jack arrived at Maila's door for the Disneyland event with a jaw swollen up like a blowfish. He had a toothache. Maila, who'd waited too long to be denied this occasion, insisted she had a surefire fix. She brought out a glass of whiskey and told Jack to take a sip and hold it against the offending tooth, then spit it out. Before leaving for the amusement park, she used an empty perfume bottle as a flask, in case Jack needed more painkillers.

The day was a scorcher. Upon arrival at Disneyland, Maila and Jack joined the crowd to wade through the gates. Then they were herded to Main Street for the dedication, to endure a stream of speeches by local dignitaries.

The crowd assembled in front of the podium. The heat was inescapable, and the men on the dais stripped off their suit jackets before launching into their speeches. The hot sun began to melt the new asphalt, and Maila's high heels stuck to the sticky morass. Jack, suffering greatly both from the heat and his toothache, sipped from his homemade flask.

Just as the ceremony began, Jack passed out. The crowd parted and two men carried him off on a stretcher.

He woke up on a cot in the infirmary with Maila in a chair beside him. Reeking of alcohol, an attendant determined Jack was drunk, and both he and Maila were unceremoniously escorted out of the park.

It wasn't long after Disneyland opened that Maila met Michael.

Better known to the world as film actor Lewis Arquette, who later played J.D. Pickett on TV's *The Waltons*, Michael went by his middle name when he wasn't performing. According to Maila's friend Audrey Antley: "Maila called Michael her one love, only love, her true love, her fiancé... because that is how she would describe every man with whom she had been intimate."

According to Audrey, Maila was hell-bent on riding the teacup ride at Disneyland. And not just any teacup but the pink one, which was featured in all of the ads around town. And so Maila and Michael drove to the new Disneyland park in his convertible.

Upon arrival, Maila made a beeline for the teacup ride, only to be met by bitter disappointment. No pink teacups. And so, she declared, to all within earshot, that Disney's promotional posters were fraudulent. After her loud protestations culminated in the offer of a free ride, Maila accepted a spin in another cup, albeit an inferior white one with only a pink rim.

> *I was young, and he was very, very young. Nineteen to my thirty-two were we that day. I believe he ended up marrying a stripper from the Valley. And if I had married my love, my true love, my only love, my fiancé, I would have five children who are addicts, because he was Michael Arquette, the daddy of all the acting Arquettes.*

Henry Willson was a Hollywood agent, legendary for his proclivity to wine, dine, and bed his young male clients—the pretty boys who came to Hollywood with dreams of stardom. As his modus operandi dictated, he gave each one a new name—macho names like Chad or Guy or Rock—and then went about the business of molding the awkward and unpolished young men into box-office gold.

While fiercely supportive of his stable of stars, the fickle-hearted Willson could also turn on a dime, as evidenced by the plethora of former clients reduced to valets on La Cienega Boulevard when their phones stopped ringing. Given that Maila and the agent shared a penchant for beautiful young men, it was inevitable that the two would clash.

One of Willson's latest acquisitions was just 18, new in town and wanting to break into show business. Maila was charmed by his good looks and thick Philly accent, and the two became lovers, although their relationship was never serious. Maila identified her friend only as "Crack Widener."

It was "Crack" who first informed Maila that Willson was afraid of her. Willson was at Gil Turner's liquor store when he saw Maila approaching. He reportedly said to the owner, "Shit, Gil, here comes Vampira. Where can I hide?" By the time Maila walked through the front door, Willson was cowering in the phone booth. He'd read the press that claimed Vampira used black magic to unleash evil spells upon her enemies.

Maila was amused yet puzzled. Even if she could cast spells, which was a ridiculous notion, why would she waste her superpowers on the likes of Willson?

She asked, "Is he the little fat guy with the girl singer who sued KABC for making her ugly and repulsive?"

"Yeah, that's him," he replied. "He doesn't have her no more. He don't take on girl clients much anymore. Just men."

Sheepishly, Crack admitted that, rather than end up parking cars, he felt it necessary to accommodate Willson's sexual overtures from time to time. And since Willson assumed Maila and Crack were committed lovers, he was afraid that once Vampira found out he was occasionally bedding Crack, she would hex him out of business.

If a young man was agreeable to Willson's demands, so be it. But it was something else entirely if, like Crack, he was not. Maila remembered when there was no one to protect her from the lecherous agents of her youth. She was not about to let that happen to her new friend. It was time, she said, "to stir things up and see if the scum don't rise to the top."

"Oh, that poor man. I really should send him flowers for being the first person to ever respect me," Maila mused. "Give me his address."

A few days later, a Red Arrow bike messenger delivered a black florist's box containing a bouquet of dead calla lilies to Willson's Bel-Air home. The card attached read, "Love and hisses."

Now also armed with Willson's unlisted phone number, Maila put the word out on the street for volunteer detectives. The cast-off valets on La Cienega were only too eager to help stick it to Willson. When the agent and one of his boys were en route home after a night of clubbing, one of Willson's former clients alerted Maila, who'd waited long enough for the agent to be in bed before calling. Willson always answered late-night phone calls himself. He didn't want his houseboy answering, just in case it was a potential hookup.

When Willson answered, Maila let loose with one of her signature blood-curdling screams and hung up.

Every time Willson changed his phone number, Maila had the new one before the sun went down.

It was rumored that Willson bought Pond's Cold Cream by the case, which he used as a sexual lubricant. Armed with this information, Maila decided it was time for the final humiliation and rounded up the muscle from the volunteer detectives.

In the early morning hours, after a night out with one of his paramours, Willson returned home to find his driveway was blocked by a disgraceful display: a torn mattress, bloodied with red paint and illuminated by floodlights for all the neighborhood to see. A sign board propped beside it read:

> **"She's young,**
> **She's lovely.**
> **She's engaged.**
> **She uses Pond's.**
> **Vampira knows."**

Henry's dead now, so I suppose he isn't afraid of me any more. Crack lost his accent, changed his name, and became a singing star and famous television and movie star. I overcame my wealth to become a bag lady. There's hope for us all, Darlings!

Chapter Thirteen

In September, Onni was living in Duluth with his new wife and was interviewed by the *Duluth New Register* about his famous daughter. Onni is shown holding a newspaper with photos of a bald Maila. The headline read:

"Finnish Editor... His Daughter Scares People on Television"

While Onni is critical of his daughter's cheesecake career and calls it "exhibitionism," he admits that he collects every news clipping of her that he can find. Onni follows up with these words:

"Maila was too eager to get on her own. She said, 'Pa, you don't know me,' so I said, 'Good luck.' That was fifteen years ago. Personally, I don't approve of it [Maila's lifestyle] at all. I wanted her to go into business or maybe become a fine dramatic actress. They tell me this [Maila's career] is art. Maybe it is if you look at it that way. You have to understand. It's different."

The general sense of the article is one of loss. Looking at the bald photos of his daughter, Onni frowns sternly. He states that he is not angry, only disappointed that Maila's way of life is so different from his. He tries to end the interview on a positive note by saying that even "when she was in New York, I never saw her dance. I understand she still doesn't smoke or drink."

She did, of course, but perhaps Onni had brought himself some kind of peace with the notion.

Maila had nothing but free time on her hands. Her ABC contract wouldn't expire until October, and she was still being paid. For the first time in years, she was completely free of all responsibilities, domestic or professional. But she was stone broke.

In early summer of '55, a lanky dark-haired kid arrived in town from the East Coast. He was a stage actor, like his father before him, and like thousands of other young people, he'd moved to Hollywood to become a movie star. Without much money, he was lucky to rent the janitor's room at the Chateau Marmont for 50 dollars a month. But unlike the other wannabes, this kid had one long, lean leg up on the competition, having come west with a plum role in William Wyler's next film, *Friendly Persuasion*.

Within a few days of his arrival in Hollywood, the new kid, Anthony Perkins, met Maila Nurmi at Googies. He was fresh and awake arriving for his morning breakfast; she was winding down from another all-nighter with her friends.

Maila and Tony formed a quick friendship. Since leaving Dink, Maila had found few opportunities to stretch her intellectual muscle. In Tony, she found an equal who could challenge her smarts and share a laugh.

Maila, blonde and beautiful, and Tony, dark and handsome, made a striking couple. The fact that she was ten years his senior didn't seem to matter. To some it appeared they were romantically involved, so frequently were they spotted together. But their relationship, like the one she had with Jimmy, was strictly platonic. Maila thought it a little curious that after several dates and a considerable time spent together, Tony had not yet even tried to kiss her. Boldly, Maila asked him why. He explained his lack of romance gestures toward her was because he'd always been "shy" around women.

It didn't take long for the newcomer to figure out that, if he was to be a star, he must be seen squiring someone of greater status in the Hollywood hierarchy than the erstwhile Vampira.

One night, the two attended a party for zodiac columnist Carroll Righter, and Tony told Maila, "You know, when we get there, you won't see me. I'm going to leave, and you won't see me all evening." So, it was a surprise when Tony soon returned to Maila's side. When she asked why he was not out social-climbing, he replied, "There's *nobody* here."

Maila knew full well that Tony was shamelessly ambitious in his quest to become Hollywood's biggest star. But his intelligence, charm, and vulnerability appealed to her sense of camaraderie, and she could forgive his occasional snobbishness. Tony accepted that Maila couldn't help him on his road to stardom, but she was damn good company.

Years before *Breakfast at Tiffany's* appeared on the screen, Maila and Tony found themselves standing in front of the magazine rack in Schwab's. Tony wore a grin like the Cheshire Cat's. "You'll have to pretend the neon is candlelight," he muttered through clenched teeth. "It's the best we can afford," he continued as he slipped a ring on Maila's finger.

"Oh, Tony, it's beautiful," Maila gasped, choking back a fake sob and holding the ring up to the light. The two had shopped together at Koontz Hardware for a lamp pull made of ball chain, from which Tony had fashioned the ring.

"How did you ever manage it?" Maila asked.

"It's on the installment plan," he answered.

That summer, Jimmy was back in town, having finished filming *Giant* in Texas.

Maila was saddened to learn that while he was there, he'd shot jackrabbits to fend off boredom. Marlon heard the same news and, as a fellow animal lover, was incensed. He told Maila, "Tell your little friend, it doesn't take a man to kill innocent animals." Jimmy reportedly was ashamed.

It wasn't long before Jimmy had a new woman in his life—the as-yet-unknown Swiss actress Ursula Andress, who was also seeing Marlon Brando at the time.

But he still found time to visit Maila on Larrabee, always emulating Marlon's entrance through Maila's unlocked front window. In that manner, shortly before his death, Jimmy let himself in one day and found Maila at home. Their conversation was of the surface variety—"Did you hear that song," "The funniest thing happened today," "Guess who I just met"—that sort of thing. But then Jimmy's mood quickly changed, and he became pensive.

He started talking about the arts: paintings, drawings, books. And since the intrusive Jack was not present, Maila thought it was the right time to ask something she'd wanted to know.

Dean had a painting on an easel in his home. The subject was lying in state, a candle burning in the back of him.

"Why do you want to die?" Maila asked.

"How do you know that?"

"Anyone who paints a picture of themselves dead..."

"That's very clever of you," Jimmy interrupted and changed the subject.

Maila asked the question again and still got no answer. Finally, she said, "Is it to be near your mother?"

Jimmy's response this time was immediate. "No, that's not it."

"Then what is it?"

"I don't want to die. I just want some fucking peace."

A knock at the front door told them that Jack had driven by and spotted Jimmy parked out front.

"Shit," Jimmy said, and ran for the back door. Maila offered to say he'd gone off with someone else. He paused for just a moment before shaking his head in defeat. When Maila let Jack in, Jimmy immediately suggested they go together to look for Ursula. And off they went.

The passion and frustration escalated, and Jack became repulsive around Jimmy. He mooned about like a puppy; he simpered and clawed. Yes, clawed with hunger at Jimmy. Jack then engaged in much artful conniving. How to find Jimmy, who was now trying to avoid him—how to get him alone, how to drive off all others—and he found ways. In this sense, he was a genius.

Jimmy had him barred from his dressing room. Jack came in anyway. Jimmy had him barred from Warner's lot. Jack got in anyway. Jimmy in desperation cried out, "Maaaan! How the fuck do you dooo it?" On at least two occasions, I recall being at home with Jimmy when he had successfully eluded Jack. But Jack showed up, and Jimmy would try to hide and then relent and say, "Oh, fuck, man, I gotta go."

Jimmy returned a final time to Larrabee Street, and this time, Maila was away. To announce his presence, he left a calling card stabbed to the wall in the middle of the giant empty brass frame: an ear, one nostril, and both eyes cut from one of the 8x10 glossies of himself that he kept in his glove box. The remnants of this photo were wadded up and tossed on the front porch, which Jimmy had painted a dark gray a few months previously. Maila's manicure scissors were left on the marble coffee table and a piece of her costume jewelry was used to tack the artwork onto the wall. In addition, Dean trained the pink ceiling light to focus on his offering.

"Typical Jimmy," Maila said. "What's an artist without a spotlight?"

Ear, nostril, eyes, but no mouth. To Maila, that was not an accident. Why no mouth? And then she remembered Jimmy's words when he stole the ring off the dead guy's finger. *Dead men never tell.* If that was what Jimmy was trying to convey, she vowed to ask him the next time she saw him. In the meantime, she planned to send him something equally strange and abstruse.

Problem was, Jimmy had moved, and Maila didn't have his new address, so she would have to send it to him in care of his new hangout, the Villa Capri.

From contact sheets of her cemetery photo shoot, Maila made postcards from the shot of Vampira sitting beside the open grave. On the last weekend in September, Maila took one of those postcards and wrote on the back: "Wish you were here... Love, Maila."

She put it in an envelope and sent it via messenger—a friend named Randy—to the Villa Capri.

Late on Wednesday night, September 28, the phone rang. It was Jimmy wanting to know if she'd sent him a picture, which Maila confirmed.

"Why?" was all he said.

Maila was confused at his reaction. He should be laughing. The mystery was solved when she learned the postcard was intercepted. Nick, the Villa's maître d' and a friend from whom Jimmy now rented, took it home. All Jimmy knew was that Nick told him it was mean.

Maila didn't want to spoil the joke and told Jimmy to reserve judgment until he'd seen it for himself. He said okay. Just before he hung up, Maila invited him to her "freedom party." It was to be a celebration to commemorate the day her KABC contract expired and when she would therefore retain full rights to Vampira.

Jimmy didn't accept or reject Maila's invitation. Instead, he said he wasn't sure but that he'd get back to her. It was late and he had to go. That was the last time she ever spoke to James Dean.

September 30, 1955, Maila and Jack spent the day together. Jack was driving Maila home when they spotted Tony Perkins and offered him a ride. Returning to Larrabee, the trio entered Maila's house and Jack commented that the light in the living room seemed weird, even though Maila and Tony noticed nothing strange. Jack left to go down the block to see a couple of friends with whom he had dinner plans.

Perkins stretched out on the floor cushions, directly below Jimmy's collage affixed to the wall with Maila's brooch: a dagger and scabbard connected by a chain. She and Tony were chatting when, at about six o'clock, the dagger came loose from the wall and swung like a pendulum just above Tony's astonished face.

Just as he reached up and stabbed the dagger back into the wall, the phone rang. It was Randy, who had delivered Maila's letter to the Villa Capri.

Two words. "Jimmy's dead."

Maila thought it was a sick joke. It must have been Jimmy's response to her postcard. He'd put Randy up to it. Even when Randy insisted it was true, Maila wouldn't believe it. Instead, she called Jimmy's answering service. After verifying that Maila was on the list of Jimmy's intimates, the awful truth was repeated.

"We have to tell Jack," Maila told Tony.

It was a short walk to where Jack was preparing dinner at his friends' house. Jack answered the door wearing an apron and holding a bowl of Brussels sprouts. Maila blew her way past Jack, saying, "Get out of the way—we have to come in."

> *Jack is shocked because, after all, it isn't even his place. Tony & I sit down & then I tell Jack to sit down, but he doesn't. He's still standing there, wondering what is going on.*
>
> *"What is it?" he says.*
>
> *And I say, "What is the worst thing that could happen?"*
>
> *And he says, "Your cats!"*
>
> *"No," I say. "What is the worst thing that could happen in this world?"*
>
> *"Not Jimmy," he said.*
>
> *"Yeah. Just what you said," I told him.*
>
> *He dropped the bowl of vegetables & in that moment he stopped being Jack Simmons and became Norma Desmond. "No, it's not true. It can't be true. I won't let it be true."*
>
> *Jack was a very good impersonator. The best non-professional I ever saw. But he could not process such horrible news as himself, so he became another person. This was too much for Tony, who became embarrassed & left to presumably walk home to the Chateau Marmont.*

When Jack came out of his trance, he said we needed to go tell Ursula before she found out over the radio or something. So, we drove over to her little cottage on a dead-end street which was covered with shrubbery.

It was dark by then. I'm thinking, "My God, the sun has set on Jimmy's last day. He will never feel sunshine on his face again." But I told Jack I'd stay in the car because I didn't know her that well & didn't want to cause any more discomfort. Jack left and walked up the driveway. And then Marlon appeared out of the shrubbery & came up to the car on the passenger side where I was sitting & offered his condolences.

Ursula had called Marlon screaming, "They're trying to kill me. They think Jimmy killed himself because of me & they think it's my fault. I'm frightened & alone. Please help me." So, Marlon was skulking in the bushes to peek in the windows to see if she was really upset or just putting him on.

That's where Jack found Marlon—in the bushes. And he said, "Maila's in the car."

The tragic news stunned the world. With the exception of Jimmy's Indiana hometown, no place felt the loss more than Hollywood. It was incomprehensible that so suddenly his light had been extinguished on a lonely, desolate road.

The profound pain of losing Jimmy coupled with her already fragile psyche made it impossible for Maila to attend his funeral in Fairmount, Indiana. But Jack made the trip, thanks to donations collected at Googies. As testament to his deeply anguished state, he told Maila, "I'm going to rip off the lid [of Jimmy's coffin] and get what I never had." Reportedly, the mortuary found that the coffin had been pried open the night before the funeral.

Ironically, Jimmy was buried on October 8th, the day Maila was released from her contract with ABC. They would never have a freedom party.

After Jimmy's death, Sophie again came to stay with her daughter. Maila was inconsolable and played Rosemary Clooney's hit song "Hey There" repeatedly hour after hour, day after day. Make no mistake—Maila loved Jimmy like a mother loves her son. Subconsciously, when she learned that Jimmy's mother was dead, she adopted him, and he became her surrogate to replace the son she gave away.

God, that poor baby, that poor battered blossom. Baby Jimmy. He was beautiful, interesting & fun & I'm glad I let him know I worshipped him. How come he had no friends? I mean here in his adopted hometown—everybody made a great point of letting him know they found him either disgusting or boring. People didn't understand Jimmy. He never pretended to be anything he wasn't & people didn't know how to comprehend that. They'd do or say something vicious to him & he'd run away & they'd say "He's angry." He was only hurt, like a child would be. Now I read about how wonderful they say he was. Too bad someone didn't sort of suggest it to him when he was around.

When he roomed with Bill Bast in West L.A.—his girl threw him out in favor of Bill Bast. Ouch! Bill Bast and "that girl" ganged up on him & created a little boycott. "We don't play with Jimmy" game. The girl he had in N.Y.C. in 1955 chose an insurance agent. "Bye Jimmy— I'll think of you." Pier Angeli choose [sic] Vic Damone—oooh. Ursula Andress chose John Derek. A small group of waitresses in the apartment back of Greenbelt's started a drama class in their kitchen. Everyone present was invited except Jimmy. They shut the sliding door in his face.

Fellow employees on the set of East of Eden shunned him. Gadge's [director Elia Kazan] hot shot nose picker from N.Y.!! Boo-oo-oo.

On location of Giant, Chill Wills (that wonderful guy) started a J.D. boycott. It was effective. Rock Hudson was a staunch supporter of it. Back in Hollywood—200 people on the set, those yellow bellied bastards—they refused to even speak to Jimmy during the work day. For the last 30 days of his life he went to work & no one would speak to him. Only Mercedes McCambridge and Elizabeth did. It's a wonder he wasn't blacklisted.

Jimmy Dean, Jimmy Dean, Jimmy Dean, wherever you are, I love you—I always will.

P.S. If you ever need anything, let me know. I'll find a way to get it for you.

The incentive for Maila to leave her home came while passing through the living room and stopping to study the ghostly reminder of Jimmy's last visit, still affixed to the wall. By then, the ear had dried and curled but, strangely enough, it was moving. To make certain it wasn't a draft, Maila closed the windows and stuffed a towel underneath the front door. The ear still moved.

Encouraged, Maila asked the ear a question aloud.

"What was Jimmy's favorite drumbeat? Was it two fast and one slow, or one slow and two fast?"

The ear responded by wiggling two times slowly and then once more.

Much like Marlon's experience when Einstein died, Maila was convinced Jimmy was trying to communicate with her from beyond the grave. The news was too exciting not to share.

"Ridiculous," her mother said.

At Googies, Maila appeared dressed in black from head to toe, a black crucifix draped around her neck. Unlike her mother's reaction, the story of Jimmy's wiggling ear created much interest. Several wanted to witness the phenomenon for themselves. And so, they came. Some were equally convinced it was Jimmy's spirit. Most were not. Although she was mocked by some for claiming to communicate with Jimmy from beyond the grave, Maila continued to believe it to be true.

In a 1966 tape recording, interviewed by Marlon Brando, Maila expounds on her connection with James Dean.

"You sound weepy," he said. "How do you feel?"

"How do I feel?" Maila repeated. In halting, protracted speech, she said, "I feel like Jimmy was the only human being to whom I was ever related. I feel like, before I met him, I lived in a sea of window dummies. And then I met Jimmy, and we were alive in the world together. And now he's dead. So now it's going to be harder than before I met him. I don't know, but that's how I feel. You *did* ask."

She said she was going to go to New York because Hollywood held too many memories of James Dean.

"How will you support yourself financially?" Marlon asked.

"I suppose I could do television commercials, or maybe I'll be a blues singer. I can't sing worth a damn, but I sure as hell know how to be blue."

Marlon chuckled and then asked, "How much money do you have? I can help you."

She had 210 dollars. But she would leave without saying goodbye and without accepting his financial help. No address. Nothing. She didn't want his charity.

Chapter Fourteen

In the wake of Jimmy's death, New York City offered a new beginning. A hopeful Maila moved into a third-floor walk-up in a brownstone at 136 West 46th Street. The former tenant's name, Peggy Willson, was not yet removed from the mailbox slot in the foyer.

Maila's move may have been impulsive, but it wasn't entirely ill-conceived. Of course, memories of Jimmy were too fresh in Hollywood, but Maila moved to New York to be near Tony Perkins, who was back on Broadway. She had a kind of desperate need to sustain their blossoming friendship. The bonus was that Perkins' East Coast connections could potentially bring her work in the theater as well.

Not that she longed to be an actress. She was still holding out to become an evangelist. It wasn't that she was even religious. It was just that evangelism was something she was familiar with, having listened to her father's orations for so many years. As well, Maila still held out hope of somehow being able to fund an animal sanctuary or the ability to help abandoned animals in some capacity. She hoped that as a woman proselytizing, gowned in lavender from head to toe, she could find a niche that could fund that dream.

The apartment was barren except for an enormous pile of shredded

185

lavender cellophane, used as postal packaging. The excelsior served as Maila's makeshift bed, above which she hung a photo of a Tibetan monk she'd torn out of a magazine. On the floor sat a vase with her 13 vulture feathers.

Years before, Peter the Hermit, the bearded, robed, self-proclaimed metaphysician who prowled Hollywood Boulevard by day and lived in a tent by night, told Maila her aura was lavender, "the sign of the spiritual seeker." The pile of lavender packaging that the former tenant had left behind delighted Maila. She interpreted it as a sign that she was on the right track with her evangelistic pursuits.

With the few dollars she had, she splurged on a can of paint and, in an attempt to create a sanctuary of harmony, Maila painted everything in her living space an ethereal shade of lavender. And not just the walls—anything that would accept a coat of paint, including the icebox, the stove, and her suitcase. In doing so, she believed her personal energies and the lavender splendor of her surroundings would merge to resurrect Sister Saint Francis who, wearing a lavender-hued nun's habit, would become a champion of animals.

Until the rebirth of another of her alter egos could manifest, Maila relied heavily upon Tony for companionship. He showed up at all times of the day or night for a glass of coffee, and if she were lucky, he'd bring her food. (She had no cups and no money.) Tony was assigned a specific knock so that Maila would know when he was at her door. In the unlikely event she found a more intimate kind of companionship, or simply wanted to be left alone, she would then open the door a crack and say a specific name, which would be code for "Go away, I'm busy," or "Come back later."

In New York, Tony was no more likely to take Maila out in public there than he was in Hollywood, with one exception. He wanted her to meet his friend, Helen.

Just how Helen fit into Tony's life was a mystery. Maila couldn't figure out the close relationship between the two, but he obviously idolized her. Maybe she was his surrogate mother; she certainly was old enough. The two lived together just a few blocks away. While in Hollywood, Tony spoke of her often and in glowing terms. Whatever the relationship, they were extremely close, in an almost creepy sort of way.

According to Charles Winecoff in his biography on Anthony Perkins, *Split Image*, the actor invited Maila over for dinner to finally meet Helen. While there, he gifted Maila with one of his paintings. During dinner, which Helen graciously prepared and served, Tony was rude and demanding toward Helen, treating her "like a housekeeper" in her own home. Maila was horrified at his behavior and became so upset, she forgot to take the painting when she left. When she asked for it later, Tony reportedly said, "Well, you left it behind, you didn't want it, so now you can't have it." Winecoff quotes Maila as saying, "That was the first time I realized Tony was cruel."

On the night of Saturday, January 7, 1956, Maila was barefoot and wearing her uniform of a sweater and capris, as she lay on her cellophane bed thumbing through a movie magazine. The day before, she'd scrubbed the building's painted turquoise staircase. In her diary for that day, just two words: "breakdown" and "hungry." Tony was expected to arrive within the hour with something to eat. She was starving.

Suddenly, a knock at the door. Maila looked at her lavender clock on the lavender cardboard box at her bedside. It was 10:45 p.m.

Wondering why Tony wasn't using his customary knock, Maila rose and turned the lavender fur doorknob cover and cautiously opened the door a crack. On the other side was a husky young black man with a zippered jacket and a glassy-eyed stare.

Through the crack, the man said, "Peggy?"

Maila told him Peggy didn't live there anymore.

When the man demanded to know her name, Maila attempted to shut the door, but he shouldered his way in and slammed the door behind him.

Maila was terrified and stood against the far wall while the man listened through the door for sounds in the hallway. Satisfied there were none, he reached inside his jacket, as if for a gun. But instead he pulled out a *Confidential* magazine and another with a cover of bloody bodies. He threw them on the floor and commanded Maila to pick them up and read them. She ignored his request and, with every bit of courage she could muster, said, "I was just in the middle of writing a letter to my mother."

"Write," he ordered. "Finish the letter."

"I can't concentrate with somebody else in the room."

He got angrier, saying, "I said write!"

Maila stalled for time, fearful that if Tony showed up, he would be shot. She knew that when he did show, she would say, "Don Medford is here," which was their secret code for "I'm in danger."

"You're not Peggy, so who are you?" the intruder asked.

The first name that popped into her mind was that of her high-school best friend. "Helen Kokko," Maila said.

In an effort to maintain the illusion of calmness, she offered the man coffee. He took a sip and put it down on the stove.

Maila was thinking of Tony again. Perhaps the best way to protect him would be to remove the element of surprise when he finally knocked.

"I have a friend who lives up the street," she said. "When he comes, I'll just tell him to go away."

It backfired. "Just let him come to this door and I'll kill him," the man threatened. "Sit down," he ordered.

Maila slid down the wall onto the floor, only to hear the man say, "Not there." He pointed to the pile of excelsior. "Over there!"

She complied and bent to put on a pair of slippers.

"What are you putting those on for?"

"We'll go out and have a cup of coffee. I know where there's some music."

"Yeah? And you'll yell for the cops. Besides, we're colored and white—where could we go?"

Maila suggested a place on Sixth Avenue, Rudley's. But the man wasn't going for it. He told her to take off her slippers and, with a leer on his face, told her that she knew what he came for.

In her moment of panic, Sister Saint Francis emerged. "You came here because God sent you. You go out in the world feeling that everyone's against you and you want to kill people. But you don't want to disappoint God. You must remember that you are a child of God and that He loves all of His children. We are both His children and we are both loved equally."

Maila's words took a curious turn on the intruder. Suddenly, he took on the persona of a little boy and began recalling his early life when his mother was a church usher. From the door latch, he toyed with Maila's lavender rosary. She tried desperately to keep him talking so she could formulate an escape plan. As he talked, he paced and rifled through a cupboard above the stove and found a razor blade. He picked it up and flexed it making a snapping sound.

"Whose is this?" he asked.

"It's mine," Maila explained. "I use it to sharpen my makeup pencils."

"You're a bad woman," he said and motioned for Maila to lay down on her bed of cellophane.

Before Maila could react, he pushed her down and got on top of her. His face was only inches from hers and he held the razor blade to her throat.

"How old are you?"

"Thirty-three."

"You won't live past morning."

The man was now facing the picture of the monk on the wall. He stared long and hard at the picture before he finally spat out the words, "I don't care who or what you are. I don't care if you're a monk. You're going to die."

The man reached up and switched off the lights. Plunged into total darkness with the man on top of her, Maila was afraid to breathe, believing it might be her last. Minutes ticked by, her heart pounding in her throat. Then another few minutes went by without the man moving. Then she heard snoring. Incredibly, he'd fallen asleep.

Inch by inch, she managed to wriggle out from underneath him and crept along the wall toward the door, but the creaking floor betrayed her. The man awoke with a start and came after her. Grabbing her, he threw on the lights and shouted at her to get back onto the bed.

Maila knew if she got on that bed one more time, she was dead. Instead, she simply excused herself to go to the bathroom. Amazingly, the man did not follow her. Maila closed the door behind her, leaned against it with all her weight and screamed for help, pounding on the walls with every bit of strength she had.

Enraged, the intruder crashed through the door and dragged Maila out. In a desperate ploy, Maila put her fingers to her lips. "Shh," she said, and pointed to the front door. The man, holding Maila with one arm, opened the door a crack with his other hand. With Herculean strength, Maila grabbed the door from him, flung it open, and ran screaming to the apartment across the hall. Pounding on the door, she pleaded for help.

There was no response.

The man caught up with Maila and ripped off her sweater. She broke away and got to the head of the stairs before he caught her again. Using the weight of her body, she hurled both of them down the stairs. A jumble of turquoise paint flashed before her eyes, and all Maila could think of was that she was glad she'd washed them. Because of the adrenaline coursing through her bloodstream, she felt no pain. Together, the two tumbled until they landed in the second-floor hallway.

The man began to choke her and Maila remembered telling herself she was not ready to die. Images flashed across her mind. She saw herself in a hospital bed surrounded by nurses telling how she was rescued. Simultaneously, she saw a picture of herself in a crime magazine—the caption read, "The body was found in this position."

She played dead and went limp. It worked. The man carried her back up the stairs, and when they reached the top, Maila threw herself out of his grasp and back down the stairs. Her assailant grabbed at her and demanded that she get

Maila showing bruises after struggle with intruder, 1956 Bettmann via Getty Images.

back on her feet. Halfway up, she threw herself down again. This time she landed on her back, and when the man was upon her again, she was able to roll to the main entrance vestibule. With her left hand, Maila reached up to the long handle of the building's front door. It opened into the stairwell of the foyer. Just a few steps up, on the sidewalk, she saw three people walking by.

"Help! Police!" Maila gasped.

Instantly, the attacker backed off. Maila got to her feet and ran up the stairs toward the passersby, shrieking and sobbing. "Please, save me!"

From the doorway, she heard the assailant say, "Helen, why are you doing this to me?"

Maila bolted down the street toward the lights from an Italian restaurant and ran inside, expecting bullets to come crashing through the window at any second.

An employee was sweeping the floor; he looked up from his task at Maila, nude from the waist up, only to remark, "We're closed, lady."

She ran into the ladies' room and locked herself in. She never learned who called the police.

Officers arrived and escorted Maila back to her apartment, waited while she got dressed, grabbed a single vulture feather, and drove her to the 16th Precinct.

It turned out that shortly before Maila moved in, her apartment was burglarized, and the intruder used the phone to make a long-distance call to Columbus, Georgia. That man was 23-year-old Ellis Barber, whose arrest record included two attempted rapes.

At the police station, Maila pointed out the face of her attacker from a book of photos. In a chilling coincidence, she learned from Barber's police record that his street name was "The Vamp."

After identifying Barber as the perpetrator, Maila rode with three police detectives to search for him. At 5:30 that morning, he was spotted walking in Times Square. When she saw him, Maila collapsed in fear onto the floorboard of the car.

The suspect was taken into custody, booked, and jailed. On January 20, 1956, Maila appeared in felony court as a witness against Barber. He pled not guilty to the charge of attempted rape and was transported to Bellevue Hospital for a mental assessment and observation. What happened to him after that, Maila never knew.

The next day, she heard that the super of the building hung out in a bar on 6th Street, and for a couple of bucks, he tipped off the bar's unsavory clientele whenever a single woman moved into one of his buildings.

The press clamored for the story. They wanted to see Maila's bruises and hear the story in every terrifying detail. The fact that she was a human being meant nothing. The fact that she was still terrified and undergoing a great deal of emotional distress did not matter. They wanted to hear about the battle between Vampira and the Vamp.

And so, she temporarily put aside the emotional trauma of her life-or-death struggle to accommodate the media. Perched on the edge of a desktop, wearing an off-the-shoulder sheath, heels, and a full face of makeup, Maila's entire back was mottled with unseen contusions. She demurely lifted the hem of her dress and pointed to the bruises on her legs. But to look behind the eyeshadow, the perfectly applied mascara, and the curled hair is to see the emotional pain reflected in her eyes. "Here you go," she seemed to say. "Isn't this what you want?"

They got their story because it wasn't Maila who'd battled for her life. It was Vampira. The bruises were superficial and would heal, but the internal ones would remain for the rest of her life.

After the story was revealed and after the last photograph was taken, Maila picked up her lavender suitcase and boarded a Greyhound for Los Angeles. It was January 22, 1956.

Returning to Hollywood, Maila trusted she could endure its memories if only to feel safe. But no sooner did she arrive than did a story explode onto the scene—one that would have lifelong ramifications.

Whisper, a sleazy cousin of the equally scandalous *Confidential* magazine, ran

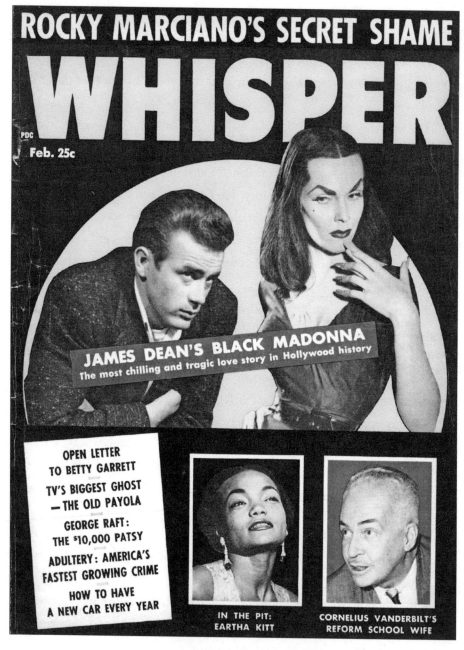

Whisper Magazine: February 1956

a cover with a superimposed picture of Vampira and Jimmy together. Stretched across the photo, a banner screamed:

JAMES DEAN'S BLACK MADONNA
The most chilling tragic love story in Hollywood history

Inside, the five-page spread told a tale of love, betrayal, voodoo dolls, and black magic. It declared that Jimmy and Maila were lovers until he became a star and dumped her. It further claimed that Maila, a self-proclaimed witch, cast a death spell upon the actor. Accompanying the story was a photo of Jimmy's cutouts on Maila's wall and a blow-up of the postcard she sent to Jimmy via the Villa Capri a few days before he died. However, the original message was intentionally altered to sound more sinister. Instead of "Wish you were here," it read, "Darling, Come And Join Me."

It became one of the magazine's most successful covers.

For those disinclined to read *Whisper*, the headline of the *Daily News'* February 5th Sunday supplement picked up the slack by exposing Maila's torment to the nation:

TV's female Dracula battles rapist-strangler after fleeing from hoodoo she feared killed James Dean

It was as though there was not a real human underneath the costume; there was only Vampira.

So they had me do a John Wilkes Booth & kill a public hero. The teenagers' hero—in this case—a movie idol & my only friend in the world besides Mother. They said I killed him with black magic & not only did the scandal sheet magazines print it, but the Hearst Syndicate as well as in the Sunday supplement, thereby spreading the news of my vengeful character worldwide.

A kind of dialectic hysteria erupted. From James Dean fans came death threats, while necrophiliacs sent love letters. Maila couldn't avoid being attacked, either physically, as she had in New York, or emotionally in Hollywood. Additionally, she was flat broke, which left her little choice but to move in with her mother into the one-bedroom apartment on Carlton Way, a block south of Hollywood Boulevard.

Maila slept on the sofa. Her mother was already at work one morning when the phone rang, interrupting her thoughts of suicide. She debated upon whether to answer. Maybe it was a sign. A job offer meant she would live. Another death threat meant to go ahead and save that person the trouble of killing her.

She answered.

It was neither. It was Hunt Stromberg, Jr.

"I read about you in the Sunday paper," the voice said in mock delight. "Congratulations on finding a way to stay in the headlines, even as I tried to bury you."

Chapter Fifteen

Stromberg would have enjoyed learning that the mere sound of his voice drove Maila to suicide. Then, maybe her intellectual property would be up for grabs and he could finally own Vampira. His timing certainly could not have been better.

But instead, it had the opposite effect. Maila would not let Stromberg's voice be the last she ever heard. In that moment, she vowed to survive. To live.

The relationship between mother and daughter was often contentious. Even though Sophie had been sober for four years now and religiously attended AA meetings, the die had been cast for Maila, who'd spent too many years as the daughter of an alcoholic. Sophie had always been short on patience and quick to anger. When a young Maila tried to make her first cake, she misread the recipe and ruined the cake, accidentally wasting the ingredients, and her mother slapped her across the face as punishment. The bowl crashed to the floor, and Maila was made to clean up the mess.

When Sophie got sober, she changed. She quit dyeing her hair and wearing makeup, and she gained a few pounds. She could still be gruff, but her outright anger seemed to have dissipated—or it was no longer on display, at least. Instead, she complained incessantly about her daughter. "Maila keeps ungodly hours. She hangs out with creeps. She doesn't help with the groceries. She spends all her money on taxis. Her behavior is shameful."

The opening scene of R.H. Greene's *Vampira and Me* offers a glimpse into Maila and her mother's interaction—a peek so subtle that it's easy to miss. There's Maila at midday, glamorous in a cocktail dress, her look accessorized with just the right jewelry, shoes, and clutch. And then there's Sophie, nattily dressed in a black suit, with a blue sweater draped over her handbag. It isn't hard to imagine the conversation: Sophie insisting that Maila take a sweater in case it got chilly, and Maila refusing it because it would spoil her look. As it turned out, Mama was right because later in the film, we see Maila wearing that sweater. Sophie was essentially Maila's handmaiden. She cooked, she cleaned, she washed Maila's clothes in the kitchen sink, she fed Maila's cats. If she did all that, she wasn't going to do it in silence.

For all she did, Sophie never came to understand what made her daughter tick. And she never gave up trying to shove Maila's square peg of a psyche into the round hole of domesticity.

Occasionally, a man would arrive to pick Maila up for a real date, and Sophie would have to make excuses, as Maila was already out with someone else. When Dink showed up to take Maila to a Screen Writers Guild dinner, Sophie's heart soared, hoping the two would reunite and thereby set her free from being Maila's self-imposed guardian. But their date was only one of convenience. Dink was expected to attend, and Maila liked parties. Afterward, she commented, "Dink is obviously more amenable to social functions when it suits his own needs."

Anthony Perkins continued to phone or visit as it suited him. If he was out of town, he promised letters that never arrived. And always there was an excuse: He forgot to take his address book, or if he did, he accidentally dropped it in the pool, or maybe he sent her letter to the wrong address. If Maila's diary entries are any indication, she may have justified Tony's inconsiderate behavior in the hopes that, no matter how implausible, a romantic relationship may unfold.

February 16, 1956:

> *Date at Thrifty with T.P.—one hr & 10 min. only—he played it*
> *sensuous. He left to rehearse with Piper Laurie. Is Osgood Perkins'*
> *little boy playing hard to get?*

Tony and Piper Laurie starred in a television show, an adaptation of F. Scott Fitzgerald's *Winter Dreams*. The reviews were terrible. Columnist Jaik Rosenstein was especially brutal, and Tony called Maila to complain. Maila assuaged his bruised ego, and on Tony's birthday soon after, as a gift to Perkins, she called Rosenstein and "gave him hell."

So it went between Maila and Tony. Dates were made, and if nothing better came up, he'd be there. If something better did, he'd cancel at the last minute. For example, they planned a dinner date at Ah Fong's, a celebrity-frequented restaurant on the Sunset Strip, and ten minutes before he was due to pick her up, Tony called to say he couldn't make it. He was at a party at the home of Mercedes McCambridge, where those in attendance were being "insufferably mean" to him. He needed Maila's soft shoulder to cry on. But from a distance, and over the phone.

Tony was being touted as the next James Dean and was soon on his way to Lone Pine, California, to begin filming *The Lonely Man* with Jack Palance. One afternoon, while Maila's miscast Romeo was away on location, there was a knock on her door. Maila was still asleep, and her mother was already home from work. Afraid it was a crazed fan, Sophie peeked through the window blinds and went to rouse her daughter.

"There's a man at the door," she whispered. "Get up."

Answering the door, the man on the porch looked familiar. He was an acquaintance, Paul Marco. "I got a script for you, baby," he said buoyantly.

The script was for a film, *Grave Robbers from Outer Space*.

The name piqued Maila's interest. "Whose is it?" she asked.

"Eddie Wood's," Marco said.

"No, no, no," Maila shook her head, "I don't think so." She wanted to go back to bed.

"Lugosi's doing it."

"I heard he was ill."

"Don't matter, Eddie's got stills."

Maila adored Bela Lugosi. But Ed Wood was poison. It would be professional suicide to work for him.

"No... no, I can't do it," Maila repeated.

Marco would not be deterred. He reached into his pocket and pulled out a wad of money.

"This is for you," he said fanning out two hundred one-dollar bills on the coffee table. "I'm prepared to offer you all of this for just one day's work."

Maila stared down at the money. Her 17-dollar-a-week unemployment check was just about to run out, with three dollars in her wallet and down to the last can of cat food in the cupboard.

"Come on, Maila. It's a union picture."

"No more than a day's work?"

"That's right. Two hundred bucks in cold, hard cash. How you gonna pass that up?"

"Okay, leave me the script. I'll read it."

According to Sophie, the script lay on the table for months, untouched, because Maila's luck suddenly changed for the better.

First, KHJ-TV expressed interest in reprising *The Vampira Show*. And just as quickly, another incredible opportunity arrived, albeit from the misfortune of a man whom Maila greatly respected and admired—Bela Lugosi. Lugosi was set to perform in Las Vegas when he became seriously ill, and in a second, the famed star was replaced by television's First Lady of Horror. Vampira signed to perform live on the opening night of *Come As You Are*, a variety show hosted by Liberace, the highest-paid entertainer in show business at the time.

Maila was transformed. Just as in the glory days at KABC, there would be interviews, rehearsals, fittings for a new Las Vegas gown, and lots of press.

Before she could plunk a nickel in a slot machine, Maila got yet another job offer.

April of 1956 marked the launch of a new production company, American International Pictures or AIP. They wanted Maila to bring Vampira to San Francisco to plug their first film, a sci-fi thriller, *It Conquered the World*, starring Peter Graves and Beverly Garland. The two-day stint promised lots of press, appearances, and a photo shoot. Coming just before her Las Vegas debut, the timing could not have been better. For her efforts, she was paid 350 dollars, which was more than she earned for an entire month at KABC. Suddenly, Ed Wood's two hundred dollars seemed like chump change.

AIP's approach toward filmmaking was make them fast, make them cheap, and target a teenage audience. Adults were staying home glued to their television sets while the teen market remained virtually untapped. San Francisco was a whirlwind of activity, appearances, and interviews. Maila was pleased to discover her hotel accommodations included free long-distance phone service, which she made liberal use of to call Tony Perkins in Lone Pine. With her career back on track, she felt she had substance to lend to their conversations.

Early the next morning, a chauffeured hearse was ready and at her disposal. The day began with a scheduled appearance on a televised cooking show. Next, Vampira was a guest on an exercise show. From there, she made a cameo at a downtown restaurant. Her appearance created a near mob scene, as San Franciscans had never seen Vampira live.

That evening, Vampira appeared in a theater lobby showing a horror film. She wasn't in the film, but none of the actual stars were available, so she stood behind a red velvet rope, signing autographs and talking to fans who'd waited around the block for a chance to meet her. There was a final stop at a nightclub before the day ended in her hotel's newly refurbished penthouse suite.

A red chaise longue was prepared for Vampira to relax upon while conducting a press conference with columnist Paul Kopay. Simultaneously, a celebratory cocktail party was happening, where red-jacketed waiters scooped Bloody Marys from crystal bowls.

AIP was a low-budget distributor, and it was unprecedented for them to go to such expense to promote one of their movies. Their extravagant efforts paid off when they made the front page in the entertainment section of the *Las Vegas Review-Journal*. AIP was so pleased with the results of their two-day media blitz, Maila received a 350-dollar bonus.

Then little more than a desert oasis, Las Vegas attracted more than a quarter-million tourists annually. If the gambling or world-class live shows weren't tempting enough, visitors of the era could also marvel at the architectural wonders of the nearby Hoover Dam or at a nuclear mushroom cloud blossoming over the desert horizon at the Nevada Test Site.

Perhaps less explosive, but no less sensational, a bombshell of the blonde variety made her way into town. Up Highway 19, Maila Nurmi rode shotgun in an old Dodge piloted by Jack Simmons. Upon arrival, Maila directed Jack to cruise the Strip past the Riviera. And there it was, on the hotel's marquee stretched high above the boulevard:

LIBERACE
Come As You Are Featuring Vampira

The Riviera, nine stories tall, the first high-rise on the Las Vegas Strip, offered 291 rooms and an Olympic-sized swimming pool. It forged a departure from the standard garden-style two-story hotels that dotted the boulevard.

Maila, meanwhile, booked a room at the Old West-themed Last Frontier Hotel, which sat side by side with the newly constructed version of itself, the New Frontier. The older hotel started its life in 1942 when the Strip outside of downtown consisted of only sand, and it claimed the distinction as the second hotel on the Vegas strip. But by the early 1950s, the Last Frontier compound included an amusement park, a church, and a casino nightclub. By 1955, just a year before Maila arrived in Vegas, the larger upscale version opened its doors. The decaying Last Frontier hotel was soon to be demolished, but it was still accepting guests for those who chose economy over amenities.

While clean and unpretentious, there was only a single bed. Before they'd left L.A., Maila and Jack made a deal. She would share her room in exchange for a car and driver. It never occurred to either of them they may have to share a bed. It would be an inconvenience they'd have to tolerate. The bigger problem was that the closest cup of coffee was all the way over at the New Frontier's restaurant.

They walked over for coffee and to fill up their thermoses for the morning. Near the entrance was a 12-foot-tall sign in the shape of a young man playing the guitar. A banner stretched across the man's hips announced:

In Person
ELVIS PRESLEY

Before rehearsal the next morning, Maila got a tour of the swanky Riviera. Marble floors and wormwood paneling greeted guests. The hotel restaurant was split in half, one side servicing indoor guests, the other opening onto the pool area. Liberace occupied a bank of penthouse suites, large enough for three pianos and decorated with enough flowers to keep every florist in Vegas in the black. From his suite, nine floors up, the view of the city and the expanse of the desert beyond was spectacular.

Maila was astounded by the Riviera's extravagance and opulence and was no less amazed when she saw its entertainment venue. The Clover Room, where she and Liberace would perform, did not disappoint. The showroom was elegantly draped in platinum-gray velour, which provided not only aesthetic appeal but also superb acoustics. From the black ceiling, a thousand lights twinkled, mimicking a starry desert sky. But the focus of the room was the 40-by-60-foot stage— impressive as any Maila had ever seen, with its six separate elevations and four revolving turntables.

With a few nights free before opening night, Maila was free to see the other acts in town. Liberace graciously invited Maila and Jack to join his entourage to see Katherine Dunham and Lillian Roth at the Sahara. But for Maila, seeing Johnnie Ray sing at the Desert Inn later was the highlight of the evening. She'd had a crush on the singer ever since her days at the Savoy. And she was all the more delighted when, after the performance, she was invited backstage with Liberace to meet him.

And then, there was Elvis. On April 23, 1956, Maila wrote:

> *Date with Liberace for Elvis Presley opening. New Frontier.*

When the show began at 8 p.m., Maila was seated with Liberace and his family. After the Freddy Martin Orchestra played, the emcee announced Elvis, who came on stage wearing a turquoise dinner jacket and matching blue eyeshadow.

> *I thought to myself, "Well now, this is going to be quite the show." Never before had I seen a straight man... & I assumed he was... wear eyeshadow & eyeliner & was that mascara as well? I mean, I was with Liberace & we had very good seats. I was momentarily stunned, but he certainly got my attention when he began to sing & play his guitar. And to move his body in such a way as I'd never before seen. I was, quite frankly, agog with delight.*

The audience was not nearly as enamored, and Elvis was met with only scattered, polite applause. Then, from the back of the Venus Room, someone booed, and then another and another. Maila was pained by the reaction. At the intermission, she thanked Liberace for his hospitality and claimed a headache before leaving with her apologies.

She cut through the pool area in the back. Deserted and dark save for the illumination from the underwater lights, a beam of light suddenly streamed

Maila with Elvis, 1956. Michael Ochs/Michael Ochs Archives via Getty Images.

across the darkened concrete. The double doors of the hotel restaurant opened to reveal Elvis, now wearing a canary-yellow jacket.

His eyes unaccustomed to the dark, he didn't realize he wasn't alone until Maila called out, "Over here."

They met halfway at the pool and pulled out some chairs to sit down.

She told him she'd seen his performance and that, as a performer herself, she knew how terrible it was to hear the audience's reaction.

Elvis responded, "You know, every night before I go on, I talk to God and He always answers me. But tonight, he didn't answer. And when them curtains opened and I seen all that white hair and them glasses, I knew why."

That's because it was the first time in history that teenagers could claim a musical style all their own. Many parents didn't understand rock and roll and feared it would lead to losing control over their children. Most adults thought that kind of music was a fad to be bravely tolerated until it passed into obscurity. Other more conservative families believed it to be spawned by the devil himself and should be obliterated from the earth. Elvis' hip gyrations only fueled those beliefs of the mostly middle-aged audience.

"They're sheep," Maila continued. "They've never seen anyone like you. *Life* magazine is going to discover you, and then everyone will want to kiss your shoes."

"It's comin' out next Thursday," Elvis said.

"I know you're older an' all, Ma'am," he continued, "but you've been awful kind. If you care to come back after the second show, I'd be proud to take you to my place and play a song for you or something."

In an audio interview, Maila claimed she didn't take the young singer up on his offer. One can hear it in her voice, the shy, coy denial. She wasn't that kind of girl. Except it was Elvis.

She did meet up with Elvis after his midnight show. His room was crowded with band members, handlers, managers, and other girls. Maila sized up the female competition and determined that she was wiser than all of them put together. The room was filled with people smoking and gave Maila the perfect excuse to grab Elvis' hand and suggest they go outside for some fresh air. People were playing guitars all around the room, and Elvis grabbed one on his way out. Maila thought, "Oh, good, he's going to serenade me."

On their way over to the Last Frontier side of the complex, Maila silently prayed Simmons would be gone when they arrived. God must have been on sabbatical, because when Maila opened the door, Jack was in bed, asleep.

"Jack, what are you doing here? Go back to your own room."

To Elvis, she said, "You'll have to excuse him—he gets confused when he drinks."

Maila introduced Jack as her assistant and chauffeur, and Jack made a hasty retreat, probably to resume sleeping in his car.

Finally alone, the two sat on the bed. Elvis strummed a few chords but said he couldn't sing because his throat was dry. Maila offered him a choice of coffee from her thermos or a warm bottle of soda. He opted for the soda.

Elvis asked if she played guitar. She didn't.

Would she like a guitar lesson? She would.

On the bed, Elvis wrapped his arms around her and positioned her hands on the guitar. It was no use—Maila couldn't concentrate on her music lesson. He chorded, and she strummed, but what she truly wanted was to hear him sing. And when he did, his choice of song was completely unexpected. He sang a church hymn, "The Old Rugged Cross."

Hardly a romantic prelude, but sweet nonetheless & albeit clumsily & awkwardly we began to make real music together. The overture was thrilling, the crescendo was breathtaking, the climax fell flat. Elvis, for all his great beauty & magnetism, was sexually inexperienced when I knew him. Was I to believe his on stage pelvic swivels & thrusts were only a tease? He made love like an adolescent school boy. I realized, he was not yet a man, still a boy with pimples, barely twenty-one. Nonetheless, he had this alluring energy about him. Indefinable really—but an undeniable presence. I knew he was going to be a big star. That the world would recognize him as a musical genius. God sent me to cheer Elvis... and I did.

Maila always was a sucker for a genius.

Chapter Sixteen

On April 24, 1956, the Riviera's much-anticipated opening night arrived. Both the dinner and late show were sellouts. For the uninitiated, the program referenced Vampira's accomplishments as such:

> *Life referred to her as a "Scary Femme Fatale." In television, she presented blood curdling and spine tingling commercials for a local sponsor. More recently, she was a "Frightful" success with her Charles Addams caricature on the George Gobel Show. This marks Vampira's first "Diabolique" entrance on a theatre stage in a role that is "Terrifyingly alluring."*

The show comprised a series of musical vignettes through the ages, as Liberace took the audience on a tour among the Persian Room at the Plaza Hotel, Chicago's Orchestra Hall, the Orpheum Theatre, the Imperial Palace of Vienna, and finally to "King George's Court," circa 1456.

The show was divided into 12 acts. Vampira addressed the audience from the perspective of a 500-year-old undead corpse, assuming the role of the moderator of musical mayhem, rising from a coffin to begin each of her segments. Essentially, she was playing the same role as she had on *The Vampira Show*. But now, instead of providing a humorous respite from horror movies, her performances allowed for behind-the-scenes preparations and costume changes. Until Liberace reappeared, elaborately dressed and escorted by feathered and sequined chorus girls, Vampira was on.

Maila performed six sets each night and participated in the finale. A minute of film survives from the Las Vegas show and depicts Vampira and Liberace waltzing; he's dressed as a court jester. These snippets are most likely from a dress rehearsal of the finale, as Vampira is wearing her original, zipper-in-the-front costume, not the custom-made dress she wore in the live show, with red rhinestones to simulate blood drops.

The Sands Hotel and Casino was located where the Venetian now stands. For Maila and Jack, it became their Googies by proxy. It also served as the after-the-show home base for Liberace and his entourage, which always included his brother, George, and their mother, Frances. Elvis and his band also made nightly pilgrimages to The Sands after their last show of the evening, along with singer Johnnie Ray.

When *Movie Mirror* magazine came to town to do a photo shoot and story on Elvis, Maila was with him at rehearsal. In one shot, a smiling Elvis has his hands around her throat in mock strangulation. It's interesting to note that Maila found creative ways to cover her fine, limp hair; on this day, she chose a scarf.

After the rehearsals and photo shoots, there was still lots of daylight to enjoy. Maila and Jack met up with Elvis and his band to check out the Last Frontier Village next door to the hotel, an Old West–themed boardwalk featuring clothing stores, restaurants, and souvenir shops. An ensemble in a window caught Maila's eye and she pulled Elvis into the shop to try it on and get his approval. A photo shows Maila holding hands with Elvis and wearing the outfit: Western-style pants and a matching vest. Later, they took a ride on the scooter cars, purposely crashing into one another.

The day would have been perfect except that Jack was beginning to wear thin on Maila. She noticed money was missing from her purse. Whether Jack took it or she simply miscounted, she didn't know, but she well knew his history of petty thievery. But perhaps it wasn't so much that she suspected Jack stole her money as it was that Jack and Elvis were becoming friends too, and now he was spending more time with Elvis than she was. This after she was the one who introduced the two. Maila kicked Jack out of their room.

Sulking in her room alone after her late show, Jack burst in. She may have thrown him out again had he not come with such an exciting offer.

He'd been at the Sahara with Elvis, and the band heard a group perform a song that they went nuts over. Elvis was so fired up, he wanted to start putting his own spin on the tune right then and there. The hotel would never tolerate a rock-and-roll band disturbing their other guests in the middle of the night, so they were going out to the sand dunes to sing and goof around. Did she want to come along?

It wasn't far, just east of the Strip where the neon façades of the city surrendered to the desert. The wind off the mountains swept through the valley, blowing the shifting sands into dunes. Jack and Maila drove out to the site, where a few cars were already parked in a semicircle, forming an ad hoc stage.

The vast expanse of the desert was a crazy place for an impromptu jam session—the acoustics were lousy, and the seating was nonexistent. The only light emanated from the canopy of stars above as well as the headlights from the cars, all trained on the future King of Rock and Roll. But there was plenty of beer, and those in attendance grabbed a bottle and plopped themselves on the hoods of their cars. Sometime during that night in the desert, some semblance of a classic rock and roll song was born.

Elvis sings "Hound Dog" for the 1st time on sand dunes. 2 A.M.
April 30.

Maila in Vegas, 1956. By Bernard of Hollywood, courtesy of the Jove de Renzy Collection.

It was dawn before the caravan headed back into town, sleepy and a little drunk, unaware they had just witnessed music history being made.

A few nights later, Maila was at the Sands. Johnnie Ray was seated at Liberace's table when Elvis stopped by to chat, and Maila made a drastic attempt to get his attention.

> *Elvis came over & I grabbed his divining rod. His fury knows no bounds. Elvis made a speech to me about, "The next time I go out with you, etc." All the times we were together, he never let me see his pee-pee so I told him he had no guts. He now hates me & is proclaiming it loudly. Fabulous activity at Sands and Liberace drove me home.*

Maila was trying to embarrass Elvis publicly in retaliation for him ignoring her toward the end of his Las Vegas gig—and it worked. She played by her own rules. What she didn't count on was that Elvis would stay angry with her until he left Las Vegas. The night he left, Elvis gifted Jack with a watch. Maila would have to settle for just her memories.

In later interviews, when recounting her time with Elvis, Maila would say she "gave him hell" for treating his girlfriend poorly. She did, but the "girlfriend" she was referring to was herself.

By 1956, Bernard of Hollywood had expanded his business to include a studio at the Riviera Hotel, and on May 7th, Maila was scheduled for an early-morning photo shoot. Bruno Bernard photographed his subject extensively in and around the hotel, in full view of those guests who'd chosen to rise with the sun. Maila was dressed in black from head to toe.

But not as Vampira—as a dominatrix in a hooded black latex catsuit, clinging to her body like a second skin. Other shots from the same morning show her in the hotel's beauty salon beneath a hair dryer and splayed on the pool's diving board. But by far, the raciest photos were those shots taken in one of the hotel rooms. Here, Maila in her catsuit wields a cane upon a hapless man wearing striped pajamas. It seems Maila took more than her personal effects and the bed from the apartment she'd shared with Dink. These were her ex-husband's "prison PJs," and the victim wearing them was none other than Jack Simmons.

At the wrap party for the show, Maila signed a written agreement to appear on Broadway with Liberace the following November. The showman, obviously pleased with Maila's performance, gifted her with a personally inscribed, rhinestone-encrusted compact.

Elvis' anger at Maila and then his conspicuous lack of generosity had hurt her pride. When he appeared at the Shrine in Los Angeles a few months later, Maila sent him a gift by messenger: a jar of hair dressing. The note she attached read: "A good pomade for soreheads."

Shortly afterward, the columnist Sidney Skolsky was standing outside of Schwab's when he spotted Maila crossing the street.

"Hey, Vampi," he said in his strong New York accent. "Whatcha got? The creeps! Where do you find them?"

Skolsky reported gossip in a monthly column called "From a Stool At Schwab's" that ran in *Photoplay*, a film magazine. He also had a radio show, and his daily and monthly gossip columns were syndicated in newspapers worldwide. Skolsky rented an office on the second floor of Schwab's Pharmacy (home to several peepholes), so he could surreptitiously spy on the goings-on below.

Because Sidney was always digging for the new kid on the block, he knew that I was the first one to inform him whenever true, new talent hit Hollywood's turf. He trusted me. First there had been a funny boy named Marlon Brando who'd turned out to be a big movie star. Then there was the geeky Dean kid. He shot to stardom. Now there was Osgood Perkins' son, this tall, skinny kid who was already being talked about for an Oscar.

So it occurred to Sidney that I knew something. Tonight, he asked, "Who's going to be the next James Dean?" I responded, "There's no such thing, Sidney. Not possible, but I know what you mean & I've just met him. He's never been to Hollywood & he's got a funny name. He sings. I met him in Las Vegas. His name is Elvis Presley."

Sidney just laughed and said, "Left field, Vampi, Left field. You're getting over-confident."

After Las Vegas, Maila had good reason to believe her success there would parlay into bigger and better things. The resurrection of *The Vampira Show* on KHJ was only the beginning.

Ed Wood's script still sat on the table where she left it and niggled at her like a memento left over from a bad love affair. She'd agreed to do it in a moment of panic, but now she wanted out. She didn't need it anymore.

What she *did* need was to hear from Tony Perkins. He'd promised to write to her while she was in Las Vegas but hadn't. She called him to ask why. Almost immediately, Perkins hung up on her, only to call back a few minutes later with a story to tell.

Anthony called ten minutes later & said he HAD written a letter & sent a photo. He was divinely sweet. He had a special photo taken in front of Ah Fong's for me & it's now in the dead letter office – Pity – his letters are such treasures.

It was obvious that Tony took a few minutes to trump up a story about a nonexistent letter and photo, knowing Maila would be heartsick for having missed them. But even if she suspected it was a lie, she wouldn't allow herself to believe it.

More phone calls from Tony followed. He called from the set of *The Lonely Man* in a state of near panic, announcing, "The little pig people are here and they're taking over! If I end up dead, you'll know why." Before Maila could respond, the line went dead.

Then more calls, each perfectly timed five minutes apart and each with a message more urgent than the last. "The pig people are real. They're going to kill me. Help!"

Then the phone calls stopped.

> *I was terrified he was truly in danger, but Tony didn't like working*
> *on The Lonely Man & hated the cast and crew. He said the entire*
> *production was like a chapter out of George Orwell's Animal House*
> *[sic]. I can only guess—someone pissed him off & his cowardice*
> *confronting them directly meant I would take the brunt of his rage.*

She must have at least suspected Tony's utter disregard for her feelings. But even as his burgeoning career meant their time together would become increasingly infrequent, she couldn't let go. As he began work on *Fear Strikes Out*, Maila decided it was better to try to maintain a friendship of broken promises and lies than to risk the pain of abandonment.

The Vampira Show redux premiered on May 18. Although KHJ was a less popular station than KABC, her salary was substantially more than what she earned at KABC, at 350 dollars a week. To make the deal even sweeter, car salesman Fletcher Jones, who'd sponsored her show on KABC, was again on board as sponsor.

But Maila was still unhappy with the writers and the look of the show. KABC owned the original props, so Vampira's authentic Victorian sofa was replaced by a cheap imitation; the same went for the poison bar. Gone, too, was the tombstone coffee table.

Maila may have been able to reconcile herself with the shoddy props if her old show's writer, Peter Robinson, were still writing the scripts. But KHJ had other ideas. Maila claimed they hired writers who were unfamiliar with her character, and she declared them all to be "inept idiots."

Idiots aside, Maila was sure the KABC execs would be watching, and so she was determined that the premiere of *The Vampira Show* would be memorable right out of the gate. She had no intention of following the script, which she found uninspired. Fresh from Las Vegas, she was brimming with her own new audience-tested material, and she launched a cannon into America's living rooms.

"I must tell you about my sister. She's dead now, lucky girl. It seems she was lynched for raping a snake."

The shit, as they say, hit the fan.

Ouch—censorship—seems I said a dirty word. Rape—FCC—a watered down Vampira follows?

It did. Her note from rehearsal the next day:

New. No cleavage edict—propriety, etc.

From that point on, Vampira was made to wear a scarf that covered all of her décolletage. It looked like she was wearing a muffler. She thought of it as punishment and privately referred to the censors as "beastly bullies." Shortly thereafter, she delivered this poem on-air.

Years ago I was interned
And sentenced to be burned
By a mob of beastly bullies.
But when they threw me on the pyre,
I refused to catch on fire,
Thank God for my asbestos woolies!

Maila continued to be most focused on Tony. He was never in town, away either filming or in New York. But he called enough to keep in contact, alleging that a week of promoting *Lonely Man* resulted in 17 interviews. Then it was back from New York to begin work on *Fear Strikes Out*, wherein Tony would portray American baseball player Jimmy Piersall.

It seems Maila was just going through the Vampira motions at KHJ. The station was afraid of provoking the wrath of the censors. The writing stunk. The set was sterile. The shock value that first endeared Vampira to the public was banned. By cutting corners, the program had suffered.

She persevered, Friday night after Friday night. Curiously, even as the ratings floundered, Maila's salary was raised to 425 dollars a week.

After signing off with her trademark farewell, she always changed into her customary capris and a sweater before bolting down the street to the farmers' market to get something to eat. And it was there, while Maila stood on the sidewalk, wolfing down a chili dog, that a man approached her.

"You're Vampira, aren't you?" The voice was rich and deep.

Still in full makeup, Maila lifted one dramatically arched eyebrow.

She studied the man with the gray spit curl and the sequined tuxedo and then wiped the chili sauce from her lacquered lips before answering, "Who wants to know?"

He was the son of a mortician and self-professed psychic who began his career hawking vitamins on early television. He went by a single name: Criswell. Upon realizing he could not sustain a viewing audience with a discussion of the merits of vitamin B-complex supplements alone, Criswell began peppering his presentations with outlandish predictions of natural disasters, UFOs, and end-of-the-world scenarios, claiming the visions came to him while sleeping in one of his many caskets. As a result, Criswell acquired a following and, for a time, enjoyed a bit of success.

That night, however, Criswell was acting as an emissary for his good friend, Mae West, who was a devout Vampira fan and never missed her show. Miss West wanted to meet her.

"We've met," Maila responded impassively.

Whether it was cosmic happenstance or something else, it seemed predestined that Maila and Criswell should become good friends. They shared a common stripe that set them apart from the Hollywood hoi polloi. As it turned out, it didn't matter that Maila thought West was a "contemptible bitch," even as the old gal turned out to be her ardent fan. Criswell maintained a simultaneous though separate friendship with both women. West sold her cast-off, scarcely used cars to Criswell for a dollar and personally prepared Swedish meatballs for him, delivered via chauffeured limousine. On those occasions, Criswell phoned Maila: "Get over here," he said, "Mae's cooking tonight."

As for Maila, it was a bit of sweet revenge that "the bitch who got me fired off Broadway is cooking my dinner."

Chapter Seventeen

The first summer after the death of James Dean arrived, and America's youth discovered their idol had truly been a game-changer. There would be no going back to the stodgy, conventional matinee stars who had captivated their parents. A new generation was on the horizon.

The James Dean hysteria continued to grow. And although no one could replace him, young moviegoers hungered for another angst-filled rebel. Someone who could capture their imaginations, to live out their dreams on the movie screen. Someone who reflected their conflict, their own inner turmoil, their need to rebel as a way to find their own identity. Hollywood needed to find another James Dean—and fast.

That summer, the city teemed with young men hoping for a shot at stardom. They arrived by the thousands. Among the James Dean wannabes was a kid who had hitchhiked from Missouri named Chuck Beadles.

At 22, Beadles could easily pass for Jimmy's brother. Same size, same unruly thatch of light brown hair, same blue eyes, same slouchy posture. But that's where the similarities ended. While James Dean had projected a bad-boy image, Beadles really *was* bad.

Jack Simmons spotted Beadles on the Sunset Strip leaning against a lamp post, taking a drag off a cigarette. Even in the darkness of the wee morning hours, Simmons could tell the guy was the spitting image of his late friend Jimmy. In fact, he was afraid to approach the guy—afraid that he might actually be Jimmy, and even more afraid that he wasn't.

Before the sun came up, Jack and Chuck were roommates, and the last person Jack wanted to share Chuck with was Maila, who he knew would waste no time in stealing him away. He had to keep his new friend a secret for as long as possible. Once, Maila caught Jack coming out of a grocery store at night. Chuck was waiting in the passenger seat. Just as Maila approached the car, Jack sped away, with Maila yelling, "Who's that with you in the car?" Jack didn't want to share.

For his part, Chuck was obsessed with James Dean and intentionally curated himself to look like him. He dressed like Jimmy, learned to walk like him, and even tried to emulate his speech. He'd read everything he could get his hands on about Jimmy—he knew about the Night Watch and was anxious to meet Maila. Jack had to face the truth, that Maila and Chuck would inevitably meet, so he decided he may as well make the meeting as memorable as possible.

To her friends, Maila asserted that Jimmy was communicating with her from beyond the grave, and Googies gossip was rampant with stories that Vampira's home was haunted by the spirit of James Dean. So, Maila was predictably accused of trying to gain publicity from her best friend's death. The idea that she had a self-serving motive was not only hurtful but false. The truth was that she sincerely believed Jimmy was corresponding with her from beyond the grave. It started with the wiggle of a paper ear, progressed to tales of ashtrays spontaneously combusting, and continued with stories of Jimmy communicating through songs on the radio.

And there were séances.

On that night of all nights, the Fourth of July, Maila wasn't in the mood for a séance. She didn't understand why Jack and their friend Troy were so insistent that they try to contact Jimmy's spirit that very night.

A few years later, Troy became James Darren and went on to a successful career in films, music, and television. But then, he was one of hundreds of young unknowns starting out in Hollywood, a young man with whom (Maila claimed in an issue of *Street Gossip*) she'd earlier had a casual affair. It was during his first trip to Hollywood, before he'd returned to Philadelphia, supposedly married, and returned to Hollywood. At the beginning of Darren's career, his agent, Henry Willson, had given him the stage name Troy. Willson had a treasure trove of names he routinely passed out to his beefcake clientele. Darren always hated it and eventually rejected it, and the name ultimately stuck to another of his clients, Merle Johnson, who became Troy Donahue. But James Darren was known as Troy at the time.

Maila was opposed to conducting séances with her mother home, who called it "hocus pocus nonsense." But she finally agreed to do it. Sophie had to work early in the morning, so she would be asleep, and if they were quiet, it should be all right.

When Jack and Troy arrived, Maila was ready, clad in black with a crucifix around her neck. Candles lit, soft music played, and incense burned.

"What stinks?" Jack said upon entering.

"My incense. I'm burning sage," Maila explained.

"No, this really stinks!"

Troy was holding his nose.

"It must be the Old Dutch Cleanser," Maila replied. "It makes it burn brighter."

So, to appease her guests she went to find some perfume to spritz around the room. The trio settled around a marble coffee table, and the séance began.

Maila clutched the crucifix around her neck and invited Jimmy's spirit to join them. Immediately, a scratching sound came from the coat closet near the front door. Then a louder scratch, a thump, and finally an undeniable bang.

Before Jack and Troy could utter a word, Maila leaped from the floor to investigate.

In the dark room, the only thing that was certain was that someone was inside the closet. Could it really be Jimmy?

But the spell was broken when she heard a man's voice emit a very un-Jimmy-like laugh. Maila realized the smell was only a ruse to get her out of the room so the man, whoever he was, could hide in the closet. Even in the candlelight, there was no denying that he looked astonishingly like Jimmy.

> *It occurs to me that the way Chuck arrived into my life was highly symbolic.*
>
> *His mother, with whom he'd been very close, had died suddenly 2 yrs. earlier. He'd not made a permanent replacement & missed her terribly.*
>
> *He was brot [sic] to my house to partake in a pseudo occult happening, a séance. During which, while the lites [sic] were out—he hid in a closet, its walls were padded (with coats). He sat silently alone in this womb like place until the door opened (the vagina?), emitting him into my life. A sort of psychic re-birth. Yes?*

Jack's fears were well-founded. Almost immediately, fireworks ignited between Maila and Chuck. And why shouldn't they? It was the Fourth of July.

Much to Sophie's dismay, she awoke the next morning to find a strange man lying beside her daughter in bed. There was only one bedroom in the shared apartment, which belonged to Sophie, so Maila's bed was in the dining room. The bed's canopy was draped in velvet and tulle, which flowed from the top and puddled on the floor. To get to the kitchen, it was necessary to pass very closely to the side of the bed. By the time Sophie arrived home that afternoon, Maila and her new friend were gone. But again, the next morning and the next, there they were, cuddled up together in the bed in the dining room. Sophie was disgusted and angry, and she couldn't wait for her son, Bobbie, and his family to arrive in Hollywood in order to take her back to Oregon for the summer.

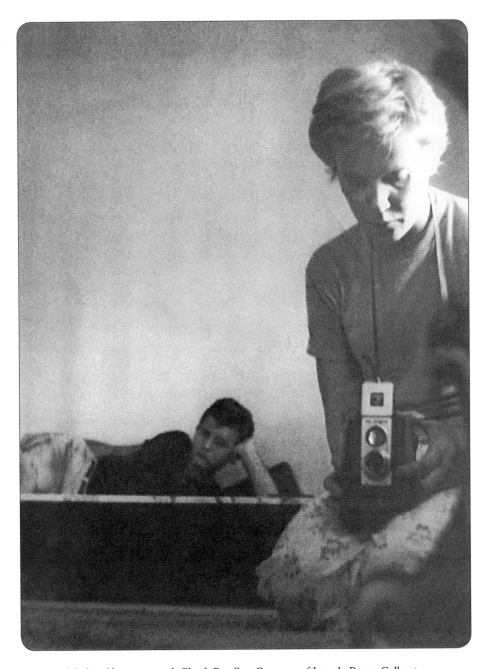

Maila self-portrait with Chuck Beadles. Courtesy of Jove de Renzy Collection

223

Maila's new lover was just 22 to her 33. She'd had other young lovers, but this relationship was different. It got serious. Very quickly.

From the beginning, Maila's tenure with KHJ was doomed. The ratings were so poor that on July 27th, her perennial advertiser, Fletcher Jones, pulled his sponsorship. Subsequently, *The Vampira Show* only completed 12 of the 13 scheduled shows, and by August 3rd of 1956, it was all over.

After KHJ canceled her show, Maila began to experience what she called blacklisting—the same term she'd used to describe her parting with KABC.

Chuck & I were just starting to be refused service in better places—I remember the Bel-Air Hotel for one. It all baffled me.

Maila learned from Marlon Brando that he'd be starring in a film called *The Young Lions* and that rehearsals would begin shortly. The part of Gretchen, the German captain's wife, had yet to be filled. Maila had read the script and she desperately wanted an audition for the role. Now that she was officially unemployed, every time she talked to Marlon, she pressured him to get her an audition. Time and time again, he put her off, until finally, on August 16th, he called with a proposal.

Marlon called me. Begs me not to do The Young Lions. Offers money.

On the nights when Chuck was gone, Maila and Marlon talked on the phone for hours. Maila confessed to him that her new romance was already in trouble. To assuage the pain, she'd once again shaved her head, this time into a modified buzz cut. It's possible that Marlon may have thought Maila was too distracted and under too much stress to devote herself to a movie role.

It was true. For the most part, the honeymoon was already over. Their relationship was like the nursery rhyme about the little girl who had a little curl right in the middle of her forehead. When it was good, it was very, very good. But when it was bad...

Chuck wasn't interested in finding a job or getting a car, and some nights, he didn't bother to come home at all. If he were home, Maila said she never knew which Chuck she would find: a sweet Chuck, an angry Chuck, or an uncommunicative Chuck. He began to hang out with a group of musicians whom Maila called "his gutter playmates who drank codeine."

The savings that Maila had left from her KHJ engagement were dangerously low. Suddenly, around the same time, Chuck had plenty of money to party, and he wasn't about to say where or how he got it. So, he offered to pay the rent. Maila refused, suspecting it was ill-gotten, possibly from selling dope or rolling a drunk.

Then Chuck was arrested. Maila knew nothing of Chuck's nefarious activities, and she was fearful the next knock at the door would be the police coming for her.

All this while I am deeply mourning James Dean (whom I am reported to have murdered with Black Magic). I am talking on the phone with Tony, Michael, and even Dink—but mostly with Marlon. It distresses me that Chuck has adorned himself with Jimmy's image, for I assume I am to Chuck, then, only a symbol. I have mixed feelings for Chuck. Reverence for his idealism, philosophy, & tenderness and disgust for his moral schism and his hero worship of Jimmy, which seems to me irreverent coming from a pipsqueak like him.

Chuck has those same mixed feelings for me—reverence & or adulation because I am a motherly celebrated heroine & disgust because I am a holier-than-thou Victorian prude whose temperance bars heroin.

After months of counseling over the phone, Marlon convinced Maila to see a psychiatrist. On October 17th, 1956, she took a bus to Westwood Village for a session with Dr. Harry Kluger. Marlon was picking up the tab, and Kluger's services weren't cheap. Twice-weekly sessions at 60 dollars a pop for two years. Across an entire page in her journal, Maila did the math.

Wow! Who would spend $20,000 on me? Marlon would.

It took but four meetings for Kluger to assess Maila's mental health. It was so vague as to be virtually worthless: She was diagnosed as "emotionally disabled." The question remained: Would two years of therapy even help? It would never be known because after only nine sessions, Maila quit, saying the sessions "were too painful and the bus ride too long."

She didn't throw Chuck out, as well she should have. In the way she had before with Dink, if the relationship was troubled, she blamed herself and believed that if she tried harder to please her man, he wouldn't leave her.

Chuck didn't like it when I spent money—even for rent & even then, there had better be some $ stashed in the snowshoe. I sent a birthday gift to Markie Winslow [Jimmy's cousin, who he called his "little brother"]. I knew that if I was still mourning Jimmy's death, what must it be doing to this poor child? Chuck got insanely jealous—a double whammy. Not only had I spent money unnecessarily, but I'd done it in remembrance of Jimmy. He wanted to be the only one—he wanted to BE Jimmy.

That Halloween, Chuck underscored this point at a masquerade party that he and Maila attended at the home of astrologer Carroll Righter.

I went as Veneria (the name I gave to Chas. Addams' little girl.) Chuck insisted on satirizing the latest "James Dean is not dead" madness—which was then sweeping the nation. He's not dead—only maimed somewhere—after plastic surgery, he will return (so the rumor legend went).

So Chuck got into a "Rebel Without A Cause" outfit & got bandaged out of sight—all but unruly hair & horn-rimmed glasses. All evening he did a sulking, "I want to be alone thing" in a corner. People were terrified—they pretended to ignore him—but of course were uncomfortably aware of him at all times. Only brazen Susan Harrison (who was in Sweet Smell of Success) tried fervently to tear away the bandages.

The press was brutal, printing that Vampira had shamelessly mocked the death of her friend, James Dean. For her participation in such an offensive display, Maila was named to Hollywood's Worst Taste List of 1956. Her outrageous public behavior only contributed to the growing shadow cast upon her professional reputation. Another nail in her career's coffin.

But that wasn't the worst of it. Sophie wouldn't be returning from Oregon until her high blood pressure was under control. Doctor's orders. Until then, she was to stay put. When Maila learned she couldn't depend upon her mother to tend her cats while she was performing on Broadway with Liberace, she did something unbelievable: She reneged on her agreement with Liberace. To be sure, it was the feeblest of excuses. The more likely reason was probably buried somewhere in her relationship with Chuck.

During the last heartbeats of her dying career, Maila managed to make a few appearances: a home show, a booth stint for *TV Radio Life* magazine at a convention, and a DJ show. She participated in the National Safety Council's safe driving campaign, "Don't Be a Droopert," co-starring "Doodles Weaver," and later a benefit for blind kids at the Deauville Club in Santa Monica.

Disney's *Sleeping Beauty* had already been in production for several years when Maila was hired for two days' work as the "live-action reference model" for Maleficent, the self-christened "mistress of all evil." On November 12th and again on November 16th, she reported to wardrobe and worked with casting director Jack Lavin. She was instructed to scream, and she did a twisting, turning movement that he particularly liked. Although Eleanor Audley contributed Maleficent's voice, the character's body movements and facial expressions are all Vampira.

The household's income dwindled down to Maila's 17-dollar-a-week unemployment check. Her stock was so low, she performed for free, hoping the exposure would resurrect her spiraling career. She appeared at a mayor's proclamation, wherein Mayor Norris Poulson presented her with the keys to the city.

Maila was practically unemployable to all except the lowest echelon of filmmakers. As incredible as it was, it turned out that she'd traded a slot on Broadway with Liberace to stumble around a cardboard graveyard for Ed Wood.

Wood's project, which Maila had again tried to ignore, was finally a go. Lack of financing caused it to be put on hold until the director could schmooze the money out of someone. That someone was J. Edward Reynolds, the pastor of the First Baptist Church of Beverly Hills, who agreed to give Wood the cash— under the conditions that the name of the film be changed to *Plan 9 From Outer Space* and that all of the actors participate in a total immersion baptism.

When Maila caught wind of this latest turn of events, she was furious. Criswell, Maila's prognosticating pal, was cast in the role of narrator for Wood's *Plan 9*. She went directly to see him, whereupon she told him that a baptism was not in her contract and she would not participate in such a spectacle. Appearing in Wood's film was insulting enough.

"Bring me to him," Maila shouted at her friend, barely able to contain her fury. "Bring me to Wood right this minute! He will know that I am already baptized! And confirmed! My name is in a time capsule, buried in the cornerstone of the Finnish Lutheran church! And if he insists on pursuing this travesty and force me into a baptism, I will sue him for stealing my goddamn immortal soul."

She did not have to participate in the baptism, but had Wood insisted, she vowed she would do it wearing her dominatrix catsuit.

On November 27, 1956, Maila and Chuck found themselves boarding a city bus, on their way to Quality Studios, where Maila would begin filming *Plan 9*. Chuck carried Maila aboard and plunked her down in the nearest available seat, settling in beside her. Her tight black mourning weeds made walking impossible.

The best part of working on Plan 9 was riding the bus in full drag.

Maila sat in silence, her gaze fixed straight ahead, polished talons clasped firmly in her lap. Beside her sat Chuck, sullen and dark.

"Fuck off!" he hissed to anyone who dared to stare at them.

The bus stopped at the 5600 block of Santa Monica Boulevard. Again, Chuck picked Maila up and carried her off the bus. Carrying her around was the least Chuck could do—she was the breadwinner.

> *I was making a movie in which I co-starred with a dead man. I truly believed my only saving grace in making this film was that nobody would ever see it. I'd received permission to perform mutely. My lines were so insipid, so inane, I couldn't even speak them privately to myself in my own home. Before I agreed to do the film, Marco checked with Wood to be sure.*

> *"That's O.K, baby—you don't gotta talk," he said. "He's just buying your name anyway."*

Quality Studios was a misnomer. In reality, it was an abandoned back-alley garage in a seedy part of town. Tucked behind the old Harvey Hotel, it shared the same block as the notorious Gold Diggers Lounge, with its clientele of hustlers and hookers.

Plan 9's graveyard set was like an obstacle course; the carpet, which played the part of the grass, was lumpy and uneven. Wearing platform shoes, Maila had difficulty maintaining her balance. As a result, Vampira appears unsteady at times. Maila suggested to Wood that she go barefoot, but the director wanted her to be taller. Reluctantly, she complied and performed the role in what she described as "Maila in an alpha state."

During filming, Maila was treated with marked respect by the crew, even as Chuck's hostility accelerated in direct ratio. He was rude to everyone, and when he learned that Maila was needed on set the next day as well, he became even more agitated. In frustration, he paced and muttered to himself. He was especially irritated with Wood, who made frequent use of a bullhorn and stopped action incessantly. Finally, Chuck threatened to "shove Wood's megaphone up his ass and break his goddamn neck." Before he had a chance to explode, Maila sent him off with a few bucks to have drinks at Gold Diggers.

Chuck didn't come to the second day's shoot. He put Maila on the bus, and a crew member drove her home. That night, Maila, whose image was collected and revered by hundreds of thousands, perhaps even millions, went home to Chuck.

> On the nite (sic) of Nov. 28 the shooting over I came home & removed the black wig—the long fingernails—the eyelashes—the tall-making shoes—the bust pads—the waist cincher—the firming elasticized panty hose. And what was left of me "after the ball was over," as it were, cried to Chuck—pleaded at his deaf ears "Why don't you love me? Where did I go wrong?" I sobbed & I crawled. Never before was I so desperate—but I didn't seem to penetrate his coldness an iota. He was like stone. When he turned to look at me standing there naked & bereft, his eyes revealed that I was the most repulsive being on the planet. I must try harder to win his love. But I may as well have sexually assaulted a doorknob—at any rate, I was washed up... I was no more.

Chapter Eighteen

Like a dying man inexplicably rallies a few days before death, so it was with Maila and Chuck. Just before Christmas, their relationship resurfaced for one last gasp.

> *Early December found us warming to one another again (the mean musicians had gone away)—we Xmas-shopped lovingly—money was low, but we finagled a little.*
>
> *To help stretch his shopping money I gave him something to send to his grandmother. A rhinestone-studded compact I never used, that Liberace gave me.*
>
> *I went out almost not at all socially—& Chuck went out with "friends" of mine who later told me he looked for girls & was deeply in puppy love with a waitress at Googies who looked like his dead mother.*

By Christmas, the money was gone. Chuck was his usual petulant self. Maila was determined to cheer him up by making him something special: doughnuts, which he loved.

But the hot oil bubbled over and started a grease fire, which quickly traveled up the kitchen curtains. Chuck saw what was happening and fled out the front door.

"Get the cats!" Maila screamed, but Chuck was long gone.

Wielding a broom, Maila brought the flaming curtains onto the floor, but the fire spread. The battle was lost. Frantic, she and the cats managed to get out, but not without injury.

Vampira, Guest Burned in Blaze at Apartment

The newspaper reported the fire was caused by a cigarette left burning in a sofa, using phrases like "flaming pyre" and "smoke awakened the ghoulish girl." Chuck escaped unscathed, but Maila was not as lucky. She suffered second-degree burns on both of her arms, which were bandaged to just below the shoulder. A photo shows her wearing a shapeless housedress, a dim smile, and dark circles under her eyes, cradling one of her cats, Ratface, between her filthy bandaged arms.

It is almost impossible to reconcile this fair-haired, hollow-eyed snapshot of Maila with Vampira, the dark goddess in *Plan 9 from Outer Space*. Even more startling is that these two versions of Maila appeared three weeks apart.

> *He (Chuck) was now his worst & angriest self. The Dr. told me*
> *not to use my arms but Chuck said I had to clean the wet charred house*
> *or he would leave me. So I swept. He left anyway—the musicians—the*
> *codeine—my money—was gone.*

The day after Christmas, with Chuck gone, Jack brought a fully decorated Christmas tree over for Maila. She wrote this poem the same day, a parting shot at Chuck.

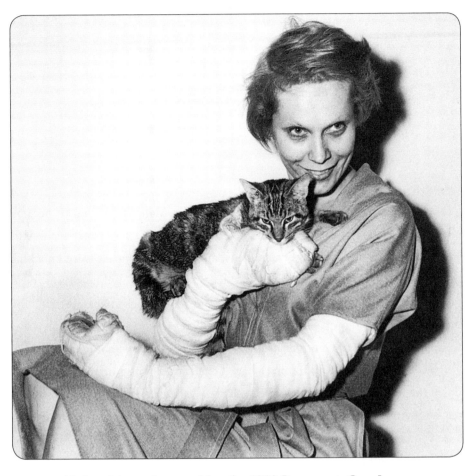

Maila and the cat she rescued from fire, 1956. Bettmann via Getty Images.

You hi-jacked my love
With attitude false
Go bray to your friends
Of my pain heart-felt
Attach your trophy
My heart to your belt
Tell them it's one

Of the many you've won
Laugh with them gaily
At what you have done
They laugh already
They found out today
The heart that I gave you
Was papier-mâché.

Sophie came back to Hollywood to care for Maila, returning to her job cleaning rooms at the Beverly Hills Hotel. Meanwhile, the newspaper account of the fire included Maila's physical address, and soon, the crazies were knocking again. Late at night on the windows and doors. The more rabid fans threw dead animal carcasses onto their porch. Someone pushed a chicken head through the mail slot. After five requests for police assistance in as many nights, Sophie was warned against making nuisance calls. The police couldn't be bothered.

More than once, Sophie must have ached for a bottle of vodka to choke down the fear, but she never weakened. Instead, she listened to the radio, sipped tea, and wrote letters. Sometimes until the morning, when it was time for work.

Chuck was gone but letters arrived for Maila from jail. He'd been charged with assault and battery as well as writing bad checks. He begged her to marry him and wanted to "make it up to her and take her to Chasen's," famously the traditional venue for the Academy Awards parties, when he got out. His letters were ignored.

By March of 1957, the bandages were off, and Maila had resumed her habit of sleeping all day, while her mother worked, and then staying out all night.

The carousel I was riding made the world outside its rim seem a
blur to me. Dizzy & giddy I was, up and down while round & round,
music, lights, laughter, laughing comrades... coming into focus out in

that blur beyond my frivolous world—a pair of eyes. The person behind them interjected a comment into our conversation.

We were in Googies; a group of hangers-on surrounded me. She pushed her way as close as she bodily could & she leaned forward leveling her eyes into mine. They were the first real thing I'd seen in a month. It had taken all her courage to draw my attention to her and she was frightened. But she'd like very much to have a ride on my carousel. We moved on & she was out of sight.

"Who's that girl?" I asked the nearest hanger-on.

"One of the girls around here. She's always alone. She cut her hair like yours."

"She's got to get out of this town," I said. "I hope she moves away & marries & has babies."

One of the swingers said her first name but I forgot it. The name wasn't important.

The hangers-on didn't suspect what I'd seen in those eyes. I had seen them only one other time, one other place. 15 yrs. ago, in my own mirror. It was her incurable vulnerability that struck a chord. Truly a lamb upon this blood-drenched ground among the wolves. How I yearned in that moment for her salvation. But it was a hectic party and I was the hostess, so I forgot the girl with the eyes.

The girl with the eyes was Diane Varsi. In 1957, Varsi was cast in the role of Allison MacKenzie in *Peyton Place*, for which she was nominated for an Oscar as Best Supporting Actress. Three other movies ensued, and in 1958, she shared a Golden Globe with Sandra Dee and Carolyn Jones in the category of New Star of the Year—Actress. Gossip columnist Luella Parsons wrote that Varsi was "Hollywood's female Brando," and she was compared to James Dean. The following year, she took her infant son and left Hollywood—as well as her husband—and then disappeared for several years.

By April, Chuck was out of jail, and another letter arrived with yet another marriage proposal. He hadn't slept in three nights thinking about her. He'd given up drinking, and would she meet him for coffee?

Vampira Has Prowler Suspect Held

Charles Beadles, 22, of 5842 Carlton Way, was arrested on suspicion of burglary after his asserted former girlfriend, television's Vampira, reported him prowling in her apartment at 5906 Carlton Way.

Chuck now lived just a half-block away. On April 23, 1956, Sophie caught him running out of the apartment when she arrived home. And in case anyone wanted to harass Maila, here again was her published address! Or, rather, Vampira's address. More dead animals on the porch followed.

Chuck was jailed again and wrote another letter in which he clearly seemed deranged. He wanted to cut the cord in his ankle and wondered if Maila would come visit him when he was hospitalized—and if she did, he asked her to bring toothpaste. At the end, he asks her to meet him in the closet before signing off that he is "going to the bottom."

After that, Chuck disappeared.

Due to extreme exhaustion, Sophie had to quit working and filed for disability. Her medications were having no effect on her blood pressure, and she was ordered to rest.

A letter from Sophie arrived at the Niemi house in Astoria, Oregon, in June of 1956. It was written on Vampira stationery.

> *I hate this paper! 2a.m.?*
> *Dear Kids,*
> *No sleep yet. Maila is out so I thot I would write you kids another sordid letter.*

Today my whole world came crashing down around me. I got a letter in answer to my application for disability unemployment. They disqualified me on the grounds that I earned only $507 in the last quarter of '56. In the same mail Maila received a $80.80 refund from Govt. income tax. The $320.61 she confessed was for '56 taxes. She works next weekend, gets $100, gets $33 a week unemployment, making $600 for June.

How can I ever get well with this kind of treatment and worry over insecurity? She told me how when she was a child & wanted to draw I would discourage her—also for her monologues. Every nite after school I listened to her readings & poems. All she cares about is running around. I (as bad as I feel) try to keep the house half way clean & buy food for her cats altho I can hardly make it to the store.

I called the hotel today about my last check for 2 days & the housekeeper wanted to know when I was coming back. I tried to stall her cause if bad comes to worse I will have to drag myself there tho I don't have the strength.

Maila never eats at home anymore. I buy bread & butter & sand. meat & cold drinks for myself. No wonder I lost 9 lbs. in 3 wks. 117 now.

I am going to try and borrow $50 from Dink if Maila lets me for 6 mos. He has a girl friend—a Finn-Swede—lazy as they come. Dink has been good to Maila but she hates him.

The kids she travels with now have cars, so M. buys gas & oil & feeds them in restaurants. Sometimes she is gone 48 hrs & never calls & I have to make excuses on the phone for broken dates. Or they come to the door, which I'll answer if I know them, and she is already gone with someone else.

These last mos. have been the hardest of my life. Even the 9 mos. in '43 & '44 that I went thru with her were not like this. I sometimes wonder if that 13 yr. old son of hers got her terrible temperment. He could be an idiot too.

I'm glad Sandra is doing so well with her flute. I had dreams of someday buying her a sax if she wanted it. Now it's a matter of survival with me.

I hope you can read this—if not burn it.

All my love—Mother

Sixteen days later, Sophie was dead, and it was the only time I saw my father, Bob—formerly Bobbie—ever cry. By the next morning, my parents and I were loaded in our Rambler, making the 24-hour trip to Los Angeles.

When we arrived at Carlton Way, the door was locked, so Dad retrieved the key from under the mat. From the front door, you could look straight through to the dining room, where it looked as if a circus tent had been erected. It was my Aunt Maila's canopy bed. All black velvet and orange and lavender tulle.

After some time passed and Maila had not returned, we left to find a motel and get something to eat.

When we returned a few hours later, Maila was home, but she was not alone. Three men sat on floor pillows around a marble coffee table, sipping coffee. It was unexpected and a little disconcerting for us to be in the midst of strangers when there were family matters to discuss.

My Aunt Maila was a sad girl in rags. Her short blonde hair was uncombed, and she wore no makeup. Her outfit consisted of a navy-blue men's sweater over a black shift dress. The sweater hung off her frame; its sleeves ended below her fingertips and required constant adjusting. Her shoes were dirty, well-worn white flats. With a tear-stained face, she made cursory introductions. They were Jack Simmons and Troy (James) Darren. Jack was dressed in black. The handsome Troy was equally well groomed in a light-colored shirt and khakis. The third man was more reserved and had short dark hair, and he seemed as though he wasn't a part of the zippity-doo-dah duo of Jack and Troy. I've forgotten his name.

Even in the undesirable circumstances in which he found himself, my father conducted himself in a cordial, calm manner. His primary purpose was simple: pay his final respects to his mother and see to it that she received a proper burial. Beyond that, I know he held out hope that through their shared grief, he and Maila could salvage a piece of what was once a family.

Jack and Troy displayed a kind of nervous energy and chatted continuously between themselves while the mystery man moved to the window seat and silently sipped his coffee. Maila couldn't seem to sit still. Whenever she got up to refill her coffee, Jack and Troy trailed after her like chicks behind a mother hen.

The next day, my father expected to spend time with Maila to discuss their mother's funeral arrangements. At Maila's request, Criswell was delivering the eulogy and choosing the pallbearers. But there were still last-minute details to take care of in preparation. When we arrived, Maila was once again in the company of the same three men—or perhaps they never left. Everyone had changed their clothes except for Maila, who still wore the same sad sweater and shift dress.

We still did not know the particulars of Sophie's passing. Any questions my father had would have to be asked in front of the trio of men he barely knew.

Maila explained that it was two in the morning when she arrived home to find her mother dead.

"I should have known, Bobbie," said Maila. "Gabriel drove me home that night."

"Should have known what?"

"The night I found Mama, I came home in a taxi. It was Gabriel—he drove the cab."

We all stared at her blankly.

"Gabriel! Gabriel is the angel of death. Don't you see? It was an omen! The angel of death came and took Mama away. At any rate, I shall never set foot in *his* cab again."

Jack began to cry and wiped his eyes on the end of the long scarf he wore. Sitting next to Jack on the floor, I too began to cry. Without a word, he offered me a corner of the scarf to wipe my tears. Maila stood in the middle of the room, waiting for her audience to settle into their perspective seats. I scooped up one of the cats and together we sat on an orange canvas director's chair that stood against the wall near the end of Aunt Maila's bed. She had our full attention.

Maila turned and exited out the front door before quickly reentering, calling out to Sophie that she was home. Even though it was daylight, she turned on a lamp, as she must have *that* night. She stepped slowly across the room, calling, "Mama? Mama?" She stepped closer and closer to me, where the cat sat on my lap. Eventually, she stood directly in front of me.

"Mama, Mama. Wake up! Are you sleeping?"

Maila's words became more and more frantic. Her electric blue eyes were riveted to the wall directly above my head. Unseeing.

And then I realized... *I was sitting in the chair where Gramma died!*

Before I could react and without warning, Maila let out a horrific, piercing scream of anguish. The cat flew off my lap, ripping a bloody trail across my arm.

Aunt Maila covered her face with her hands, collapsed in a heap on the floor, and began to cry. I didn't stick around to see what would happen next—I bolted out the front door. I didn't stop to think where I was going; I just ran down the sidewalk, lined with palm trees.

I don't know how far I ran, perhaps only a block or two, before I realized my arm hurt. I had to go back, but when I reached the apartment, I couldn't bring myself to go inside. Instead, I followed a wooden fence that separated the house from the neighboring property, which led into the back yard.

I stood there, looking at the tiny rivers of blood that splayed across my arm, when I became aware of laughter coming from the other side of the fence. I peeked through the slats and saw people next door swimming in a pool. Their laughter was somehow comforting, reminding me that the world I knew was still the same, regardless of what I'd just experienced inside the apartment.

Then I heard my mother calling my name. Inside, she tended to my injury while I watched my father try to coax his sister away from the men, who continued to stick to her like cat hair on velvet. He was going to the mortuary to see their mother and asked her to go with him.

"I can't," Maila said. "It's too painful."

The funeral was the next day, and we waited outside the mortuary for Maila. She arrived with her entourage—her hair remained uncombed, and her dark sunglasses stood out in stark contrast against her pale face. She wore the same shift, the same dirty shoes, and the same men's cardigan, although this time, she wore it inside-out.

When we entered the mortuary, Maila insisted that her three amigos join us in the family room. My father, who had taken to privately calling his sister's sidekicks "Tom, Dick, and Harry," felt they had no reason to be with the family. He didn't know if Sophie even knew these men, and if she did, he didn't know whether she liked them.

But to keep the peace, Dad remained silent.

Sophie's service was modestly attended by her coworkers from the hotel and AA members with whom she'd been close. There were many beautiful floral arrangements, the largest of which was sent by Criswell's friend Mae West. Dad was pleased with Criswell's eulogy.

Unfortunately, even Criswell's booming baritone could not distract from Jack's strident boo-hooing. They were not just polite sniffles but loud and prolonged sobs that echoed off the chapel's tray ceiling for the entire duration of the service.

We were a reluctant patchwork of seven, piled into the family car for Sophie's burial in Inglewood. My father turned to a now completely composed Jack and said, "Judging by your performance in there, you'd make a damn good professional mourner."

Jack beamed, clueless as to the insult. "Oh, my God. You really think I could?"

The day that Sophie Niemi's children said goodbye to her, on July 1, 1957, they said goodbye to one another as well. They would never see each other again. As for me, it would be another 32 years before I saw my Aunt Maila.

Chapter Nineteen

In the space of a few short years, Maila had survived losing Dink, Jimmy, and both of her television shows, along with a brutal assault in New York, a fire, rabid fans, media lies, and Chuck's emotional battering. But the death of her mother was the *coup de grâce*.

Sophie was the one person in the world who always had Maila's back, who shared in her every torment. Sophie was the only one who never gave up trying to put Maila's Humpty Dumpty life back together again. Less than two months before she died, Sophie and Maila were at NBC for a segment of *Queen for a Day*, as Vampira made an appearance on their Mother's Day show. Maila took a small amount of comfort in knowing that her mother had watched her perform live at least once.

The fact that Sophie had died alone caused great guilt in Maila. For a time, she claimed Sophie was frightened to death by a crazed fan who came calling in the night. The denial eased her conscience. But the truth was that Sophie couldn't erase the damage done to her body from years of alcohol abuse—her heart simply gave out.

After learning of his ex-wife's death, Onni sent a heartfelt letter to Bob.

What has happened, we can't change. Let us just try and remember her beautiful sides, which were many, and let us say: let her rest in peace.

When you children were small in Lanesville and Fitchburg, we had many moments that I still like to remember. But when I visited Finland in 1926, she had already strayed in unpleasant adventures— and it went on for decades. I had dedicated my life to temperance, and it was my livelihood. Those ideals were despised in my home... but it's good that her restless spirit may rest now.

How did Maila take this? Is she married? And what does she do? Or does she do anything? She hasn't written me in years. Did she ask about us?

When she was the most vulnerable and lonely, Maila moved from the Carlton Way address to a place on Keith Avenue and Ramage Street, two blocks off of Santa Monica Boulevard, to try to get her life back together. Her new home was close enough to walk to Googies, but she bought herself a bicycle for longer errands.

A few gigs rolled in here and there. On November 12, 1957 she signed a contract with CBS for an appearance on *Playhouse 90*, a drama series. The under-five-lines classification paid her $108.50 plus 10 percent. As Vampira, she emceed a benefit for Jack Benny at the Hilton and appeared at a business banquet at Romanoff's.

John Brinkley became the new man in Maila's life. John was a writer and B-movie actor who starred in *Teenage Doll* and *A Bucket of Blood*, among other films produced and directed by Roger Corman. Corman became successful thanks to his make-'em-cheap-and-make-'em-fast approach to pop cinema.

John and Maila were friends from at least 1955—he sent her a letter from New York in which he seems to be sharing an apartment with another of Maila's former paramours, Michael Arquette. He talks about receiving a scholarship to study with modern dance pioneer José Limón, and mentions a meeting with Stella Adler, Marlon Brando's acting coach. What's curious is that John suggests Maila send "Mr. Brando a copy of the slogan" in the letter so that he will not be "ignorant when it does come." The slogan reads, "God did fuss to make you us."

At Christmas of 1957, there is no hint of a romance in a letter from John, although it sounds as if they may have been roommates at the Keith address and that John was booted out by an disapproving landlady. The text of his letter implies that the landlady perhaps didn't approve of tenants of the opposite sex sharing living space without the benefit of marriage.

> *If your land lady (I use the word loosely) questions you about the presence of any new occupants or the whereabouts of the old one, explain to her that I was working on a science fiction epoch for Roger Corman and instead of returning to mother earth proceeded on an obstinant [sic] search,...*

In closing, he apologizes that he may not have the "status" of Jack Simmons but asked Maila to let him know if she'd like to see a movie or go have a cup of coffee.

Allegedly, Maila and John Brinkley were secretly wed on March 10, 1958. In a letter dated a month after her supposed marriage, my father, Bob, indicates that they'd been in contact by telephone and he knew about John. The primary purpose of the letter was to finalize an agreed-upon, equitable split of their mother's final expenses. At the end, Bob offered an invitation.

> *Although it does not appear likely we would again be in L.A. this summer, I can't help but think that perhaps there is a greater possibility of you and John coming north. Our accommodations are not akin to some of the Hollywood set-ups, but let me (us) assure you that we*

would be glad to have you here. The very fact of the matter is that you are overdue for a visit to Astoria. Please give every consideration to a possible visit here.

While my father seems to acknowledge the disparity of their lifestyles, he sincerely wanted to reestablish a relationship with his sister. But it was not to be. Bobbie led a traditional life as a family man with an established career. Maila couldn't relate to the mind-numbing monotony of that kind of existence, no matter how much her mother had touted it. At the time, chaos was the fuel that powered her life, and a respite from the exhilarating roller-coaster ride that was Hollywood was not in the cards for her.

If Maila and John really were married, it seems to have been a marriage of convenience—because within a year, Maila was engaged to another man.

I see a fuming, bubbling mass of matter rotating as it ferments. A myriad of maggots borough [sic], slither and writhe on its outer surfaces and in and about through subterranean passages. Slime-covered though we are, we cling still tenaciously to the unrelenting sordid (or possibly sweated) mass. For it is our world. The only world we neurotics know. Sometimes we find ourselves on its outer surfaces where, if we pick the film from our eyeballs, we can see the sun. Not feel it, of course. Just see it. For we are unable to feel anything but the constant anxiety we know, which consumes us and never leaves us. Save rarely to make way for a frenzied manic sort of hysteria.

Nan, the night cashier at Googies, was what Maila called the "procurer" of all sorts of needs. Whether it be an apartment, some pot, a lover, a roommate, a car, or an old stove, Nan was your gal. She and her best friend, Ann, were inseparable—and on Sunset, the duo became known as Nannie and Donut Annie.

246

They hung their clothes at The Honey Hole, a cozy, little Hollywood bungalow rented by a charismatic & witty black supper club singer named Bobbie Lucas. Bobbie filled his bungalow with an astonishing assortment of diverse bundles of human exotica, very few of whom ever did any lucrative work. They flopped everywhere—on the patio, in closets, the bathtub, the carport & on the roof.

Nannie and Do-Nut Annie sometimes rested their weary bones at The Honey Hole and almost always paid their share of the rent & often joined in the violent fights over who ate whose mayonnaise out of the fridge.

Nannie was an actor fucker & worked out of the Player's Directory, an actor's registry with their picture & agents' phone #s. In her personal black book, she made fascinating comments in the margins as her work progressed. (She was working from A to Z.) Example: Mr. 4 x 4 meant he was 4" in diameter but sadly only 4 inches long. Annie was Nannie's shadow. She took seconds.

The young, single Hollywood actors were a tight bunch, and parties were frequent. Nannie, whose lover was Troy Donahue, was privy to where the best parties were. And Maila, at 36, had lost none of her passion to party.

On one particular night, the party was at her friend James Franciscus' home. Maila knew James from the film *I Passed for White*, in which he'd starred and she had been an extra. Nan and Troy picked Maila up for the party. In a 1966 recorded audio tape, Maila described the events of that night, circa 1958.

I was drunk, champagne drunk. And skinny, too, & out of my cage.

Henry Willson's boys are here in their dark, blue suits. How straight they stand in a neat circle. Talking quietly. Such gentlemen.

Henry must be due. They're all on their good behavior. There's Henry now. How neatly the circle sweeps like a line of golden girls toward the entrance to greet Henry.

Tuesday [Weld] came to the party with a black kitten. She's got it with her in the bedroom because of the noise. She's got Raphael [Campos] in there with her, too. Well, it's not true what they're saying. I went in & checked. I'm the inspector at this party. I haven't been in a dog's age.

Rafael dances me out to the patio. Dear, sweet, comfortable Rafael, who always takes care of me. Nan does, too. Where is she? She isn't having trouble with Troy tonight. They brought me. She made him bring me.

Now, am I going to disgrace them by hanging from the chandelier by my knees—again! No. There's an arm. I'll hang from it. "Hey, catch my feet."

He did. I put my hands on his shoes. We danced. Upside down, was I. He threw me around like a bean bag. He was a marvelous dancer.

"I'm Carleton Carpenter," he said.

I stepped back a pace and squinted. I saw a tall, skinny silhouette.

"If you are, it's too good to be true," I said.

"But I am."

"Then I love you. I've always loved you."

An actor-singer known for his work in MGM musicals, Carleton Carpenter stuck by Maila for the rest of the party. Nan and Troy beamed like proud parents.

When it was time to leave, Carleton asked for Maila's phone number.

"Next time," she responded. "We found each other; we love each other. Don't be greedy."

She spent the night on the couch in Nan and Troy's La Jolla Avenue apartment.

Two months went by without a call from Carleton. Maila was bewildered. With friends in common, getting her phone number was a snap.

For the first time in a long while, she had a gentleman who occupied her fantasies. Ever since she first saw Carleton Carpenter on the screen with Debbie Reynolds in the 1950 flick *Two Weeks with Love*, dancing and singing "Aba Daba Honeymoon," he had been Maila's movie-star crush. He was her type: a tall, skinny hayseed with a big Adam's apple, just like Tony Perkins. Not only were the two physically similar, but they shared a common intellect and sense of humor as well.

Maila worked the late shift at an answering service. Her coworker Winnie Ruth's son, photographer Paul Jasmin, just happened to be Carleton's best friend. One night, a call came through on the switchboard. "I have someone here who wants to talk to you," Winnie Ruth told her.

It was Carleton Carpenter, with a business-like, patronizing tone. "He sounded irritated, as if I was pestering him." He hung up without asking for a date or her phone number.

A few weeks later, Winnie Ruth called Maila at home to invite her to a small dinner party. Paul was cooking spaghetti for a few friends. Carleton would be there and wanted Maila to join them.

On the appointed evening, Maila arrived on her bicycle. Feeling awkward, she retreated to the kitchen to help prepare the meal. After dinner, Carleton took her into a small candlelit side room next to an aviary. He held her hand and spoke to her tenderly, all within eyeshot of those in the living room.

After the party, once again, there was no word from Carleton for another few months.

Then, out of the blue, Carleton called Maila, asking for a date. He took her to the Keyboard nightclub where his friend Virginia O'Brien was singing. The two sat at a table, held hands, and had a few drinks. Shortly, they were joined by a mutual friend, the songwriter Earl K. Brent.

As O'Brien sang, Brent leaned over to the couple and asked, "Do I hear wedding bells from you two?"

Carleton, still holding Maila's hand, asked if she was still with John Brinkley. The music, the drinks, and the dimly lit aura of the Keyboard all rendered Maila oblivious to all—save for the crystal-blue eyes of her dream man.

"No," she said.

"Then there's no reason why we can't?"

"No," Maila said.

"Then we are," Carleton said, whatever that meant.

The next day, a friend called Maila.

"Did you read Harrison Carroll's column? You're engaged! Carleton Carpenter has announced his engagement to you. Right here it says, 'Carleton Carpenter's friends will be amazed that he is engaged to be married to Vampira.'"

There it was. Her fiancé was engaged to marry not Maila Nurmi but Vampira—because everything about her was a joke. Even her engagement.

After the announcement in the press, the newly engaged couple was frequently spotted in public. Carleton hired an astrologer to map out their charts for compatibility. They frequented Bailey's Bar and together named their future daughter Clancy. Carleton did his best to impress, taking Maila to a private screening of *Fearless Fagan*, in which his co-star was a lion, as a display of his courage. He cooked for her in his home—his family's recipes from back home in Vermont, along with freshly baked bread.

Just before Christmas, the two quarreled. Maila complained that Carleton was ignoring her in order to spend time with a new friend, Anthony Perkins. Maila's opinion of Tony had drastically changed and she was more than a little jealous. Maila had finally realized that Tony was gay, so why was he hanging around her new man? She regarded him as deceptive and unnecessarily cruel—as such, her nickname for him was Sinbad.

The fight over Tony ended with Maila calling Carleton a pig. Days later, on Christmas morning, Maila found a case of Kitty Queen cat food on her porch, wrapped up as a Christmas present. The note attached read: "From your friendly neighborhood piglet."

He was a millionaire. And here I was, practically starving to death, and for Christmas, he bought me a case of cat food. The whores get the furs and sports cars. Me, I get water pistols, jewelry made from plumbing parts, and cat food.

Maila's farewell note to Carleton read:

You and I were deliriously happy until Sinbad Perkins cruised himself into your heart and stole you away from me. It's just as well, lovie—you needed somebody tall. When you speak of me—and you will speak of me—you can say that Vampira is playing nightly with herself at Bailey's lounge.

Chapter Twenty

Maila continued to seek acting roles and was cast in a one-line unaccredited role in 1958's *Too Much, Too Soon*, starring Errol Flynn and Dorothy Malone. The line: "We're almost out of ham sandwiches."

Next came a series of three quick flicks for producer Albert Zugsmith. Like Ed Wood, Zugsmith was banking on name recognition, so once again she was not billed as Maila Nurmi but Vampira.

In *The Beat Generation*, Zugsmith wanted a real beatnik. Maila fit the bill and won the role of The Poetess, appearing in jeans and a sweater and affectionately cradling a white rat. While her part is small, it is significant in that it affords the viewer a glimpse of the real Maila, without the Vampira getup. *The Big Operator*, starring Mickey Rooney, featured Maila as Gina, a shopkeeper. She was billed as Vampira again this time, and again, her role was small. *Sex Kittens Go to College* was a trashy exploitation film with Mamie Van Doren, Tuesday Weld, and Brigitte Bardot's little sister, Mijanou. Maila played Etta Toodie, a goofy computer lab assistant. This film displays how much Maila had physically deteriorated in the year since she worked on *The Beat Generation*—her teeth show signs of decay, and although she wears an oversized lab coat, she looks emaciated.

Maila in The Beat Generation, *1959.*

An excerpt from an Allied Artists press release from 1959 reads:

> *Maila Nurmi, who as Vampira, is one of the current television*
> *rages in Great Britain, has completed her comedy role in Sexpot Goes*
> *to College (Albert Zugsmith), and leaves for London next week for 16*
> *weeks of personal appearances with Liberace. The London Palladium*
> *has booked her for eight weeks, and the remaining eight weeks will be*
> *in every principal English and Scottish city.*

She didn't go. The reason remains unknown. But if Maila's frail appearance in *Sex Kittens* was any clue, she was struggling with her health. To make ends meet, she took on cleaning the homes of friends for 99 cents an hour.

It didn't mean that Maila wasn't still looking for work in films. In 1962, she appeared in *The Magic Sword* for Allied Artists, where she took on the dual roles of a beauty and a beast. As a sorceress, she's an apparition through a misty fog, while as the hag, she's a hideous, grotesque creature with a protruding eyeball.

After that, she couldn't find work.

> *Maybe that's what I was meant to be... a char woman like my*
> *mother. I am the daughter of Sophia, the Finnish chambermaid—the*
> *cleaner of Marlene Dietrich's toilet bowl. 'Elizabeth's bowls have*
> *no ring,' they exclaimed—in Beverly Hills and Brentwood. Elizabeth*
> *was my housecleaning name. And it was true. No rings. I cleaned the*
> *infamous Hollywood Whorehouse: It was very popular with the 'IN'*
> *crowd. A famous bandleader/actor married to a top T.V. red-headed*
> *comedian used to arrive in his limo, have a girl & then go off into the*
> *night. He was a $100 customer!*

Maila soon lost her patience with her female clients and declared, "No more women! I'll clean only for bachelors." She'd always preferred the company of men—as a teenager, she told her brother that if she ever married, she intended to keep her last name because her initials spelled M.E.N.

But her housekeeping wages barely paid the rent. The question of where she could earn more loomed large, and the answer came in the unlikely form of the Italian Adonis, Fabrizio Mioni.

Mioni and Troy Donahue were close friends, although Maila only knew Mioni casually. Mioni, meanwhile, was an Italian national who wanted to stay in the country to continue his acting career. So, Donahue's love interest, Nannie, put the word out that Mioni

Fabrizio Mioni, 1964.
Michael Ochs Archives via Getty Images.

needed a wife, and so Maila agreed to a marriage of convenience in exchange for a small monthly stipend.

I visited Mioni at his home once and found him to be a delight. Because it had been 50 years since his marriage to Maila, whom he called Elizabeth, he could recall few details from the time he knew her. He commented that, "Before I married Elizabeth, I had to clean her up. She was a mess. I paid for new clothes and a full beauty salon treatment, head to toe, because I knew there would be press."

On June 20, 1961, Maila became Mrs. Fabrizio Mioni. After the ceremony, the bride and groom returned to their respective homes and lives. She kept the name Maila Elizabeth Mioni for the rest of her life.

The new Mrs. Mioni moved to 8642 Melrose Avenue, a few blocks from her old apartment on Keith Avenue. Her new place routinely teemed with society's misfits: a boy singer, an unemployed circus acrobat, a drugged-out painter, a few down-on-their-luck hustlers, and a pregnant unwed mother who spent her days pulling her hair out with tweezers, one by one. They came and they left, in a state of perpetual flux. From this assemblage of kindred spirits, Maila forged together a kind of temporary family.

And so here at the eighty-six-forty-two club, this mortuary on Melrose, has two faces. One it wears when I'm housing a destitute swinger & another when I am alone & allowing my soul to ripen.

I mean to say a swinger has got to be pretty destitute to land at Maila's. Not only has he or she got to be down & out, but he's gotta be bad news. A swinger never voluntarily commits himself to a state institution, jail cell, what have you. And that's a drag because he doesn't bring with him any vibrations or physical activity to appreciatively change the tenor of the morgue. Gradually, time heals his wounds, his tempo picks up. He's swinging once more. Usually after a couple of weeks of all night talks & intermittent visits to the Handy Burger with Maila, his own life begins to re-mold. He's cool now. Some possible score or other is in sight. Sports cars roll up, honk. Gone.

In full swing, the apartment was alive with music, TV, gas, electric lights, and sometimes even a working phone—an accomplishment seeing as no one had any money. Scores of visitors dropped in, dropped out, and got ready for dates. The empty beer cans piled up as the temporary tenants watched Johnny Carson.

On the morning of September 19, 1962, the Red Cross came to Maila's door with a message of a family emergency and a phone number to contact her brother. Bobbie told Maila their father had suffered a heart attack and died while mowing his lawn in Palm Beach, Florida. He was 73.

256

On the day of Onni's funeral in Florida, precisely at noon, Maila excused herself from her house guests.

> *I told them I'm going next door to the vacant lot. Noon was the*
> *approximate time they were shoving him under, as best I understood it.*
> *I took a white candle with me, lit it & prayed. I thought it shocking my*
> *brother hadn't offered me plane fare to Florida. Now I'm all alone in the*
> *sunlight, God's orphan, & must focus on the goodbye to the gentleman,*
> *the loving Rock of Gibraltar, I'd known so intimately a long time ago.*

The brother and sister were so estranged, neither knew the other could ill afford an unexpected trip across the country. Bobbie took out a bank loan in order to travel from Oregon to his father's funeral. He returned from the funeral with an extra suitcase filled with his father's clothes that his stepmother had demanded he take. Even his socks. Onni's clothes and the red spinel engagement ring that Sophie had given him were the sum total of everything he inherited. Onni's merry widow got the rest.

Returning home, Maila found her two female guests in a state of frenzied exuberance. "Guess who has your phone number! Just guess," they squealed in unison. "MAX-imilian Schell!"

> *So that's what they were doing. Busy on my telephone, tracking*
> *down the hotel of a visiting movie star, so they can leave a number*
> *& hope he calls back so they can offer him their bodies. All while I'm*
> *praying for the soul of my only & last father. The chief horror was their*
> *expectation that I would share their jubilation.*

In 1964, Mioni was granted a divorce pursuant to a final payment of one hundred dollars. And almost as quickly, the swingers were gone, and Maila was alone again.

For awhile there, I thought I was Ninos de l'Enclos reincarnate...
opened up my wings & let the young chicks nuzzle in my down. Ninos
de l'Enclos no more. No more actress. No more gypsy. I sit quietly at
forty, no more noses under my wing. The down wore away. In 1953, I
went to a masquerade party & the costume I wore stuck to me. I was a
professional vampire or something. For eleven years, I tried to scrape it
off, peel it off, burn it off with acid. Finally gave up trying.

Although no longer a working actress, Maila retained her firm allegiance to the horror genre. In January of 1965, she attended the premiere of Roger Corman's film *The Tomb of Ligeia*. A photograph of Maila with its star, Vincent Price, illustrates that she was still a remarkable beauty and quite capable of putting on the dog. But desperation had returned to Maila's mortuary on Melrose. The heat and electricity were turned off, and the hungry bear of poverty was again scratching at her door.

On a warm May night in 1965, Maila was asleep on a rug in her living room when she was awakened by knocking. The sound came from next door. She heard her landlady's voice: "Yes, Maila lives here. But she cleans houses. She's asleep."

The voice of the unseen visitor sent chills through Maila. It had been eight years, but there was no doubt that the voice belonged to Chuck Beadles.

He was sitting on her front steps when she arrived home from work the next day. His physical resemblance to Jimmy was no longer obvious, and he no longer emulated Jimmy's style.

He stunned me. A republican crew cut, killer eyes, Fascistic
looking... he wore a gray business suit & wrist watch. He looked like he
owned slaughterhouses... and he had a car, a red one.

The red car was the most egregious offense committed by the new Chuck. Ask any pretty girl or boy in town—only perverts drove red cars.

"I came back to make it up to you," Chuck told Maila. She didn't know whether to throw herself into his arms or run away. Instead, she stood her ground, remained silent and eyed him suspiciously. His tailored suit, his expensive watch.

"You told me once, 'Just act as if you've got it,'" Chuck said. "Look at me, Maila, it works."

Maila's head and heart were at war. Instinctively, she knew Chuck was still bad news, but the love she had for him never went away. She listened to his grandiose proclamation that he would love her, protect her, and never again abandon her, and she took him up on it.

And so, the couple reunited. It started out well—they'd drive over to Century City to see the wonder rising from the old Fox movie lot. They window-shopped, read books together, and recited poetry to each other. Kipling's *If* became their poem. In deference to Maila's lifestyle, Chuck adopted a more casual appearance, but insisted that his shirts were crisp and his slacks were pressed. And he always wore his status wristwatch.

They often went for long walks in the evenings. As they strolled down Norwich Avenue one night, Chuck zeroed in on a stranger passing by. "Look, see that guy?" Chuck asked playfully. "What does he do for a living? How much money does he have in the bank?" It was a guessing game.

Well, it was dark. I saw him chiefly in silhouette as he passed us. "Oh, him," I said. "He's a bookkeeper. He has a savings account, no checking... $900."

"How the fuck did you know that? That's my job. I've been doing it for 10 yrs. I had good teachers—but how the fuck did you know?"

"Is that right, Chuck? Am I really right? He has $900? How do you know that? How can you tell?"

Well, that poor unsuspecting man. We were discussing his books as mater [sic] of factly as if we were his accountants.

"You got a real talent there," said Chuck to me with great admiration. I was delighted to have pleased him.

Most evenings, they went across the street to Bailey's, drank screwdrivers, and listened to Al Hibbler on the jukebox. But before long, Chuck grew restless. He complained, "I'm just hanging around watching people croak."

Over drinks one night, the two conjured up a plan they believed might work. Melrose Avenue was beginning to blossom with trendy boutiques, and with them came a noticeable influx of traffic into the neighborhood. Maila's ground-floor apartment with its large front window could be repurposed from living quarters into a shop by day and then still remain private at night.

Chuck was energized anew and promptly sold his red car for a blue Chrysler Valiant. With a profit of eight hundred dollars, he used the capital to launch their new business.

It was a simple summer, but I was in ecstasy. I've never been happier. We cleaned up the place and we painted. We had cards printed for our shop. We found and restored furniture. Chuck was great with his hands.

The business cards read:

SHEER MADNESS OBJECT [SIC] D'ART

The business foundered, and it began to have an effect on Chuck, who again became impatient and agitated. His mood was buoyed after two men came in and raved about the feel of the place. They loved everything that Maila and Chuck accomplished to make their shop inviting and asked if they could help them replicate the same aesthetic in their own shop.

Maila and Chuck worked for three days to fix up the men's new store. They painted the place inside and out. Chuck built window boxes and Maila planted flowers in them. But when it came time to pay for their efforts, the men reneged on their agreement.

Chuck became enraged.

> *He broke into the store after hrs. Broke all the merchandise—*
> *threw black paint on the walls we had painstakingly painted. He went*
> *to their home & roughed them up. The next day, he went to their store*
> *& demanded $150 for our stolen time—& threatened them again. We*
> *didn't get the money, but Chuck literally drove them out of town.*

It wasn't only the unscrupulous shopkeepers who suffered Chuck's wrath. He became more out of control by the day. If Maila got a phone call, he would jerk the phone out of her hand and threaten the unsuspecting caller in gangster lingo. He disappeared for hours at a time and one day returned with a silver coffee urn with tags from an exclusive Beverly Hills shop. He boasted that he stole it from a window display in broad daylight and insisted that it be sold in their shop.

When Maila demanded an explanation, instead of being contrite, Chuck exploded. "Look at me," he shouted. "You see this watch? It cost a fucking fortune. I'd rather go shopping without shoes than this watch." Somebody certainly paid a fortune for it, but it wasn't Chuck.

Suddenly, the impact of Chuck's words hit Maila. His watch was a tool to avert suspicion, If you looked like you had money, you were a responsible citizen. For Maila, it was an aha moment: Society considered poverty a motive for theft.

She never forgot it. Then she felt a surge of anger and betrayal because it was then that she knew Chuck was stealing to support a drug habit. Nothing had really changed—he was still the same old Chuck. It would be only a matter of time before he was committing bigger and more serious crimes to support his habit, if he hadn't already.

*I felt deeply defiled. He didn't know me from gutter people. I
didn't know how to steal, screw, or push dope for a living & I wasn't
about to learn.*

Maila knew she had to devise a way to make Chuck leave and to believe it
was in his own best interest to do so. She couldn't think straight, terrified that he
would either hurt her or himself. She was frantic and told Chuck the drugs were
driving her crazy. There was no bedroom in which to barricade herself like she'd
done with Dink, so she retreated to the bathtub, with pillow and blanket, and
refused to come out, not even to eat.

The impasse was breached when Chuck surrendered. He promised to quit
cold turkey. As a show of faith, he flushed his stash down the toilet and headed
to Santa Monica to a place called the Church of Synanon.

The Synanon organization was a controversial drug rehab cult, founded and
run by reformed alcoholic Charles Dederich. In 1965, rehab was nonexistent,
and Synanon was touted as revolutionary in its philosophy of junkies helping
other junkies overcome their addictions. At the time, the only other recourse for
addicts was commitment to a mental hospital.

The next day, to Maila's great relief, Chuck left for the Synanon drug rehab
program. Now she could clear her mind and think. Was it possible the time there
could change Chuck? Or would he return the same?

As it turned out, it didn't matter. The next day, Chuck was back on Melrose.
Of his experience, he said, "Fucking jerk-offs, the whole joint is nothing but
bullshit and bad vibes."

However, during Chuck's very short absence, Maila had formed an alternate
plan should his rehab program backfire. Her fear of him gave her the permission
to lie to his face.

"The cops were here looking for you," she told Chuck, without knowing if
he'd actually done anything.

As soon as the words left Maila's lips, Chuck panicked—and his reaction left no doubt that he was in big trouble.

He cried in desperation to me—clutching both my hands and trembling. "I'm sick—oh, I'm so sick. I can't tell you what's wrong, but it's the worst thing it could be. Pray for me."

She was terrified but didn't want to know. What could possibly be the worst thing?

Immediately, Chuck prepared to leave. She watched him load his belongings into the Valiant but couldn't bear to see him drive away from the apartment they shared, and so she rode along with him a short way. On the corner of Melrose and La Cienega, at Leo's Flowers, Chuck pulled over to the curb. He wanted to buy her flowers.

She wanted lilacs. But on this last week in October, there were no lilacs, only pumpkins, and Maila chose the smallest one she could find.

They walked outside together for the last time. She told him she would carve her gift into a smiling jack-o-lantern boy, to remind her of him. Then he drove off, and Maila watched Chuck's car disappear into traffic.

Yes, I was blue & valiant, too, waving him off. But I was glad he was going. This time it was I who didn't know what was being forsaken. My only friend in the world & I deliberately drove him off.

He headed for Hollywood, Florida, where he claimed to have family. For a few months, they exchanged letters. He pledged his undying love and enclosed a little "survival money." And then, the letters stopped coming.

One thing can be said for Chuck—he gave Maila more material things, in ratio to his assets, than any other man had. But he couldn't give her the one thing she needed most from a man: integrity.

After Chuck left, Maila reopened her shop and renamed it Vampira's Attic. She tried making chandeliers, spending days scraping metal, until one day, she passed out. She thought it was a metal allergy but refused to see a doctor because Chuck, so often a fugitive, had indoctrinated her with a general sense of fear and mistrust. He'd sowed the seeds of paranoia, which flourished in Maila after his departure.

At 42, Maila felt she'd lost her last hope for love. Whether that would have been true or not, rather than risk the pain, Maila decided to remain celibate for the rest of her life.

Chapter Twenty-One

The lingering specter of Vampira, while benign under almost all circumstances, still carried with it the potential to spark a disturbed mind. Like the crazed fans who came to Carlton Way to terrorize Maila and her mother, the Melrose apartment had its own set of lunatics. Years after Vampira had mostly faded from the press, a few deranged fans still pursued her. When she found razor blades embedded in her front door, Maila went to the police, and they thought it was a joke. She felt there was no one to protect her from whoever was dogging her every move and believed that, if she were to survive, she would have to save herself.

She credited Chuck with teaching her survival skills. He told her that when times were tough, he'd slept in unlocked parked cars. And so, during the full moon, when the crazies were their most frightening, she slept in unlocked cars for three nights until the moon began to wane.

America's Golden Age seemed to end with the assassination of President Kennedy, and another era began the following year with the Civil Rights Act of 1964. Bob Dylan preached "The Times They Are a-Changin'" and encouraged an altered mindset to escape the complacency of the '50s. The change demanded a shift in consciousness. Courses were altered, adjustments made. The dawning of a new history was in the making.

By 1967, the Summer of Love, the beats had morphed into a different kind of cat. The hipster—or hippie—counterculture flowing down from San Francisco's Haight-Ashbury district espoused free love, peace, and harmony. Young people traveled in groups, lived in communes, shunned personal hygiene, and grew their hair long. The influx of hippies brought a stronger police presence on Melrose.

> *I was a Bohemian. I was a Beatnik. But I was never a Hippie. I was too old, so I became the mother of Hippies. So the other nite, I was on my own porch—musing—when I noticed a telephone pole totally submerged in outdated posted notices. So I cleaned it off. Before I'd had time to pick up & properly discard what lay at my feet, one plain clothes man & a police car with 2 officers pounced on me. Trying to harass me the plainclothesman (dressed as a hippie) asked me if I was aware there is a $500 fine for littering? "And what," I asked, "is the reward for cleaning off telephone poles?" He answered "Would you like to tell it to 'the man?'" He was trying to intimidate me on grounds that I probably smoke marijuana & therefore was quaking in my boots at the term "the man." That sneaky imperious hypocritical pig incensed me.*

Intermittently, for several years, Maila noticed a peculiar numbness in her legs and brushed it off as a pinched nerve or sciatica. It certainly didn't concern her enough to see a doctor, which she still distrusted. But then it got worse. Some days her legs felt so heavy, she could scarcely move, getting out of bed only to feed her cats. Even then, the numbness caused her to stagger and stumble as if she were drunk.

While explaining her symptoms to a neighbor, Maila was alarmed when her friend implied she was poisoned by "that stink hole over on Wilshire."

Three miles southeast, the La Brea Tar Pits was the source of a heavy stench, especially when the winter and spring rains caused the basement sump pump to work overtime. To Maila, it seemed entirely plausible that nearly a decade of living near the west end of the wash was indeed poisoning her.

Eventually, Maila's symptoms were serious enough for her to seek medical help. The diagnosis was not poisoning but rather pernicious anemia, a serious autoimmune disease that, if left untreated, could result in permanent paralysis or even death. "Pernicious" in this sense means "deadly." Before treatment was available, it had been a fatal disease.

The condition was irreversible, and the prognosis was frightening. The myelin sheath that protected the nerves in Maila's lower spine was damaged. However, if she complied with a lifetime regimen of vitamin B12 therapy, good nutrition, and exercise, she could regain limited use of her legs.

The causes of autoimmune diseases are mostly speculative. Scientists simply don't know with authority what causes this kind of anemia. But certainly, the years of starvation Maila endured, both intentionally and due to poverty, contributed to her illness. And cinching her waist down to 17 inches, thereby displacing her internal organs, probably didn't help.

Twice weekly, Maila was wheeled to the lab for blood draws. It was there one day that she received a phone call at the hospital. The voice on the other end of the line caused a surge of karmic energy to rush through her body. It belonged to the man who'd memorialized her image as a bloodless zombie on film: Ed Wood.

The vampire was near dead of pernicious anemia & was in a charity ward of the hospital—very few aware of her whereabouts—& when she left her ward to visit hematology—she received there a phone call. Not on the phone in the front office of hematology either, but the inner sanctum where the blood is kept!

Before Maila had a chance to ask how he'd found her, the director launched into the reason for his call, once again offering her two hundred dollars to appear in his new film *Necromania*.

Only two hundred dollars. It had been 13 years since she'd worked for Wood in *Plan 9* for the same amount. Apparently, Wood's films were immune to inflation.

"I can't walk," said Maila.

"You don't have to walk, only sit. In a coffin, and scream. Criswell's letting us use one of his. What do you say, Maila?"

"I say Greta Garbo is more capable to sit and scream than I. And far more accessible as well. Goodbye, Ed."

It would be the last time she ever spoke to Ed Wood.

Maila was transferred to the Fountain View Care Center for rehabilitation. Now, flat on her back, she had lots to process and plenty of free time to do it. She enlisted the help of friends to feed her cats, pay her rent, and close her shop.

Beginning in June of 1970, she kept meticulous records of her progress. At first, she needed a wheelchair to move around. Even then, some days she couldn't move her legs at all and remained pinned to her bed.

With nothing but time on her hands and the ever-present need to create, Maila's poetry written while she was at Fountain View demonstrates that her sense of humor remained intact.

> *The patience of Jobe* [sic]
> *I must now illicit* [sic]
> *To keep tidy this bed,*
> *And try not to piss it.*

After a month, she was evaluated for eligibility for Social Security disability benefits. Physically, she would have ambulatory challenges for the rest of her life. Her doctors found no evidence of memory loss.

Maila was released from Fountain View in July with a diagnosis of pernicious anemia with subacute combined degeneration. Without a walker for the first week on the outside, she was relegated to either crawling or scooting around on her butt.

Maila had been placed in the care of an old friend from her early modeling days, Elizabeth Cozgriff. Elizabeth was a longtime friend of Maila's. When she recovered, they often traveled to Las Vegas to let their hair down. In their younger days, the women had packed their fanciest duds for their trips to Vegas and called themselves "the wild girls." According to Elizabeth's granddaughter, Darcy O'Brien, they still enjoyed their jaunts to Las Vegas in their 40s, but without the need to flaunt and flirt.

Dogged in her determination to walk again, Maila had to learn how to bend her feet, maintain her balance, and eventually maneuver stairs. On good days, she registered small successes like being able to get her own pitcher of water. Bad days, she was bedridden with legs of lead. By the first week in August, she managed to walk five blocks with the aid of a walker.

Her progress was rapid. On October 10th, after five months of treatment and just 15 weeks out of Fountain View, Maila reopened her shop on Melrose and took in 22 dollars. A few weeks later, she walked an astonishing 55 blocks.

Her spine wasn't the only casualty of her years of malnourishment. Her teeth, which had begun to darken several years before, were loose and decayed. During her months of rehabilitation, hellish toothaches prompted her to pull several of her own teeth. By this time, most of her top teeth on the left side were gone.

Ironically, the pernicious anemia improved Maila's financial health. Although at the young age of 47 she would require the use of a cane for the rest of her life, her monthly disability checks guaranteed her an income. If she was careful about where she lived, they could at least cover her rent.

Melrose was bustling in a way Maila had never seen. Street vendors set up shop on the sidewalks, their inventories largely harvested from a new kind of place: the swap meet. Inside the walls of drive-in theaters, junk collectors and bargain hunters joined their collective karmic energies and spawned a trash-to-treasure paradise. Everything from auto parts to macramé plant hangers could be found at a swap meet, and at rock-bottom prices. But the huge crowds converging upon these junk fests created a parking nightmare. So, for those looking for a steal of a deal without the hassle, there were the street sales in West Hollywood.

It was just what she needed to resuscitate Vampira's Attic. Jack Simmons provided the wheels and the muscle to load up his car with the goodies that Maila selected from swap meets and then tote them to her house.

She set up a table at Santa Monica and Havenhurst. Shelley Winters was a regular, as were Carol Lynley and Carol Burnett. She saw Joan Crawford and Diahann Carroll stop by. Once, Jeff Donnell—George Gobel's TV wife and Aldo Ray's real one—sold at her own booth next to Maila. The Santa Monica street sale was also an art fair. In addition to the junk dealers, the vendors were jewelry makers, potters, painters, and leatherworkers, among other kinds of artists.

Maila dealt in old clothes. She'd set up a table, heap it with her jumble of rags, and sit in the sunshine, drinking in every ebullient moment of the day. When her legs were good, she'd load up a wheelbarrow and push it up and down the street, creating a portable boutique. The other vendors became her surrogate family. To them she was Melrose Rose, the curator of crap with distinction. Laughter and music filled the air. Every weekend at the street sales was like a carnival. Every street musician there was a Mozart, every sale a triumph, and every shopper a temporary friend.

> *I went into business for myself with 3 cents—yeah, 3 cents. I was broke & paralyzed on my right side.*
>
> *The swap meets arrived at a glorious time, within walking distance. My sporadic paralysis had been diagnosed, and they were shooting me up thrice weekly with Vit. B 12, "the happy vitamin."*
>
> *Happy went with me to the Happy Meets. Early swap meet vibrations were super positive. People buying & selling and others*

anticipating a miraculous discovery in the next batch of rubble. I met

many new friends, as dogs were allowed to attend.

Maila was the happiest she'd been in years. She'd regained enough strength to maneuver with the use of a cane, she was earning money, she was having fun, and perhaps best of all, her crazy stalkers were gone.

Now in "progressive ambulation," she could walk 15 minutes to the most happening nightclub on the planet, Whisky A Go Go on North Clark Street and Sunset Boulevard, where girls danced in cages suspended from the ceiling. The venue hosted groups like the Byrds, the Doors, the Turtles, and Buffalo Springfield, and its live house band was led by Johnny Rivers. The Whisky was arguably the birthplace of Los Angeles' rock and roll scene.

But Maila didn't come for the music or the drugs. She came for the fashion. Bell bottoms, vests, jackets, and hats; rhinestones, feathers, ribbon, faux fur, scarves, chains, and bandanas. The eruption of colors and textures worn by the attendees at the Whisky were a wishful fashion designer's dream.

I didn't want to sell old clothes. I wanted to make inspired clothing,
so I designed & remodeled rags—funky, like the hippies & kids I saw
at the Whisky.

I got only the best rags. The kind rich people threw away after
only wearing them once or not at all. I knew the woman who was a
good friend of the big shot at our Goodwill. The trucks, when full,
would make one secret stop before arriving at the main depot. Pickings
were good for those of us who knew the right people in the right places.

The kids from the Whisky came down the hill in groups to check out Maila's offerings. It was amazing to see how much extra cash she could get from adding a couple of feathers, ribbons, and some beads to a Goodwill find. She specialized in sewing velvet pantaloons, which she sold by the dozen to the musicians and their fans at the Whisky.

> *I sold these plumed Shakesperian berets to The Grass Roots &*
> *for sundry Beatles inspired musicians. They picked through my clothes*
> *to find the vanity garments. I did a tie-die [sic] for Grace Slick, a dish*
> *cloth bikini for Melanie, and a necklace I crocheted with twine & added*
> *some beads for Joan Baez. Frank Zappa, wife & their baby, Moon,*
> *came by a few times and bought things. Oh, & Brooke Hayward. She*
> *was still married to Dennis Hopper then, I think.*

> *Also, the clothes & backdrop for a 3 Dog Nite [sic] album cover.*
> *I won the praise of [costume designer] Thea Van Runkle, who told me*
> *I was the most creative person she had ever met. It was rite [sic] at*
> *the time she was nominated for the Academy Award for the clothes in*
> *Bonnie & Clyde. It helped my business immensely. I raised my prices*
> *from a median range of $2.50 to a median of $4.00 for a dress.*

> *I thought I was rich.*

By the summer of 1973, the increased traffic on Melrose spawned more new businesses: boutiques, restaurants, and antique shops. Subsequently, the rents doubled, and Maila could no longer afford her apartment. Melrose Rose left behind her newfound family of street vendors as well as the not-so-sweet memories: Carleton Carpenter, Chuck Beadles, the La Brea Tar Pits, and the deranged fans who stalked her doorstep.

She moved 43 blocks east to what she called "the heart of the barrio" in East Hollywood. Her new apartment was inside of a tiny, flat-roofed house at 713

North Heliotrope, still just a block from Melrose Avenue. The entire space was about the size of a guest bedroom in a Bel-Air mansion.

A Mexican restaurant stood on the corner. The fact that they served not burgers and fries but instead tortas and frijoles did not concern Maila—it was coffee and conversation she was looking for. The owner, Hilda Álvarez, remembered Maila from the first day she turned up at the Sombrero.

"Then, we have not too many blonde customers, and I'm thinking how it was strange to see the pretty blonde lady sitting alone, just drinking coffee. And then she comes in the next day and every day. Always alone. Never did she order anything to eat, just coffee. So finally, I go to her and introduce myself. And she says her name is Helen Heaven."

The two ladies hit it off, and soon "Helen" was allowed in the kitchen to clean up at night for a free meal. The Álvarezes soon became her surrogate family.

Hilda and her husband had three young children, and Maila interacted with the kids as if she were their grandmother. She especially enjoyed helping them with their homework. Because English was Hilda's second language, it was a godsend. Maila was a private tutor for her children. She was so much a part of the family that when the Álvarezes went out of town, Maila took care of the kids.

Even then, "Helen" carefully guarded her past and remained somewhat of a mystery. So when Hilda saw a big white limo pull up to her place and saw a man get out, go up to her door and then quickly leave again, she was curious.

"Marlon Brando was giving Helen money. She showed me his check for three hundred dollars. Mr. Brando, he sent a driver over once a month for a few years, and then no more. It just stopped."

Marlon could be quite generous to friends in need and was one of only a handful of friends whom Maila trusted to keep her location a secret. His largesse was intended not only to help Maila with living expenses but also, if need be, to hire an attorney to try to stop the release of *Vampira*, a film starring David Niven and Teresa Graves. But by the time she'd called a lawyer, it was too late. The film was released in the UK and scheduled for its U.S. premiere.

The movie was renamed *Old Dracula*, however—not because of Maila's efforts, but to take advantage of the success of *Young Frankenstein*. However, it retained the name of Graves' character, Countess Vampira. (In 1975, Niven wrote a memoir of his life during the Golden Age of Hollywood, *Bring on the Empty Horses*, the title of which was the obvious inspiration behind Maila's quote, "Bring on the empty hearses," in the foreword of this book.)

The '60s and '70s marked the beginning of the exploitation of Maila's intellectual property that would continue for the rest of her life. She would never live to see a dime from those who profited from her character.

On the phone with Marlon, Maila railed against those who were "picking her bones." She claimed ABC's *The Addams Family* matriarch, Morticia, was more Vampira than the original drab character that Charles Addams had created. Natasha, the gothic cartoon spy from *The Adventures of Rocky and Bullwinkle*, essentially *was* Vampira, while Hanna-Barbera later featured a character actually named "Vampira" on their monster-themed Saturday morning cartoon *Drak Pack* in 1980. And Disney secured a spot on Maila's mental hit list with its Cruella de Vil character from *101 Dalmatians*.

With Marlon's financial assistance, Maila was able to have a telephone, which served both parties well. For Maila, it meant security as well as accessibility in the rare circumstance there should be an offer for an interview. For Marlon, it fed his appetite for lengthy, late-night phone calls, since he never physically visited her anymore. As usual, Marlon was prone to ramble on about politics and his personal philosophies, but occasionally, he strayed into a discussion of his love life, which never ceased to irk Maila. When she chided him for "always dating such pointless broads," she obviously excluded herself.

In the early years of her self-imposed exile, Maila was interviewed by screenwriter Venable Herndon for his book *James Dean: A Short Life*, and in 1976, at age 53, she appeared in the documentary film *James Dean: The First American Teenager*, talking about Jimmy and their youthful exploits. She was horrified by the way she looked. Seeing the gaping holes left by her missing teeth just shattered her confidence, and she resolved to stop smiling when photographed.

Next came a feature article in Andy Warhol's *Interview* magazine and an appearance at a book signing for Richard Lamparski's book *Whatever Became Of...?*, which discusses her quiet middle-aged life in East Hollywood. At some point in the mid-'70s, she lectured at a James Dean Fan Club convention in L.A.

> *For twenty years, I kept myself within five days of being camera-ready. And then I thought, how sad is this? I kinda figured out that nobody was going to call.*

By 1976, when Marlon's financial support ended, the phone was disconnected, and all offers for appearances and interviews ceased. And it wasn't only that her lifeline to the outside world was severed—she lived without the creature comforts most of us take for granted. She had no bed, no television, no electricity, no furniture save for a couple of plastic patio chairs. In 1977, she poured her heart out in an essay titled "Cat Piss and Tears."

> *Elder maiden ladies in the year 1977 often find themselves socially, sexually, & sympaticoically [sic] "high & dry." The high & dry spinsters are not organized. The hallmarks of the unofficial club are, however, quite evident on each of the sisterhoods.*

> *(1) Facial edema (result of long 'secret' hrs. spent teary eyed.)*
> *(2) Mild to dramatic scent of cat urine permeating her clothes.*
> *(3) She seems to be an obsolete personage who shuns both drip dry & dry cleaning. Nor does she subscribe to any of the dazzling new "Wet Looks." But rather more to the "Dust Bowl Look" of the depression era. The only wet-looking things about her are her psychedelic plastic*

reticule & her armpits. *Baudelaire, were he among us today, could tell us what is in that reticule. Puss 'N Boots—kitty litter—tea bags— perhaps melba toast. He would know.*

It's indelicate to ask the ladies themselves, we think. Yes, we think. But they would love to be interviewed. They are so very lonely. Nobody much speaks to them anymore except the census taker, the social security re-evaluator, and the Wilshire strangler. So their limited lives are an on-going wet war. Wetting their blankets with tears & drying the cat box with kitty litter. It's on & on for these anonymous ladies.

Yet, it's not all that bleak for the old girls. Somewhere between the 1st & the 5th of the month (her extravagant period), she may well wet her whistle with a glass or two of Ripple.

Twice as much for the non fickle few
Ripple is their heaven sent dew;
Trickle, trickle, trickle,
Ripple, ripple, ripple!
(Poor dears, even their drinking song has an obsolete unlovable cadence.)

That same year, 1977, my father died unexpectedly at the age of 55. I called Information in Los Angeles for every name I'd known my aunt to have used: Maila Nurmi, Elizabeth Nurmi, Libbie Niemi. I even tried to contact Dean Riesner. Finally, like my dad did when there was a death in the family 15 years before, I enlisted the help of the Red Cross to find my Aunt Maila. No luck. She had disappeared off the face of the earth.

Maila wouldn't learn of her brother's death for nearly 12 more years.

Chapter Twenty-Two

By the late 1970s, the punks had arrived in Los Angeles. Many lived in and around Maila's neighborhood and she was fascinated by what she saw. Young people with spiked hair, tattoos, and body modifications wearing studded leather jackets and ragged jeans held together by enormous safety pins. Men as well as women with their faces painted in an elaborate theatrical style. A longtime makeup enthusiast, Maila marveled at their creativity and expertise.

One man, Tomata du Plenty, stood out among the rest. Born David Harrigan, he was the frontman for the punk band The Screamers. He and Maila met in a parking lot near her home; she was out for her daily walk and he had just left a rehearsal. His music was anti-establishment and represented the iconoclastic philosophy of the punk subculture, which was very similar to Maila's own personal ethos. The two shared a common wit and artistic passion and became fast friends.

Long Gone John was a part of the music scene as well and another of Maila's friends. He made sure to check in on her, took her on errands, and worried if she was getting enough to eat. John later became the founder of the successful record label Sympathy for the Record Industry.

Aside from the Álvarez family, Tomata, and a few of his acquaintances,

Maila rarely cultivated new friendships, but she still hung on to Jack Simmons. Their bond survived because of their mutual abandonment by James Dean. At the beginning of Maila's self-imposed exile, Jack came around weekly to chauffeur her on errands. But some weeks, depending on Maila's mood, Jack was turned away when she wouldn't answer her door. Maila complained that Jack was emotionally abusive. In all probability, Jack, concerned for her welfare, doled out unsolicited advice that she didn't appreciate. But according to Hilda, Maila was alternately either ambivalent or disdainful of Jack.

By 1979, Hilda was divorced and remarried, and the Sombrero was sold. Her new husband was a French chef, and the couple made plans to open a new restaurant, Heliotrope House, across the street, serving continental cuisine. Maila was offered the chance to decorate the place. In preparation, Maila and Hilda planned entire days together scouring swap meets and yard sales.

As the grand opening of Heliotrope House approached, the dining room was readied in accordance with Maila's Victorian-inspired vision. Pillows were plumped, furniture arranged, artwork hung, plants poised, and candles lit.

At some point, Hilda took it upon herself to hang three small pictures on a wall. Upon arriving at the restaurant that day, Maila immediately took notice but didn't say a word.

The next morning, when Hilda came to open up the restaurant, the front door wouldn't budge. The entrance was blocked. Going around through the back, Maila, who had a key, was already there and stood in the empty dining room, fire in her eyes.

"Helen moved everything in front of the door," Hilda told me. "And when I saw, I just started crying."

The dining room was bare to the walls. Every table, every chair, and every plant had been shoved into a massive, tangled heap in front of the door. No small feat for a woman who walked with a cane.

"You destroyed it," Maila screamed at Hilda. "You destroyed it all! It was my design! How dare you paint on my canvas? How dare you?"

Hilda was furious as well and ordered Maila out of her restaurant, warning her to never return.

Weeks passed, and then Hilda noticed Maila sitting in a chair out on the sidewalk in front of her house. They looked at each other but no words were spoken. The next day, Maila was again out on the sidewalk, and this time, the women exchanged a few words. As the days passed, it became apparent they both missed their friendship.

Hilda invited Maila to come inside for a cup of coffee. It took a few more days for Maila to process the idea before she could bring herself to return to the restaurant. And when she did, the incident was never mentioned again. In that moment, Hilda accepted Maila for who she was, and over the next 30 years, there was never another cross word between them.

In the early '80s, Jack moved to Long Beach, where he and his partner, Phil, enjoyed some success in real estate. After that, his scheduled visits to Maila became monthly. Because she had no phone, each visit was prearranged via a call to Heliotrope House, whereupon Maila either confirmed it or rejected it. After nearly three decades as friends, Jack was aware that Maila's confirmation in no way guaranteed she would be available.

Even so, he faithfully made the two-hour round-trip trek from Long Beach to East Hollywood every month. When Maila didn't answer her door, he would check to see if she was drinking coffee at Heliotrope House. Sometimes she was and sometimes not.

Eventually, her collection of personal memorabilia and unsold items from her shop outgrew the little box apartment on Heliotrope Street, and Maila moved around the corner to 4358 Melrose. She called the new apartment her warehouse.

Using her Vampira's Attic inventory added to her various yard sale accumulations, Maila set up shop again. The warehouse served as both home and business.

Carla Brown, a 50-pound English Pointer, entered Maila's life when her owner died. When Maila heard that the dog was destined to be euthanized, she adopted her. Every day, they went for a walk, westbound on Melrose, Carla wearing one of Maila's thrift-shop scarves around her neck. With Carla beside her, Maila felt more secure in their rough neighborhood. At 3 p.m., there was no whisper of the unrest that would almost certainly erupt in the night.

The Satans and the 18th Street gangs were waging a bitter battle for supremacy. Maila and Carla walked near the underpass of the Hollywood Freeway, where gang members sprayed reverse swastikas on the concrete and sniped at motorists on the off-ramp. Tire marks were still visible in the spot where a driver had been shot in the head.

They passed the laundromat, where a sign from management hung asking customers to remove bullets from their pockets, as they damage the washing machines. They passed the gas station, where three attendants had been killed in the past year and a half.

The route to the Mini Burger is concrete and asphalt all the way, and Maila apologizes to her companion. No grass. On weekends, they head over to Los Angeles City College where there's plenty. It's paradise.

> *We arrive at the mini burger. I feel guilty because I'm hungry and buy two mini burgers & a cup of coffee. $1.25. That's twenty-five cents over my daily budget. Carla gets the four bun halves. I feel guilty giving her refined bleached & poisoned flour & also because she's forced to live in that goddamned heatless, damp tomb of a warehouse. It seems I carry a lot of fucking guilt around. Poor Carla, her tough luck to be stuck with me. I'm ashamed. Please forgive me, dear one.*
>
> *I got the (juke box) music for free and there's no tipping in this place & I paid no bus fare to get here. Plus I've lost 2 ounces today so my day is made. I feel secure. Tonite I may spend only 20 minutes rather than the usual 45 barricading my doors. If Carla were a Great Dane, I could*

save 25 barricading minutes each nite & 15 unbarricading minutes each morning. But I say, "Who can afford a Great Dane?"

In 1980, a resurgence of interest in Vampira was sparked by Michael and Harry Medved's book *The Golden Turkey Awards*. The Medveds tapped *Plan 9 from Outer Space* and its director, Edward Wood, Jr., as the worst movie and director of all time.

As a result of the publicity from the book, the Vista Theatre scheduled a screening of *Plan 9*. At this news, Maila thought the time was right to take her frozen asset, Vampira, out of cold storage.

On April 12, 1980, Maila sent a handwritten letter to Marlon Brando's accounting firm, Brown Kraft and Company, on San Vicente Boulevard. The rough draft, in part, read:

> *On April 9, your messenger reached me with a gift from Marlon Brando, your client, for which (I) thank you. Enclosed please find a note of gratitude I would like forwarded to Mr. Brando as I do not have his address.*

She used this two-hunded-dollar gift from Marlon to make Vampira T-shirts to sell at the *Plan 9* screening at the Vista. The turnout was surprisingly large and included actors Diane Keaton and Warren Beatty. That night, Maila watched *Plan 9* in its entirety for the first time. The occasion was 24 years in the making.

John's Place, a storefront comedy theater, stood next door to Maila's apartment on Melrose. Over the last two years, John Deaven, the proprietor, and Maila had become sidewalk friends. When one day Maila wore one of her T-shirts, Deaven was delighted to learn that his neighbor was once the celebrated Queen of the Cobwebs, Vampira. He asked if she was willing to make a short 8mm film dressed in character. It was perfect timing and would serve as the beginning of her plan to resurrect Vampira.

The cast of the comedy troupe immediately set about to write *Bungalow Invader*. As promised, Maila donned a black wig, applied her spooky makeup, and put on a black tattered dress, albeit more modest and roomier than the original— and minus the waist cincher. For her efforts, she was paid 350 dollars.

In February of 1981, a local entertainment trade magazine, *Drama-Logue*, did a cover story with several stills from the film. *Bungalow Invaders* was described as "a silly romp through the many rooms of a Hollywood bungalow using many windows, much screaming and burning candelabras." The next month, *Los Angeles* magazine picked up the story and ran it in their "People Scape" column.

At KHJ-TV, Walt Baker, the station's program director, read the article and began a search for Maila Nurmi.

It was an intricate process, as she had no phone and her address was a secret to most. Ultimately, another Melrose shop owner came to Maila's door with a message to call Walt Baker, who wanted to meet with her. Twenty-five years after being fired over her snake-raping comment, Maila returned to KHJ.

She was nervous. Deaven had succeeded in concealing her cane and her missing teeth. But what would Baker think when he saw her?

If he noticed, he didn't let on, greeting Maila in the second-floor corridor at KHJ.

"You're Vampira," Baker said. "I'm honored to meet you. You're a very famous lady!"

He informed Maila they were looking for a horror host and had tested a waiter who didn't work out.

"We want your fame," he said. "We'd like for you to play Vampira's mother."

"No, I'm afraid I couldn't do that," Maila said. "Vampira was born magically. She has no mother."

Baker ignored her response and launched into a story about his wife, who, as Hobo Kelly on television, retired the character when she wearied of the role. "No one could play it but her. Just like no one can play this character but you."

"Mr. Baker, with all due respect, that simply is not who Vampira is."

"You remember we had Larry Vincent," Baker continued, nonplussed. "Larry's gone now. Cancer. But if you aren't interested, Moona Lisa is waiting in the wings."

Both Vincent, known for his character Seymour, and Moona Lisa, a mildly Vampira-inspired character, were former KHJ horror hosts.

"Fine, then," Maila conceded. "If your only alternative is that I play Vampira's mother, which is out of the question, then do what you must. But I'll tell you what. I will find a girl and train her myself. And if you like, to lend credence to the show, I'll be on it from time to time as other characters."

"Then you'll appear on the show?" Baker sounded hopeful.

"Yes, as odd relatives and such. I have a wonderful new character who's like the Elephant Man. You know, it'll be like *Carol Burnett*, or like *Laugh-In*, with guest regulars."

"But you'll have to appear frequently. At least at first. Maybe every other week."

"Yes, that would be fine," Maila said.

Baker asked about money, reminding Maila they were a small independent station without network affiliation.

"I'll do the acting for AFTRA minimum. But for the use of my character Vampira, I want a flat four hundred dollars each time you air a segment. Out of this, I will pay my girl."

"How will you find her? The girl for the part, I mean."

She suggested a contest from which she would choose someone who was innately self-absorbed yet intelligent, with a great sense of timing. Looks were secondary; the visual image was achieved with makeup. Most importantly, Maila maintained, it was imperative that she be allowed six weeks to train the girl properly.

Baker asked if she could write the scripts.

"No, I'm not good at entire segments. One-liners are my forte. But I could assist the writer."

"Do you have old *Vampira Show* scripts?"

"Yes. I have a few. Very few. It's a format that's relatively easy to clone. Once you get the puns in your blood, they spew out."

Baker's mind was racing ahead. "Larry Thomas is not at the station," he said. "We'd have to find him and pay him extra. That'll be expensive, but he's worth it."

Inwardly, Maila cringed. Larry Thomas was the script writer for Vincent's Seymour character.

> *I found his writing truly adolescent. "Seymour" utterly appalled me. Everything about it, the set included, was embarrassing beyond peer. Hadn't I sheltered Vampira for a quarter of a century? Did he really think I was going to allow hack artistry to wash over her now? I tried, in the name of diplomacy, to couch my horror at this suggestion, all the time I was thinking—how am I going to get away from here?*

The more she thought about the meeting with Baker, the more uneasy Maila felt. At this point, Maila wasn't convinced KHJ was completely serious about resurrecting Vampira, and so she thought that maybe instead of a horror hostess, the role should be for a man. So, she encouraged her neighbor, John Deaven, to audition for the role of horror host. As a comedian, he seemed an appropriate choice.

Deaven wasn't hired. But during his audition at KHJ, he told Baker that he and his friends had pooled their energies and monies to get Maila camera-ready for *Bungalow Invader*. Now Baker was armed with the knowledge that Maila had no money. He may have already assumed as much, seeing as Maila had no phone.

When KHJ had indeed interviewed Deaven as a prospective horror host, Maila began to believe that perhaps the station was sincere in their plans. If she could have chosen anyone to be the new Vampira, it would have been singer and dancer Lola Falana, who then enjoyed superstar status as the highest-paid female performer in Las Vegas. So Falana wasn't available.

284

But there was someone else—a young, talented bass player named Patricia Morrison, whose look was a blend of punk and goth. A dark priestess. Still in her teens, she was already a veteran of several popular punk bands and recalls the first time she met Maila.

"I was amazed at how gorgeous she still was. Those cheekbones and piercing eyes—wow. It was obvious she could be trouble very easily, but I liked that too. A rare thing, someone who speaks their mind and the consequence be damned!

"I remember she was hired by channel 11 [sic] to find someone to be a new horror host, based on what she had done. She contacted me via [Long Gone] John, suggesting I may be good for it. I was in two minds, as I was in a band and thought, in my youthful way, that that was my destiny. But because it came from Maila, I was interested in the idea or at least open to it, as to me she was the prototype of that gothic look that we now all know so well and is easily recognized worldwide.

"She was the original, and to me, no one has come close and I doubt ever will. I felt safe if she was going to be involved. I would never have wanted to carry on from her and do it wrong, but it never went any further than her registering her interest in me."

Soon after Deaven's meeting with Baker, a message arrived at the Heliotrope House for Maila to call Baker immediately and set up another meeting before he left on vacation.

She looked forward to this meeting, for it would resolve any questions of the station's intent. Maila came with sketches she'd prepared for potential characters, and she found Baker full of conviction and ideas. *The Vampira Show* would air Saturday night at six and again on Sunday afternoon at four. Vampira had never aired in prime time. Maila's hope was restored.

This second meeting generated so much promise that Maila was comfortable showing the sketches she'd made of her favorite new horror character, Wretch. Without so much as a glance, Baker dismissed them and waved in a tall man standing in the hallway. "Maila," he said, "this is Dick Johnson. He's going to produce your show."

He entered Baker's office and shook hands with Maila.

She was told that only a meager two hundred dollars were budgeted for Vampira's costume, but that now Maila was to appear on the show every week, and her duties would include that of associate writer and producer.

For Maila, the most exciting part of this meeting occurred next when Baker handed her a piece of paper that read: "Search for Vampira—Procedures."

The plan would run from July 13th to July 24th and be broadcast Mondays through Fridays on KHJ's *Mid-Morning L.A.* talk show. Each day, the top five contestants would be chosen from a submitted photograph and a written essay titled "Why I Think I'm Vampira." Each girl would provide their own costume, makeup, and transportation to the studio and appear on the morning show. Before their appearance, each would be given a short audition script to study, which would appear on the teleprompter during the on-air audition.

The contestants would be judged by Maila Nurmi, Dick Johnson, and Larry Thomas on their delivery and imagination of scripted material, their appearance as Vampira, their personality, their improvisation skills, and their pre-show interview. From each days' top five contestants, one would be chosen as the winner and announced during the final segment of *Mid-Morning L.A.*

Baker left for Ireland in May, and Maila had but one meeting with Dick Johnson. The meeting was a rehash of old news—except for one thing.

"Walt said we're going to audition for a girl rather than having a contest."

Maila didn't like it, but she was certain Baker was clear that she would choose the girl and train her. Whether it be by contest or not, she would sit through their auditions. That was fine.

Three weeks later, Johnson called the Heliotrope House with the message he, too, was leaving on vacation and Cal Brady was now in charge of preproduction.

Maila met Cal, a lighting and set man, in Walt Baker's still-empty office. She was told to assemble scripts, stills, sketches, old publicity tear sheets, and anything she thought would be relevant to the recreation and production of *The Vampira Show*.

"Bring them to me right away and leave them at the information desk marked 'urgent,'" he instructed. As Maila was leaving, almost as an afterthought, Cal informed her that Larry Thomas, Seymour's writer, was now in charge. Maila, as associate writer, again held out hope that once Larry Thomas learned about Vampira, the scripts they produced together would work.

As luck would have it, when Maila returned to KHJ with a thick folder of the requested items, there was Walt Baker standing just inside the door.

He was obviously startled to see her, as he hadn't bothered to tell Maila he was home from vacation. He reddened and asked, "What are you doing here? Are you here to see Dick Johnson?"

Maila told him she had the materials that Cal Brady requested.

"I'll take that," Baker said, as he turned on his heel and walked away.

Shortly thereafter, Baker and Maila talked on the phone. Now he was insistent that she appear every week as Vampira's mother. It was as if he'd heard nothing of her plans for Wretch or her other characters. For perhaps the first time in negotiations involving Vampira, Maila compromised.

"Okay, I'll go this far. I'll do her voiceover if we never see her."

"Good," he agreed. "We can show Vampira answering the phone and hear her mother's voice as we see the girl's face."

"Yes," Maila conceded. "As long as I never, and I mean never, appear as any Vampira type whatsoever."

It was agreed upon.

KHJ's preproduction hierarchy was mind-boggling. Within six weeks, *The Vampira Show* was passed from Walt Baker to Dick Johnson to Cal Brady and now to Larry Thomas. Maila couldn't begin to figure out how to navigate the maze of executives. She waited ten anxious days with no word from any of them.

There were only eight weeks left to prepare. KHJ had all her materials, and she had nothing in writing. She called the station several times a day.

Finally, Baker called. "Come in tomorrow. The contracts are ready," he said.

Maila entered Walt Baker's office where he sat alone.

"We've found the girl," he informed Maila. "You're going to love her. She has great timing."

YOU found the girl? Maila kept the thought to herself.

He showed her a stylish, overexposed studio portrait of what appeared to be a high-fashion model. "She looks beautiful," Maila said.

"Her name's Cassandra Peterson. You'll meet her today. She's coming in. I gave her the merchandising rights."

Out loud this time. "You WHAT?"

Baker seemed surprised at Maila's reaction.

"It's between you girls. You two fight it out."

What no one could comprehend was Maila's visceral connection to her creation. In all things Vampira, Maila demanded complete and utter control with little compromise. It may be that her unyielding position that doomed the rebirth of Vampira.

Dick Johnson entered the office with a simple greeting and promptly called to a man who was passing the open doorway. "Larry," he called. "Come meet Vampira."

Larry Thomas remained standing just outside the doorway. He forced a reluctant arm into the room by way of introduction, and Maila got up and shook his hand.

The five of them were waiting in the conference room across the hall for the girl: Walt Baker, Dick Johnson, Cal Brady, Larry Thomas, and Maila. For 25 uncomfortable minutes, they waited until Peterson appeared with a smile, carrying a costume sketch of herself. "I stopped by to pick this up," she said.

The sketch was passed around the table amongst the men. No one volunteered to show it to Maila. She asked to see it.

288

The top half of the dress was an exact copy of my Plan 9 dress—down to the tear in the forearm—but the bottom part was bizarre. The sketch was of a knee-length accordion-pleated skirt like the famous Marilyn Monroe shot, but in black.

Cassandra told the executives that her friend Robert Redding was making the dress of the sketch. She went on to explain that as fans blew her skirt, colored lights would halo her blowing hair.

"Cassandra," moaned Larry Thomas, "that doesn't work with black hair. And you're not Ann-Margret."

Cassandra & all the others made no mention of legs. It was pure mammarian monomania. I brought up the subject of legs. Baker asked her, "Do you have legs?"

"Yeah," she said vacantly. "I have legs" & she raised her cotton jersey shift 2 in. to reveal her knees... no-one asked if she had thighs.

Thomas handed her a type-written page. "This is a sample of our dialogue," he said.

The phone rings. Vampira answers. "Hi Ma, what's it this time? Did the shopping cart you were pushing fall off a cliff?"

There it was. Maila was excluded from the entire process. They steamrolled right over the top of her and her precious commodity without so much as a backward glance.

They auditioned the girl, they hired the girl, and they gave her the merchandising rights. Now they wanted Maila to sign the contract. The salient points were as follows:

This agreement shall cover KHJ-TV's right to utilize your character, "Vampira," your performance within the program and your duties in assisting the writer and producer in the production of the program.

KHJ-TV pledges that at no time will any cruel treatment of animals be allowed to take place during the production of the program.

You agree that the character "Vampira" will be performed by an actress chosen by KHJ-TV. Further, that you will perform from time to time in the character of "Mother" of "Vampira".

For your performance as "Mother" of "Vampira," KHJ-TV shall pay you applicable AFTRA scale.

For the rights to the character and your assistance in writing and producing, KHJ-TV shall pay you Four Hundred Dollars ($400.00) for each program produced under this agreement.

She refused. Adamantly and with conviction. By doing so, it invalidated every signature already affixed to the contract.

"If you don't sign it within 24 hours, we'll go with another format," Baker warned.

"Go fuck yourself."

Maila walked out the door.

Walt Baker had his own version of how things went down. In an interview for *Fangoria* magazine, he admitted that he contacted Maila to discuss a new Vampira show. He also confirmed that Maila brought in her old scripts and pictures, which included set information. He concurred that Maila agreed to play Vampira's mother and do occasional guest appearances.

In the article, Baker stated, "What I really wanted to buy from Maila Nurmi were the rights to do the character Vampira." For those rights and any informational input Maila could offer, she would receive associate producer credit for the show.

Baker then denied there was ever an agreement that would allow Maila to find and train the new horror hostess, which, because a copy of such a schedule exists today, seems to fly in the face of the facts.

According to Baker's own words, "Cassandra Peterson was hired with the understanding that she would play a Vampira character."

While Maila claimed to have met Peterson in person, Baker neither confirmed nor denied it happened. Instead, he asserted the contracts were sent out to Maila for her signature, which were answered by Maila's attorney, who stated that his client was no longer interested and didn't want to be involved in the project. Baker said that this left the station no alternative but to create their own character.

Maila did, in fact, hire an attorney to write a cease-and-desist letter. On the morning of the first day of shooting at KHJ, with Cassandra Peterson as the new horror hostess, Maila said that Peterson performed as the Vampira character. Maila wanted to deliver the cease-and-desist letter in person but was advised against it.

What is known is that by the end of that first day, Larry Thomas had renamed the show *Movie Macabre* and renamed its star "Elvira, Mistress of the Dark."

Later, Maila wrote this to "some moguls" at KHJ-TV:

> Sorry I couldn't come in poison, Darlings—I abhor to barge in where I'm not invited—but my GucciLac Hearse runs on were-wolf urine—& there simply wasn't any at the pumps, Darlings...
>
> ...Oh, Hexon said they had some, but it turned out to be Vulture piss.

As for the similarities between the Vampira and Elvira characters, their sets, and their scripts, Baker said, "Our approach to the character is exclusively ours."

It was only the beginning. Cassandra Peterson and her success as Elvira would consume Maila's life for nearly a decade.

Chapter Twenty-Three

Maila prepared herself for battle with the only weapon she had. A pen. She poured out her soul in notebooks, on scraps of paper, on the backs of envelopes.

> *Now as I still count pennies for each can of tomato soup, the world has come to believe that the word "Vampira" is in the dictionary. That it is the female word for the male "Vampire." They believe that Vampira herself is in public domain & lift my product. This is America! Where, then, is this pauper's attorney?*

> *Am I, an impoverished & demoralized cripple, going to continue in this fashion while those who stole from me continue on in ill-gotten gluttony?*
>
> *In the name of God, let me speak!!!*

She tried. She really did. A soldier in an army of one, she took to the streets with homemade flyers, first on Melrose and then on Hollywood Boulevard.

During 1982 alone, and on three different occasions, she stuck her flyers on every windshield in the Los Angeles Press Club parking lot. She wrote free ads in newspapers, asking for support. Her single line in the personals read: "All who resent Elvira's brazen thievery, write to Vampira, 723 N. Heliotrope."

> *I thought the public would come to my defense in a barrage of silver bullets. No one came. Except one fan letter from Orange County.*

But she was dismissed as a lunatic.

Maila always remembered what she called "the Hollywood sign incident." The next best thing. Through the years, Maila came to believe the label "the next best thing" was synonymous with "second-best" or "not as good," and she'd come to believe she had never been quite as good as the likes of Lauren Bacall, Rita Hayworth, or Barbara Freaking. If she thought about that message from so long ago, she certainly wouldn't allow herself to add the name Elvira, who, Maila said, acted like "a stripper in a basement of an Elks Club."

The September 24–30, 1982, issue of the *LA Weekly* published a letter written by Maila—but signed "Vampira."

> *Dear Editor:*
>
> *Three Jeers! To laugh aloud when alone is, psychologists declare, a sign of madness. Knowing this, I was none-the-less guffawing aloud some supremely unvampire-like guffaws as I rollicked thru "The Best of the Worst."*
>
> *And lo—fathom my delight—to come upon (while in this sublime state) your selection of the most disappointing cleavage!! Elvira, Interruptus of the Dark!! Mistress of the Mediocre!!*

Now jubilant as well as rollicking, I hastily poison penned an ode to this same odious "vampira?" You darling, you guessed it, some bad blood lies between those lovely vampire ladies.

Sin-searly & Gr-r-hatefully your abhorring fan,

Beach balls made of silicone;
Sneering, droning monotone;
Of such things the maid is fashioned;
Then of smugness add a dash and;
Watch the silly slattern slut;
Pull her punches, preen & strut;
For Vampira's private ingrates;
Satan's puppet proudly gyrates;
And what will new tomorrows bring?
More of this disgusting thing?
Deeper necklines, pubic hair;
Don't you wish that you were there?

The above is my literary opinion.
Print it if you like—I take full responsibility—let her try to touch my Transylvania bank account!!

Vampira

When there was nothing more Maila could do to bring attention to the flagrant misappropriation of her Vampira character, she sat in her unheated warehouse with Carla and contemplated death. But because of her love for her pets, she concluded that suicide was a selfish act that would only result in her precious animal friends being sent to the pound and euthanized.

And so, she sat there with Carla, dwarfed by stacks and piles of her own personal memorabilia, secondhand finds, and unsold merchandise, but not bothering to open her shop. And Carla, whom she'd rescued from certain death, now gave Maila a reason to stay alive. Even if she could no longer love another human being, she felt compelled to love something or someone. She was teeming with love. But instead, there she was with Carla and her boxes of junk—all as abandoned and discarded as she was.

It was then that Maila began to think that perhaps she was unlovable or unworthy of love. Broken things became a reflection of herself, so she filled her life with things instead of people. That's why she could close herself up for weeks at a time, when the stress became too much, and be comfortable doing it. Maila called this "incubation," which she learned from Marlon Brando, who'd credited Einstein. He'd practice incubation during his self-imposed exile on the Tahitian island of Tetiaroa—a kind of hibernation where one shuts oneself off from the outside world to reduce stress and redefine one's goals. The process could take a day, week, month, or longer, depending upon how much negativity one needed to rid from one's mind and body.

Thus, while in incubation, there was a knock at her door. Maila made no effort to answer.

Suddenly, a bizarre sight. At the transom window above her front door appeared a young man's face, bisected by a long forelock of black hair that ended at his chin. The Misfits had come to visit.

According to band member Doyle Wolfgang von Frankenstein, after the knock went unanswered, singer Glenn Danzig climbed on Doyle's shoulders and looked into the window. There was Maila, sitting in a chair, ignoring the boys peering in at her. They slid a note under the door saying they were signing at Vinyl Fetish Records and asked if she would come and join them.

Any other elderly woman living alone in Los Angeles may have been terrified by the specter in the transom window. But Maila was intrigued. The man's hair had been combed forward into a point—called a devilock, she later learned—and it was reminiscent of her own hairdo in the '50s, when she shaved her head save for a fringe of bangs.

The Misfits were thrilled when the next day, on April 17, 1982, Maila showed up at Vinyl Fetish Records in full Vampira costume.

The Misfits' appearance was scheduled to coincide with the release of their first LP, *Walk Among Us*, upon which appeared the song "Vampira."

Maila was deeply touched by the tribute and signed autographs and posed for photos with the band.

They weren't the first band to honor Vampira in music—in addition to Bobby Bare's "Vampira" in 1958, she was also honored in British band the Damned's 1979 track "Plan 9 Channel 7." But it was the serendipitous encounter with the Misfits that lifted Maila from the doldrums of despair. In them, she recognized fellow soldiers, viewing the band as members in a growing army of creative beings changing the world with their art. Fearless rebels, all.

Doyle later said, "I found her one of the bravest and most charming people, despite the heartbreaks that came her way."

Maila was invigorated from her abbreviated incubation. She was again enjoying the company of the Álvarez family (now the Álvarez-Ruiz family) and her friendship with Tomata du Plenty, while other punks fed her creative spirit. From her treasure trove of collected antique baubles, beads, and buttons, she began to make jewelry again, an art form she'd dabbled in while rehabilitating from pernicious anemia. She'd amassed a huge assortment of old jewelry from Goodwill, yard sales, and swap meets, perhaps 60 pounds in all: a mix of Peking glass beads, rhinestones, crystals, old coins, Bakelite, and even a few pieces made from elk teeth.

The artist within Maila emerged. By disassembling the pieces, she restrung the beads to create necklaces and pins, sometimes using fingernail polish to paint the beads, other times adding a fringed tassel or the metal clip of an earring to give the jewelry her signature look. Her pieces were long and asymmetrical and resulted in a talismanic aesthetic—a kind of otherworldly charm necklace.

Patricia Morrison recalls seeing Maila selling her jewelry at Venice Beach Market. It must be said here that Morrison wore her long black hair teased high and favored black clothes and glam punk makeup long before there was an Elvira. In fact, Morrison said, "I was frankly horrified when I saw the Elvira character. Maila as Vampira represented to me a strong, cold beauty with delicious, naughty wit. I felt Elvira was 'for the boys' with the goofy comments and boob jokes. I was trying in my own way to be a strong female, and 'Elvira' did me no favours... there was a piece in a newspaper where CP (Cassandra Peterson) talked about the [sic] Elvira and said she 'got the idea from a girl in a band playing at Club 88.'"

That girl at Club 88, of course, was Patricia Morrison herself.

Afterwards, Patricia said, "I spent years being called Elvira! And even had journalists later ask me if that was where I got my image from. If you look at Elvira's image at the beginning, the hair, the leather bracelets, etc., are all very similar to what I looked like at the time, much more so than the elegance of Vampira. I hope I made Maila proud with my answers and singed a few eyebrows of naïve interviewers at the same time."

When Patricia, wearing sunglasses, approached Maila that day at the Venice Beach Market, Maila thought the girl was an Elvira fan emulating her idol. Maila, being Maila, laid into her. While Patricia can't remember the exact words, she recalls that they were "blistering!"

It was only when Patricia removed her sunglasses that Maila calmed down and chatted amicably with her. They exchanged Elvira stories. Morrison related that she went to buy her favorite lipstick at a little beauty shop in Hollywood only to be told that the last tube had just been sold to "the real Elvira." The excited salesgirl expected Patricia to be impressed. Instead, she said, "I gritted my teeth and left."

In March of 1984, Maila heard that, before becoming Elvira, Cassandra Peterson had appeared in a print ad for a male enhancement product and that it appeared in the current issue of *Hustler*. On her way back from a walk to the neighborhood liquor store, *Hustler* in hand, Maila decided she couldn't wait to get home, so she sat down on a short brick retaining wall and began to leaf through the magazine.

Maila soon became aware of a car full of kids driving slowly past her and staring. "What must they have thought of an old lady reading porn on the sidewalk in broad daylight?" Maila later said. The car came around a second time, even more slowly. Suddenly, she realized she may be in the sights of a gang looking for a victim. When the car again disappeared around the corner, she went as quickly as she could to the nearest house and hid behind their bushes. Sure enough, the car came back around a third and then a fourth time. When she felt safe enough, she walked home.

That night, there was indeed a fatal drive-by shooting near where she sat.

"And that's how Cassandra Peterson almost got me killed," Maila claimed.

At Halloween that year, Maila was slated to appear in a live show with punk band the Cramps. She was to lay in a coffin at the front of the stage; as the band played, she would emerge in Vampira costume. Something went wrong the day of the show, and the band was delayed. Minutes ticked by as she lay patiently in her coffin, while the audience grew restless. Fifteen minutes became a half-hour and then a full hour, and still Vampira lay unmoving inside the box, while the stage remained empty.

Finally, with as much decorum as she could muster, Maila opened the coffin, got up, and exited the venue without saying a word.

Considering that her nemesis, Elvira, was the star attraction at Knott's Berry Farm's annual Halloween Haunt that year, one can imagine how Maila felt that night. Angry, victimized, demoralized.

Elvira's Movie Macabre, riding a crest of incredible popularity, went into syndication. Soon to come were the licensing deals—everything from calendars to coffee mugs featuring Elvira's image were available to the buying public.

A half-mile west from Maila's place on Melrose stood the Anti-Club. Loosely described as an art house, it was to the mainstream nothing more than a dingy dive permeated with pot smoke, amp-busting music, and an anarchic spirit. Most nights, the place exploded with chaotic, explosive punk music.

After headlining at some of the most prestigious clubs in Hollywood, like the Roxy and the Whisky, the Screamers had disbanded in 1983, and by '84, singer Tomata du Plenty had set to work on establishing an art career. Maila described Tomata as the first person she'd known since Jimmy who could "hug you with his eyes." And Maila, although she would never admit it, was severely hug-deprived.

Maila's poverty troubled Tomata—he worried about her living without electricity and about whether or not she was eating properly—and he frequently took her out to lunch. Since Maila didn't have a phone and she rarely answered the door, those who knew her understood that the best and sometimes the only way to contact her was to leave a note on her door.

Hiya Helen,
Let's go eat something and talk about stuff. 1 o'clock tomorra
– Tomata and frenz?

Being an artist himself, he knew Maila would much prefer to earn money through her creativity than by getting a handout. And so Du Plenty arranged a way for Maila to make some extra cash by performing a series of monologues at the Anti-Club. On the last Thursday night of each month, Helen Heaven took the mike at center stage under yet another pseudonym: "Honey Gulper."

As the story went, "Honey" moseyed into Hollywood by way of Arkansas, bent on movie stardom, where she became the victim of too many unfortunate cosmetic surgeries and was left with nothing but her memories.

Hi guys! Is you ready? Honey invites you to take a dive backwards down the time warp water chute into the abyss before progress blighted our lives with McKnuckle burgers and deadly doubleknits. So let's sit back and soak in the warm mire, submerge and then bathe our psyches in the roiling, exhilarating mud bath called Googies. Googies, the crossroads of the world, born in the belated shadow of the Garden of Allah. Googies, the home of hilarious hipster hi-jinx and the repository for sex-starved satyrs and jazzy jezebels.

Now tip-toe with me, darlings, into this rapacious rapturama.

There amongst the obsessive star-struck masses were the real players.

The seltzer-headed alcoholics, lounge lizards, and lotharios. The platinum blondes with polluted pasts, the raunchy redheads with greed for guts, the burned-out brunettes with hostile hearts. And there, too, sitting so benignly is a pristine artless girl, bald as a newborn babe. Doubtless from an unfortunate mishap at the hands of an unscrupulous hair dresser. This lonely newsketeer now bursts with gossip to soothe your savage souls.

For an hour, Honey Gulper regaled her audience with tales from her past and earned twenty-five dollars for her efforts.

Thank you for helping to recycle an old biddie! Be patient with me, I may yet prove as useful as an aluminum can. And remember, the price of life will always be death!

Considering her former incarnation, it seemed an appropriate sign-off. The *LA Weekly*, the *LA Reader*, and the Sunday *Los Angeles Times* heralded Maila's monthly readings at the Anti-Club. The publicity boosted her spirits. But too soon, the emergence of the Red Hot Chili Peppers interrupted Maila's gig—the band's soaring success forced her to relinquish her ongoing Thursday night slot.

When Heliotrope House closed its doors and Carla Brown passed away, there was no need for Maila to stay on Melrose. Maila moved west into a converted garage at 844½ North Hudson Avenue, back in Hollywood proper. The new location was a good fit for her, in a familiar part of town.

Even as she moved into a better neighborhood, she couldn't escape her bag lady consciousness. To give her money meant she had to change her consciousness—to change who she was. She had to be forever in need, for it was need that felt normal to her. Life must always be a struggle for survival. In that way, she came to mirror her mother's beliefs. We become what we see.

My mother was the kind of person who could see an airplane already gracefully in flight and still believe that it was too heavy to fly. One of those sort of people who are forever planning for a rainy day and preparing for dire circumstances and poverty and thought it was sheer heresy to anticipate anything but destitution.

Maila loved living on Hudson. It didn't matter that her home was a garage with two tiny windows, high near the ceiling. Surrounded by boxes of her treasured memorabilia, they became part of her décor—and the boxes could well double as a chair or a table. Whatever didn't fit in the space, she stored in Hilda's garage.

The Studio Café, so named for the film technicians who routinely lunched there, was a two-block walk from Maila's new home on North Hudson Avenue, and it became her new local. Longtime proprietors Louie and Mina were always ready with a pot of fresh coffee and the latest gossip.

At the end of the street was a small deli and liquor store, and it was there that she found her new best friend, Bogie. Not the actor, but a homeless black Labrador mix, whom she adopted. Named for another liquor store further up the street, the dog was first spotted there begging for food. Along with Bogie, Maila took in a pigeon who couldn't fly. She named the bird Stinky and he lived with the dog and Maila, uncaged. Bogie later became instrumental in meeting Rick. Maila met the young Brit when they were both walking their dogs, and they sparked a friendship that lasted until Rick's premature death, 20 years later.

For a few years, regardless of her poverty, Maila's life was good. She enjoyed new friendships, and by 1985, with Tomata's help, she was performing again at the Anti-Club. In 1986, Maila appears in a full-length punk musical film, *Population 1*, in which Tomata stars as the sole survivor of a nuclear bomb and the only living person on Earth. Maila played the part of the mother.

Maila befriended other musicians as well, among them drummer Jeff Satan. The two enjoyed each other's company and often parked on Mulholland to chat for hours before the expansive view of the city. It may seem like an odd pairing; he was just 22 years old to Maila's 60-plus. But Maila was ageless and in nearly every sense these young artists' contemporary.

Jeff Satan was the drummer in garage rock band Satan's Cheerleaders, and he asked Maila to record some tracks with them, to which she agreed. Maila couldn't sing, but she could proselytize. She'd spent most of her childhood listening to her father preach against alcohol and the devil, agitating the masses with his fiery speeches.

Months earlier, while the band was walking down Hollywood Boulevard one day, they'd picked up a flyer that had been abandoned on the sidewalk. On it were the words of a fire-and-brimstone street preacher, warning those who read it to repent before the devil steals their immortal souls. One of the band members pocketed the flyer, thinking it may be useful someday, considering they were Satan's Cheerleaders and all.

That day arrived in 1987, when the band recorded "I'm Damned" and "Genocide Utopia" with Maila on lead vocals, performing the sermon from the discarded flyer. Even though it was a cold read, she sounded like she'd been preaching for decades.

The band was delighted. One band member summed it up with "That record turned out to be our 'Louie, Louie.'"

Chapter Twenty-Four

In the mid-'80s, Maila began working on her autobiography with Stuart Timmons, a young writer, historian, and gay rights activist. Stuart spent months with Maila, sometimes entire weekends, tirelessly assembling the pieces of Maila's life into a cohesive narrative for an autobiography. During the process, there was much talk about the tremendous popularity and continuing success of Elvira, over which Maila was still incredibly distraught.

Some days, Maila was incapable of forming cohesive sentences and spent hours crying. Stuart took her out to dinner almost every night to try to dispel her suffering. But despite his efforts, talking with Stuart about her life only served to dredge up six years of frustration over her dealings with KHJ. Stuart became convinced that Maila should seek legal advice. It was something she'd wanted to do for years, but without any money, a car, or even a phone at her disposal, it seemed impossible. But in Stuart, she had an advocate and supporter who was eager to help. By the beginning of 1988, Stuart was searching for an attorney to represent Maila. L.A. attorney Michael C. Donaldson was contacted. Regrettably, he declined to take on the case because he thought Maila may have waited too long to legally seek relief. But in his March 30, 1988, letter of response to Stuart Timmons, he encouraged him to continue to seek counsel and wrote that if Maila had contacted him earlier, he would have taken the case "without question." Furthermore, he stated, "Based upon the materials you have presented me, I have formed the opinion that Ms. Nurmi was indeed ripped off."

A few weeks later, Maila had her legal team—Mandel & Manpearl along with attorney Jan Goodman—to represent her in the battle of Vampira vs. Elvira, contending that any statute of limitations concerning the case had not been violated. The autobiography was put on hold, and Stuart Timmons took on the roles of Maila's assistant, paralegal, stenographer, researcher, typist, chauffeur, and confidant. His devotion to Maila came at a time when she most needed it.

Stuart hit the ground running. By April of 1988, he had composed a progress report in which he detailed his collection of Vampira photos from her television shows. Although it isn't known for what purpose, Stuart also placed ads in the *Los Angeles Times* as well as *Fangoria* and *Hollywood Studio* magazines.

The only mention of attorney fees is found in Stuart's letter. He states:

> *In reviewing the agreement Maila signed last Thursday, the phrase about the client reimbursing the attorneys for costs and expenses raised a bit of concern. She asked me to convey that she is eager to repay any such financing and does not want to discourage any expense that would help present the strongest possible case, but also that, in the worst case scenario of no settlement, she wants to keep her liabilities within her limited means.*

Limited, indeed. She was flat broke. And the meter was running.

On September 8, 1988, a complaint on Maila's behalf was filed in the U.S. District Court for the Central District of California. Cassandra Peterson and KHJ/RKO were not the only ones in Maila's sights. They had lots of company: Mark Pierson (Peterson's then-husband), Queen "B" Productions (Peterson and Pierson's production company), NBC Productions, Walt Baker, Larry Thomas (original producers of *Movie Macabre* and part owners of the Elvira character), Dick Johnson (associate producer of *Movie Macabre*), Panacea Entertainment (involved with Elvira merchandising), John Paragon (co-writer of *Movie Macabre*, Elvira's syndicated shows, and the proposed Elvira movie), and Elvira Merchandising, Inc.

The common factual allegations in the complaint state that in 1954, Maila developed a public personality and character, developed a television show in which she hosted late-night horror movies, and that she hosted those movies in a campy manner, combining sex appeal, humor, and themes of death in her scripts.

Through the years, Maila continued to monetize her character through movies in which she was billed as Vampira, was featured in commercials, records, and periodicals as Vampira, and owned a retail store called Vampira's Attic in which she sold clothing with the Vampira label. In addition, she made and sold jewelry pieces that were often signed "Vampira."

Maila further states that she is in possession of a document that seems to support her "factual allegation" that in July of 1981, she was in negotiations with KHJ and Walt Baker to revive the Vampira character for a proposed television show—typed on KHJ letterhead and signed by Baker. A copy of said document was affixed to the complaint.

There it was, every last detail—from hiring a girl to portray the new Vampira to Maila appearing periodically as Vampira's mother—with signed documents from KHJ sayng she was to participate in the selection of the actress. It also showed that, in accordance with Baker's request, Maila provided management with old Vampira scripts, samples of dialogue, photographs, sketches of Vampira and Vampira sets, trade secrets, samples of advertising used on the show, and other proprietary items. Also in the agreement, it stated that Maila would be paid AFTRA rates each time she appeared on the show. She also included the document that read that, in exchange for the rights to the character and her assistance in writing and producing the show, KHJ would compensate Maila four hundred dollars for each program produced—which Maila had refused to sign.

Rights to the character? This was the sticking point and the reason why only Baker and not Maila signed the contract. Signing away her rights to Vampira was never a part of negotiations, and Maila claimed that proviso was slipped into the contract surreptitiously. When she balked at signing, another round of negotiations was planned.

Instead, KHJ hired Cassandra Peterson without Maila's knowledge or consent. Furthermore, Peterson was given the merchandising rights, because as Baker allegedly stated, 'she asked for them.'

According to court papers, plaintiff Maila Nurmi was informed that although no contract had been signed by all parties, the new *Vampira Show* was in production.

Maila claimed there was a mad scramble on that first day of production to rename the character from Vampira to Elvira to avoid litigation. But many similarities remained.

Vampira utilized a carved wood, Victorian red velvet couch. So did Elvira.

Vampira utilized a distinctive, low-cut, tattered black dress, emphasizing cleavage and a voluptuous figure. So did Elvira.

Vampira utilized lighted candelabra. So did Elvira.

Vampira utilized cobwebs. So did Elvira.

Vampira utilized skulls. So did Elvira.

Maila alleged that defendants Baker, Peterson, RKO, Thomas, Johnson, Panacea, and Queen "B" Productions created the Elvira character and produced the series of *Movie Macabre* using the identity, character, and sets of Vampira without obtaining the permission of or payment to the plaintiff. The complaint continued with a claim for relief. The complaint was finished with an exclamation point.

In Maila's case, the relief she sought was money, and the amount of money she was asking for would take a lot of justification. Maila's lawyers came out swinging, citing not one but eight reasons why their client should be compensated to the tune of ten million dollars.

First claim: Violation of Lanham Act, a federal statute, for false designation of origin and misappropriation of Vampira character.

Second claim: Violation of California Civil Code for imitation of plaintiff's likeness and character.

Third claim: Invasion of privacy for exploitation of plaintiff's personality and imitation of plaintiff's character.

Fourth claim: Infringement of common law right of publicity for proprietary right in Vampira character.

Fifth claim: Unfair competition and misappropriation of property right.

Sixth claim: Injunctive relief, expressed as a judicial order to prohibit further damage by the defendants to Maila Nurmi's Vampira character.

Seventh claim: Accounting, expressed as a request to know all earnings from Elvira merchandising, movies, television, and personal appearances.

Eighth claim: Breach of contract, expressed as breach of implied contract.

In the original contract that KHJ had written up for Maila to sign, there was one stipulation which stood out and proved how serious and involved Maila was with the television station in re-establishing a new Vampira Show. It read: "KHJ-TV pledges that at no time will any cruel treatment of animals be allowed to take place during the production of the program." That was all Maila.

Maila asked for a jury trial and that all reasonable attorney fees be paid by the defendants.

In preparation, Maila's attorneys drew up a list of 35 potential witnesses. Among them, besides each of the defendants, were John Deaver and the former Hilda Álvarez, along with Stuart Timmons himself.

In response to the complaint, the defendants filed numerous motions for delays and dismissals, which resulted in multiple hearings before the judge. In January of 1989, the defense requested that all of the plaintiff's claims, except the first, be dismissed on the grounds that they were not within the jurisdiction of the federal courts. Only the first claim, which asserted a violation of the Lanham

Act—also known as the Trademark Act of 1946, which governs trademarks, service marks, and unfair competition—pertained to federal law.

Judge William Byrne, Jr., gave a little to both sides. He dismissed the plaintiff's final claim, breach of contract, but the other claims remained part of the lawsuit. When multiple claims in a lawsuit fall within specific guidelines, a judge can then declare pendent jurisdiction, i.e., the authority of the court to hear a closely related state claim against a party that's already facing a federal claim. Judge Byrne did just this, finding that remaining claims were "substantially related" enough that he could adjudicate the case in the interest of "economy of litigation."

In other words, there would be no need to have two court cases, one in state court and the other in federal.

In the midst of all this legal haranguing, I finally found Maila. An October '88 issue of *Star* magazine announced that Vampira was suing Elvira for ten million dollars. She was alive!

From the article, I learned the names of Maila's attorneys. An information operator gave me their address and I wasted no time writing a note to them, explaining who I was. Inside the envelope, I tucked a letter to my aunt, asking them to forward it to her.

Within four days, her response was in my mailbox. Eleven pages, front and back. I was like a kid at Disneyland. Over the moon.

She kicked it off with "Heavens, Sandy! Are you my last known relative that I know where they're at?"

She told me about her life. She almost never had a phone, and if I'd tried to call Dink, well, he was still too important—he had an unlisted number. She said she had pernicious anemia and most of her upper teeth were missing, but she had a set of false choppers she wore if she needed to strike a pose. She wrote of her love for animals, the palm trees in Los Angeles that deemed to soar into the "rarified air," and how she cultivated all living plants including weeds in her garden. She hated Johnny Carson, thought Madonna was tawdry, but loved Cher. She hemmed the skirts of that "crippled bitch" gossip columnist Rona Barrett and cleaned a young Burt Reynolds' house. She told me of her by-then-former friend, Stuart Timmons, and that he couldn't be trusted as he was trying to steal from her, and if he should ever call me, I was not speak to him.

I'd written of my father's passing, and she apologized. "To think that Bobbie died and I never knew. Shame on me."

And so, our letter-writing campaign began in earnest and continued even as the lawsuit was still going strong. Maila sent me photocopies of pictures showing the similarities between Vampira and Elvira and copies of articles from newspapers that supported her legal claims. But mostly, our letters were filled with innocuous prattlings of two people getting to know one another.

The lawsuit heated up, and motions went back and forth for months. On March 31, 1989, Judge Byrne issued his ruling. He found that "the defendant's instruction of the word 'likeness' more faithfully reflects the intent of the statute." In other words, Peterson's attorneys had convinced the judge that a likeness means an actual representation of a person, rather than a close resemblance. The Court granted the defendants' motions to dismiss and to strike the claim for punitive damages under the Lanham Act. The motion for sanctions was denied.

His decision meant it didn't matter that Elvira wore an almost identical dress as Vampira or that her set incorporated an almost identical red death's-head sofa, candelabra, cobwebs, and skulls, or that her cheesy puns were in the same vein as Vampira's. It didn't even matter that on the first day of filming *Movie Macabre*, it was called *The Vampira Show*, or that the host was originally called Vampira, not Elvira. And we know this to be true because Maila wrote it down on a scrap of paper, contemporaneously, on the day it happened, without expecting her words to ever be known or seen. The paper was found in her apartment after her death.

> *On the first day of filming at KHJ, they called it the Vampira*
> *Show & Cassandra was called Vampira!!! After I threatened them*
> *with a lawsuit, after lunch, Larry Thomas changed the name to Movie*
> *Macabre & she became Elvira, Mistress of the Dark.*

But even after all that, Maila still had a chance. According to an article in *Metro Digest* dated August 16th, 1989, Judge Byrne gave Maila until September 18 of that year to either contact the court or have her ten-million-dollar suit dismissed. The judge had already thrown out the claim that Elvira violated Vampira's right to publicity, but he ruled that she may still seek damages for possible trademark infringement.

But Maila remained silent. Her inability to trust once again reared its head and she'd become convinced that Stuart Timmons was going to steal the work they'd done on her autobiography—and once Maila booted you out of her life, you were gone for good. So without Stuart, money, or an attorney, she was done. She wrote a letter to Judge Byrne on notebook paper thanking him for his service in litigating the lawsuit and stating that she would not be appealing, as she was out of funds.

Publicly, Cassandra Peterson said she didn't understand why Maila didn't like her and wondered why she and Maila couldn't be friends. The probable truth was that Peterson didn't want to alienate her fans, many of whom were also Vampira fans.

Cassandra Peterson went on to make millions of dollars as Elvira, while Maila Nurmi didn't even have a phone.

Chapter Twenty-Five

In her letters to me, Maila never indicated when the lawsuit ended. Over the months, I sent her an audio tape of my father singing and telling silly jokes that he'd made at Christmas of 1970. When she wrote back and said she didn't have anything to play it on, I sent her my daughter's tape player. I also sent copies of letters that Onni had sent my dad after Sophie died. They were typed in Finnish, but I knew she could translate them. And clothes! Sometimes the ladies whose houses I cleaned would give me their castoffs, and those went to Maila as well. I remember she was especially fond of a pink floral raincoat with matching hat and satchel I'd sent her.

Soon, I was making plans to go to Hollywood to visit her. But I needed a car. One reliable enough to make the 2,000-mile round trip from Oregon. To pay for it, I supplemented my housecleaning job with a bartending gig on the weekends. I worked 76 days without a day off, grateful I had a mother who watched Amy, my 12-year-old daughter.

On Friday, August 25, 1989, Amy and I arrived in Hollywood in our white Plymouth Horizon. Right away, we went in search of Hudson Avenue where Aunt Maila lived—navigating our way with a paper city map.

In front of her apartment building, two women were sitting on a mound of grass under a tree, one blonde and one brunette. As I got out of my car, both women stood up. The blonde woman began to walk over to me, and it was then I realized it was Aunt Maila. No longer the distraught, emaciated woman in her 30s whom I recalled from her mother's funeral. She was 66 now, maybe 40 pounds heavier, and seemed taller somehow, with her hair pulled up into a bun. But just like before, she was dressed in black pants and a sweater, with her sleeves pushed up at the elbows.

And then I saw her eyes! Those bright aqua eyes, the same color as my father's. I knew without a doubt it was Aunt Maila.

We embraced and I introduced her to Amy. She directed us to follow her down a pathway toward her converted garage, where Bogie waited. She had no sofa in her home, just a two-seater wooden bench and a recliner. A floor lamp with fringed lampshade stood next to the recliner, and a cabinet stood to the left, upon which sat a few knick-knacks and a small television.

Squatting along the opposite wall was my grandmother's silver chest. It looked exactly as I remembered it at age ten. According to Sophie, it was intended to be left to my father, which she claimed contained the baby books, family pictures, and mementos she'd squirreled away during her lifetime. As my parents attempted to haul it out to the car after Sophie's funeral, Maila intervened and insisted it be left with her, and my dad didn't argue. Now I noticed that it wasn't really a silver chest at all but a foot locker that had been painted gray; the paint was now nearly worn away. But its contents were something I desperately wanted to see.

"Yes, that was your Grandmama's," Maila affirmed. "It's where I keep all my treasures."

A bird perched in a small square window near the ceiling, his droppings cascading down the wall. "That's Stinky Two," Maila explained, following my line of sight. "I rescued him as he could no longer fly. He shares my breakfast with me every morning."

Maila and her niece Sandra on Melrose Avenue in Hollywood, August 1989.

Portrait of Maila by Mark Berry, December 2006. Courtesy of the Jove de Renzy Collection.

The next day, Amy and I arrived at Maila's at noon. She was waiting at the curb. Because I'd told Amy that while we were in L.A., we might shop for school clothes, Maila suggested we stop at the Pic 'N' Save near her home. Once we saw the clothing at the closeout retailer, I knew my spoiled daughter would turn her nose up at them. "Worse than Newberry's, worse than Woolworth's," was Amy's assessment. She wanted to go to a shopping mall, although I assured her that it wouldn't be in the cards that day.

Instead, Maila gave us a tour of Hollywood. She kept up an entertaining dialogue, explaining the historical significance of various buildings and streets. Amy couldn't have cared less, pouting from the back seat, bored out of her mind.

Hollywood Boulevard was a disgrace: punks, druggies, homeless people, and a plethora of tourists meandered aimlessly together. Over lunch at the Hard Rock Café, Maila and I eased up and found ourselves chatting more comfortably, my sullen and silent daughter aside. Limos passed back and forth our window. We strained to see the occupants but didn't recognize anyone.

When it was time to leave, Amy and I were walking back to the car when I noticed Maila was not with us. I briefly chastised myself for not walking more slowly, as my aunt walked with a cane. But as I turned to look back to see her, I noticed that she had stopped about 20 feet back, and her face was contorted with rage.

"Fuck you, you spoiled brat!" Maila screamed at Amy. "Fuck you, fuck you, fuck you!"

My first thought was "Oh, no, I can't let this be the end of my 32-year quest to find Maila!" And so I just stood there and let her vent, not knowing what else to do. Amy just glared at her, expressionless.

Then Maila changed. "You'll be all right when you grow up," she continued, "but right now you're a pampered, selfish, little twit."

Was this a stab at an apology?

The thing was: Maila was right. Amy was all those things. She knew she was acting awfully, but she didn't care. I'd become accustomed to Amy's brattiness since she hit 11—she was a self-absorbed kid who thought this trip was all about her and her quest for clothes. When we got to the car, I told Amy to get inside and that we'd talk about it later.

If anyone else had verbally attacked my daughter, I would have lashed out. But it was Maila. My last tie to my daddy, who shared his sister's aqua-colored eyes. We were the last of the Niemis. And I was not angry at her, only shocked. I could not not let this occasion slip through my fingers after so many years.

In the car again, Amy rode in the back, Maila in the passenger seat. Her outburst was over as quickly as it began. I said something to Maila like "It's okay. And yes, she's spoiled."

Before I even started the car up, Maila pointed to a building across the street and said, "That's the hospital where all the celebrities go to dry out or die. Cedars-Sinai. They're very good at keeping the press away. That's where Lucille Ball went to die a few months ago."

We were back on terra firma.

Amy's father lived in the L.A. area, and it had always been the plan that he and Amy would visit. I called him and arranged for him to pick Amy up early the next day. Blessedly, that meant for the rest of my visit, it would just be me and Maila.

When I arrived at Maila's place the next day, she was again waiting at the curb. We were going to hobnob with the elite and have Sunday brunch at the Beverly Hills Hotel, because Maila said she hadn't been there since she was asked to leave an animal benefit hosted by Debbie Reynolds. She intimated that this happened while she was being blackballed by Hollywood.

We parked in a lot crammed with Mercedes-Benzes, BMWs, and Jaguars. Valets rushed to take my keys. The walkway to the restaurant was carpeted with AstroTurf. Ahead, I could see something shiny on the ground, and as we approached it, I saw that it was not a penny, like one might find in a grocery store parking lot, but a quarter. Of course, I took it. Maila said it was a ploy by one of the valets to see who was cheap enough to pick it up.

We were seated at a table in the back reaches of the restaurant. We'd gussied ourselves up, but we were still pegged as tourists, considering that our table was directly across from the orange juicing machine and its horrendous racket.

It didn't matter—Maila was having a grand time. Straight away, I noticed that her affect changed. She was more animated than I'd seen her and lapsed into a contrived Katharine Hepburn accent, the one she used as Vampira. As time went on, she spoke louder and began waving her arms and gesticulating, although perhaps she was just competing with the orange juicer. Coming back from the ladies' room, we ran into Barbara Eden of *I Dream of Jeannie* fame and got her autograph, which boosted her mood even more.

After we ate, we stopped at a shopping center for some ice cream, then drove past the old Carlton apartment where Maila and Grandma lived—and where Grandma had died.

Each day, I arrived at noon and picked up Maila from the curb. Although it was August in L.A. and I had no air conditioning in my little Plymouth, Maila wore sweaters and pants and sometimes even a jacket. Her jewelry was distinctive; I commented on the long strands of colorful beads and medallions strung randomly and asymmetrically, which she'd made herself.

One afternoon, she took me to her friend Ludlum's house. He was in his 70s and conducted acting classes in a garage on his property, and Maila said he threw her 20 bucks every now and then when she taught a class. She introduced me as her niece and asked Ludlum if we looked alike.

"Maybe in the eyes," he responded.

On this day, there were about six students in attendance. At the front, a rudimentary stage had been assembled, and Maila was soon guiding the class through a reading. Later, she whispered to me that the young man with the dark hair had serious emotional issues, as his mother had nursed him until he was eight. I soon learned that Maila was the queen of gossip, continually delighting me with her scandalous asides.

We took a tour of Melrose Avenue. Outside of a shop, I saw a woman reading a book in the sunshine in a black bra, a hot pink panty girdle, and combat boots. One side of her head was shaved, while a long purple braid hung from the other side. The shop's name was Retail Slut, which prompted me to go inside to check it out. They sold the requisite halter tops, mini skirts, and bandage dresses, all displayed beneath perhaps 40 naked Barbie dolls hanging from the ceiling. Maila remained blasé, but it was a whole new world for me.

As we passed a shop displaying a huge Asian urn, Maila stopped and declared, "Isn't that phantasmagorical?"

My mouth fell open. I hadn't heard that word since my father was alive. He'd be driving the car and suddenly, out of nowhere, he'd say, "Phantasmagorical!"

and then pause, and then add, "Philiosinosity!" I never asked why or what it meant.

I told Maila this and got no response, other than a steady glare.

It wasn't until I got home that I put two and two together. Even as a child, Maila was big on ten-dollar words. I'll bet one day she spouted the word *phantasmagorical* in order to impress the family, and my dad mocked her with the nonsensical ending. That silent stare I got from Maila suddenly spoke volumes.

We ate lunch and dinner out every day. We went to some garage sales and drove through Mulholland, where there was abandoned furniture on the side of the road, free to anyone who wanted to haul it away. And this was good stuff. Rich people's stuff.

Finally, after several days of getting to know one another in person, I felt brave enough to speak up. "I want to go visit Grandma's grave," I said.

Maila's eyebrows shot upwards in a look of surprise—or was it panic? She hesitated before saying, "Oh, well, I suppose that would be all right. It's been a while."

"A while." I wondered what that meant. A year? Ten? Twenty? Never? Not that it mattered—it just wasn't what I expected. And it wasn't my place to comment as to why, or how come she'd forgotten her way to the cemetery in Inglewood.

Instead, I said, "All I remember is that it seemed like a long drive from the mortuary."

We stopped to buy some red roses because Maila said they were "Mama's favorite flower." She carried red roses at her wedding on Valentine's Day. Then we headed off to Inglewood.

As we got closer, Maila became quiet and was chain-smoking, even though, as I know now, she'd quit years before. We rolled down the windows of the hot car. I glanced over at Maila all bundled up in the summertime—sweater, slacks, and a jacket—and noticed that tears were flowing down her face.

"Are you all right?" I asked.

She shook her head no. The tiny bows and feathers in her hair fluttered.

At the next opportunity, I pulled off the freeway. By the time I stopped the car, she was sobbing.

She couldn't go to the cemetery. It was too painful, she said, and she didn't want to relive her mother's death. Anyway, what difference did it make now, after all these years?

I didn't argue with her; I just turned the car around.

We pulled over and gave the roses to a woman on the street. Maila spotted a random woman with an expression of hopelessness on her face, approached her, and handed her the roses. The woman's smile was our reward.

Instead of a cemetery, we went to a restaurant, and Maila initiated a conversation about Sophie. The day before she died, Sophie had received a gift from a neighbor: four red roses she'd grown in her garden. Suddenly, I blurted out, "They were on the windowsill above the kitchen sink!"

"Yes, they were! You remember that?"

And I had. They were cottage roses, small ones, plucked from a shrub.

Maila went on to say the roses we bought for the grave reminded her of her mother's last day. "Mama loved roses, but we didn't have any, and that last day, she said that the next place she lived, she'd plant some. She never got the chance. I bought her some when she died."

"I also remember the bathroom," I added. "It was painted pink and had a green marble sink and matching antique wash stand. With a black-and-white picture of a man with a pig. Who was that?"

A slow smile crept on Maila's face. "Oh, that was Jimmy. Sweet, dear Jimmy Dean. Do you remember him?" Maila asked.

I had been too young to remember, but I'd seen *Rebel Without a Cause* and *Giant* as an adult. I was only vaguely aware that Maila had been his friend.

She suggested we drive up to the Observatory in Griffith Park to see where *Rebel* was shot. On a terrace overlooking the park, a bronze bust of James Dean was on display, crafted by artist Kenneth Kendall, who was also a friend of Maila's—every year, he, Maila and a group of their friends met to celebrate Jimmy's birthday. Although I could see the Hollywood sign from the terrace, Maila suggested there was a way to get much closer to it.

Beachwood Drive starts out as a straight road, but when it reaches the canyon, it turns into a series of tight, meandering curves. At the end of the drive, we were pretty close to the Hollywood sign, but hiking in on foot was not physically possible for Maila. As we approached a market on Beachwood, Maila asked me to stop. I went inside and bought a Coke and orange juice.

"This market was here when Jimmy was alive," Maila said when I returned.

It was a hot day, and as Maila sipped her juice, I suggested we go find some shade. She wanted to talk about Jimmy. She told me about a picnic they'd shared in the far reaches of Griffith Park, and how her favorite picture of him was the one with the pig. She said it wasn't the Hollywood Jimmy but the farm boy that he was.

On my final night in L.A., we had dinner at The Lunch Basket on Santa Monica Boulevard. Maila and I both had a beer, whereupon Maila admitted she didn't really like beer and preferred brandy. After we ate, I asked Maila if she'd like some brandy. She shrugged.

I stopped to buy a bottle of Christian Brothers, a six-pack of Coors, a couple packs of cigarettes, and a bag of pretzels. Since Maila hadn't invited me back to her place, I asked if she'd like to go to my motel room. I had two double beds and Amy wasn't there.

Because of Bogie, she declined and suggested her house instead. There, she poured herself some brandy, I popped a can of Coors, and we used a plate on the floor between to use as an ashtray.

I knew almost nothing of Maila's time in Astoria, but I was trying to find some experience we may have shared, so I mentioned the tuna canneries. Her eyes lit up. She did, in fact, work in them and remembered that time vividly.

Abruptly, she asked me, "Do you sing?"

"Nope," I answered.

"Neither do I. But your Grandpapa had a lovely voice. Sang in the church choir and at other civic functions. Played the sousaphone, too. A very musical man. I inherited only his fanaticism. But while in the cannery, I sang. Nothing to look at all day but those poor, decapitated creatures."

I knew it. Most of Astoria's female population had worked at the House of Tuna at one time or another, including me. Maila did two tours; I did eight.

"But what I was going to say is that day in the fish cannery changed my life forever."

I was all ears.

"I thought, 'Here I am, stuck in fish cannery hell,' and so I sang when all I really wanted to do was cry. There was a whole world out there of which I was not a part. And as long as I volunteered to stay there, the hellishness would continue unabated."

Suddenly, she began singing "Summertime" and reached her arms skyward. "One of these days, you're gonna rise up a'singin', and you'll spread your wings and fly up to the sky!"

I didn't think those were quite the right words, but I also didn't care.

Maila went on. "I realized then, in that exact moment, if I wanted to survive, I had to spread my wings and fly high and fast from everything and everyone I knew. I made a plan to leave and knew if I could tolerate another three or four months eviscerating tuna fish, I could save enough money to buy wings to fly away. Of course, I didn't know then those wings would carry me straight into the merciless belly of the Beast. I was unprepared. I didn't yet realize wings alone cannot slay dragons, although I tried. God knows I tried."

She got no argument from me. I'd never known the story behind why she left the family. The alcohol gave me the confidence to finally ask her if we could take a peek inside Grandma's "silver" chest.

We sat on the floor as Maila opened the lid to reveal that it was stuffed with scads of papers, letters, pictures, and newspaper articles, along with other odds and ends—some dead corsages, a couple of gloves. That kind of thing.

Maila poked around and pulled out an old photo album full of Niemi family pictures I'd never seen. My father as a baby wearing a christening dress! As babies, we could have been twins. There he was again, as a child of maybe four, wearing glasses. Before then, the earliest photos of my dad I'd seen were his Army pictures. There were Maila and Bobbie at the beach, Grandma and Grandpa standing on a porch, and the whole family next to an old car. Grandma in her wedding dress.

I badly wanted copies of these photos, but I didn't dare ask. Not yet. "There will be another time," I thought to myself.

There were letters, lots of letters. Among them were some of mine. Maila pulled out one specific letter, handed it to me, and told me to read it. It was a love letter from Marlon Brando asking her to marry him. I was stunned.

"Wow," I gasped. "You turned him down?"

"Yes, for two reasons. He was a sex addict and a hypocrite. He would have cheated on me within a week, and I couldn't have that. Secondly, Marlon was an animal lover—he dared not step on grass for fear of killing an ant—yet his money was invested in stockyard beef. So we remained friends and casual lovers. He was the most successful of our group, and when he became insistent he would marry, we all had a hand in choosing Anna Kashfi—which proved to be a huge mistake as she was psychotic."

Among Maila's treasures were a couple of pairs of Vampira gloves, with a few nails still attached, some original Vampira scripts, one of her black wigs, and a long-line bra, which I noticed had been altered.

"I had to make it smaller," Maila said. "There were no long-line bras that would fit a 17-inch waist."

Then there were the bat sunglasses. I didn't know then that they'd become iconic after Vampira wore them during photo shoots.

"I bought these in New York, before Vampira was born, even before I did cheesecake."

"You did cheesecake?" I was astounded. Neither Grandma nor my parents had ever mentioned it.

"Oh, yes, for several years, but never nude. Your Aunt Maila was even a cover girl a time or two. Anyway, I posed wearing these glasses numerous times as a femme fatale and later as Vampira. These glasses have been with me for decades."

What other secrets would I learn? Maila was full of them.

"Tony Perkins is gay but he's always been ashamed of it. He's married now and trying very hard to pretend he's not. I felt sorry for him because one should not have to make excuses for oneself. But he was very intelligent and a good friend at one time, and then he became cruel and heartless. I never understood why."

I was on my fourth beer so what the hell... I asked. "What about Orson Welles?"

"Ah, yes. He's a Taurus, like you."

A long pause.

"Aunt Maila, I know about the baby."

"I thought you would. It was only natural that Mama would tell Bobbie, and then you would hear of it. It was a terrible time in my life. I was very young and naïve. My boy would be a few years older than you are now. Every year on Christmas and his birthday, I go outside and make a wish to the heavens that he is safe, healthy, and happy."

Maila refilled her brandy. I had a million questions. But I waited to hear if she would reveal any more to me. And soon, the dam broke.

She told of meeting Orson at Musso & Frank Grill in Hollywood and the absolute thrill she felt of seeing him in the flesh, to say nothing of actually speaking to him. That he was the epitome of everything she hoped to achieve. That he romanced her and she fell hard and fast. That when he left her pregnant at 20 to marry Rita, it was the first time she'd considered suicide. Even more than 40 years later, the tears came, trickling down her cheeks, and I was sorry that perhaps I'd pushed her too far. But she brushed them away and continued.

"Mama had been in Astoria, waiting for Papa to send for her to come to

New York, and he kept putting her off. She was an alcoholic, and he couldn't stand drunks. But my situation dictated a change of plans, so it worked out that we would make the trip together. It was Mother who decided I should put the baby up for adoption, and as it turned out, it was the right decision. Who knew childbirth was such an excruciating experience? I swore then I'd never have another child."

She paused for what seemed like an inordinate amount of time. I was afraid to break the silence.

Then Maila announced that she was going to take Bogie out for a pee break. I went outside with her and the dog, and in a half-whisper, she said, "I gave him a name."

"The baby?" I asked.

"Yes. I named him Kal. No middle name. I didn't get that far. Besides, I knew he would have another name, so what was the point?"

"'Cal.' That's not a common name. Why Cal?"

"Kal with a K, not a C. I believe in giving children family names. Your Grandpapa's names were too foreign. Onni and Kosti." She chuckled. "Bobbie's middle name was Kaleva, also too foreign, so I just shortened it to Kal."

"My Dad would have been honored to know that," I said softly.

"In a few interviews, I tease that Orson gave me the clap. Allegorically speaking, which I sometimes do, people assumed I was talking of a sexually transmitted disease, when in fact it wasn't that at all. He gave me the KLAP. Stands for 'Kal Like a Potato' or 'Kid Like a Potato' because he looked like a potato when he was born."

Maila revealed that she was in love with Orson one moment and hated him the next. But they resumed their romance after he and Rita became estranged. She hoped that one day they would be married and he would take her under his wing and promote her career as a monologist. They traveled by plane, and once, while in New York, he hinted that he would marry her the following year, after he and Rita divorced. She claimed that shortly after their breakup, Welles and

324

Hayworth made *The Lady from Shanghai* in which he had Hayworth's long red hair cut off and bleached blonde, in a hairdo identical to Maila's.

"I always felt like it was his final homage to me," Maila said. "There was a famous quote from Orson in that movie, something like 'I don't know if I'll live long enough to forget her,' and I often wondered if he was talking about me or Rita. In any event, I never saw him again except for once, as he exited The Riviera in Las Vegas. He'd just finished appearing there when I arrived to perform with Liberace." She hadn't told me about Grandma's confrontation with Welles at the Knickerbocker, and I didn't push it. Instead, we continued to soak up the booze and I asked her to tell me more about her stint in Las Vegas.

"It was glorious! I had the time of my life," she enthused. I was happy we'd changed the subject. "I met Elvis! He was oh so young and handsome and incredibly talented. An absolute musical genius." We were getting drunk, and Maila's words were thick. "The way he moved those hips on stage, I was expecting a symphony, and I got Johnny One-Note."

"Aunt Maila!"

"He never let me see his pee-pee. Not once. Like he was ashamed of it, or maybe he was just shy. And he didn't know how to use it then either, but he was so damned beautiful and such a magnetic character, I didn't care."

"You slept with Elvis?" I was still in shock.

"Oh, no! We never actually slept. I was his Las Vegas girlfriend. We went shopping, rode bumper cars, played carnival games, card games, ate lunch, and fooled around. Of course, even then, Elvis had an entourage perpetually hanging around and we had to find ways to ditch them. We performed across the street from each other for two weeks. But, alas, I grabbed his pee-pee in a public place, and he never forgave me."

We were both in our cups and laughed uproariously. My 32-year-wait was worth it.

Then we just got silly and sang the Finnish National Anthem. We thought of the most difficult words to pronounce in Finnish and asked each other to repeat them just to prove to ourselves how Finnish we really were. Even drunk, we excelled. A decision was reached and we deemed ourselves 100 percent Finnish.

I was too drunk to drive. Maila had neither bed nor bedroom. And so with a sweep of her arm, she offered me a spot where she herself lay her head at night: the floor. She pulled out some pillows and blankets from behind her chair and we made our bed, Bogie lying between us. Although we were lying on a rug, I remember the floor feeling lumpy and peculiar. Years later, I learned from Stuart Timmons that the floor was dirt, covered with plastic sheeting, then plywood, and finally a rug.

I awoke with a dry mouth and a headache, but Maila appeared to be fine. We let Bogie out, combed our hair, smoothed out our clothes, and walked to the Studio Café, Maila's personal haunt, for breakfast.

A few high-backed wooden stools stood at the counter. Pastel green linoleum adorned the walls, upon which hung myriad black-and-whites of old movie stars: Clark Gable, Ava Gardner, Myrna Loy. Well-used matching Naugahyde booths completed the 1940s décor.

When Maila took a seat at the end of the short counter, I knew it was "her seat." We ordered eggs and toast and Maila introduced me to owners Louis and Mina—he cooked and she served. From his open kitchen, Louis kept up a running dialogue of gossip, while Mina interjected her two cents from the dining room. It was the perfect clubhouse for this stage in Maila's life.

My time was running out. I was leaving the next day, so after one last tour of the Hollywood Hills, it was time to go back to my motel and pack. Amy's father had returned her to me, sans school clothes. As arranged, we arrived at Maila's at 10 a.m. on the morning of our flight home, all packed up. Again, Maila waited at the curb, wearing black pants and a sweater. She came to my open car window.

Not for the first time, I asked her to consider moving to Astoria, promising to pay her expenses. She gently but with conviction said she was staying in Hollywood because she didn't want to lose her anonymity. I told her I would never forget our visit and that I'd had one of the best times of my life. I told her

I loved her and would miss her and would try very hard to come see her again.

She looked sad, like she knew this was really goodbye, and then she pulled a 50-dollar bill out of her sleeve and insisted I take it. I vigorously refused, and it went back and forth—no/yes, no/yes—until I realized I was going to lose this one. There was no way to outlast Maila.

As I pulled away, we touched hands for the last time, through the window, and I told her she'd get the money back one way or another. As I drove away with tears in my eyes, it occurred to me that for our entire time together, except for a moment when she showed me the bat sunglasses, we'd never discussed either Vampira or the lawsuit.

I never saw her again.

Chapter Twenty-Six

Two weeks after I left Hollywood, Maila met Audrey Antley. An operator who worked the switchboard, Audrey described herself as a fixture at radio KLOS 95.5 FM, specifically *The Mark & Brian Show*. One day, *Plan 9 From Outer Space* became an on-air topic of conversation, which naturally segued into a discussion of Vampira and ultimately Maila. A contest was initiated called "Where in the World Is Maila Nurmi?" Audrey heard that someone had seen her at the Studio Café, and when she checked it out, sure enough—there was Maila sitting at the counter.

As it turned out, *Plan 9* was set to play at a local drive-in, and Audrey asked Maila if she would like to accompany her. Maila accepted. Audrey picked up Maila for the double feature in a van with a sliding door.

Improbably, *Girl Happy* was the first film, starring Maila's former lover Elvis Presley as well as ex-husband Fabrizio Mioni. Mioni acted in very few movies, but there he was, sharing the big screen with Elvis in the part of a sex-crazed Italian exchange student who was trying to steal Elvis' girl.

At intermission, It was announced over the speakers that Vampira was in attendance, along with a description of her vehicle and where it was parked. Maila was offering autographs to anyone who wanted one from the back seat of the van, via the sliding doors, for the many fans who came over to meet her. During the rest of the movie, every time Vampira appeared on screen, the audience went wild.

Maila enjoyed the evening immensely and it proved to be the beginning of a long friendship between the two women. What Maila didn't yet know was that Audrey had a secret. As the two spent more time together, this fact slowly became clear. Maila started wondering how her friend could afford the numerous luxuries, such as the fur coats she often wore, on a radio operator's wages. Animal lover that she was, Maila didn't approve of the coats to begin with, but that's why she'd noticed them. Out of politeness to her new friend, she remained silent. But something didn't add up.

Ultimately, Audrey revealed her secret to Maila. She tentatively knocked on Maila's door one day and was relieved when Maila answered wearing a full face of makeup. This was a very good sign—Maila was agoraphobic and preferred walking through life unseen except for her one-hour early morning socializing session at the Studio Café. Makeup meant Maila was feeling good and social, ready to go out for the day.

"Maila," Audrey began, "I'd like to offer you a job."

"What kind of a job?"

"First of all, I need to know if you would be comfortable walking a block and a half to Santa Monica Boulevard, catching a bus on Huntley, and walking across the street and up some stairs."

"Yes, I could manage that," Maila replied.

"Good," Audrey said. "I own an escort business called Capricious, and I'd like you to help me out." She paused to take a deep breath before she continued. "I have an alter ego named Mistress Stephanie Locke. She's a dominatrix."

Dead silence from Maila, but her incredible blue eyes danced.

"It depends on what you have in mind," she replied, as a smile creased her face. "I don't think my catsuit still fits."

Audrey laughed. "No, no, Maila. I've worked several 80-hour weeks in a row, and I need help. I'd like to hire you as my receptionist to answer the phone, schedule appointments, and most importantly, call the girls so they come to work on time."

Capricious employed 11 women, whom Audrey described as "beautiful, precocious, and heavy partiers." Most were destined to become trophy wives to very rich old men. But the partying meant they often slept in when they should be at work. She needed Maila to call the girls every morning to wake them up and get them motivated to come to work. The job required four hours Monday through Friday and paid 250 dollars a week.

Maila had never earned so much money in her life. She quickly agreed to take the position.

At 10 a.m. the following Monday, Maila crossed the street at the corner of Santa Monica Boulevard and Huntley Drive to her new place of employment. Capricious occupied the top floor above The Gauntlet, a piercing and tattoo parlor, and the editorial office of the *Piercing Fans International Quarterly*.

Audrey, a.k.a. Mistress Stephanie Locke, showed Maila around the place. There were four fantasy dungeons: The Mad Scientist, the Medieval Dungeon, the Pink Sissy Room, and the Egyptian Temple Room. Mistress Stephanie explained that these rooms were the most expensive in all of Los Angeles and were available to rent by the day or the hour. Then Maila was given a list of phone numbers to dial every morning to remind the spoiled staff it was time to get out of bed and come to work.

Maila enjoyed her time at Capricious. Mistress Stephanie even allowed her to decorate one of the "victim rooms." When she arrived in the morning, the state of the reception area told her if the girls had been busy the night before or not. Leftover pizza boxes meant business had been slow, which was good news for Maila—she would gather the remains of the pizza for her dinner that night.

Before the first customers arrived, Maila often sat on the sofa with the girls at her feet, like a librarian reading stories in the children's section, and regaled them with stories of Vampira and her friendships with Marlon Brando and James Dean. The girls were spellbound.

One day, a client arrived and promptly disrobed, save for a French maid's apron. He moved about the reception area with a pink feather duster.

> *Not a lot surprises me anymore, so I guess I was more amused than shocked. His backside was completely nude. I didn't know if I should say anything to him or not. As if he could read my mind, he turned his head & said, "Mistress Stephanie ordered me to clean this room." His testicles & the tip of his penis were in view below the hem of the apron. I was desperately thirsty & chanced to go to the refrigerator for a cold drink at the exact moment the man knelt at the open refrigerator door & started to rearrange the soda & juice bottles. He handed me a bottle & I thanked him as if it was the most normal thing in the world.*

Working at Capricious was a godsend, not only for the pay but also in that it taught Maila to ride the bus again. It seems that once, years before, she'd had a friend whom she described as having a "big bottom," and while she was exiting the bus, the door had shut prematurely on her bum, dragging her for half a block before the driver stopped. Maila was scared that she could fall victim to such a tragedy, especially since she had the added disadvantage of using a cane, and that it was an accident waiting to happen. But after a few weeks of taking public transit again, her anxieties and fears had been neutralized, and she got over it.

In 1994, the film *Ed Wood* hit the movie theaters, having been adapted from Rudolph Grey's book *Nightmare of Ecstasy*. In the early '90s when Grey was doing research for the book, he and Maila exchanged frequent letters. When the movie was released, with actress Lisa Marie playing the part of Maila/Vampira, Maila was enjoying a resurgence of interest in the glamour ghoul character she created years before. She was in demand again, and it rejuvenated her spirit such that she went to a beauty salon and had her hair cut, styled, and colored. Requests for interviews, appearances and invitations to various award shows inundated her mailbox—among them, an all-expenses-paid trip to attend a monster convention

Maila with her friend, Dana Gould.

in New Jersey. The con's offer included meals, hotel accommodations, and the use of a booth from which she could sell photos, autographs, and her jewelry, as well as five hundred dollars of spending money.

She turned it down. Maila had thought she could handle the new interest in Vampira, but the spotlight on her life soon proved too much, and instead of embracing it, she began to shut down. Daily, she went through the mail that arrived at her door and threw away the invitations. Bogie died and she adopted another dog named Houdini, "half Akita and half werewolf," as she described him, and she took in a feral cat named Violet as well. With the exception of her morning visit to the Studio Café, she was a shut-in, and her pets were her life.

During this time, she thought about her life and where she wanted it to go next. She seemed to relish the "social pariah" role that she'd created for herself.

When my parents married, it was a match made in voodoo heaven.
Their union produced two children—my brother Bobbie & me. He lived
a boring & bourgeois life and managed a farm store, where he became
an expert in which came first, the chicken or the egg. In celebration of
his birthday, every May 27th, I count my friends which number about
a hundred, six of which are humans. I as well survived to adulthood
and became a social pariah. I guess you could say I was the lucky one.

Then an invitation arrived at her door that piqued her interest too much for her to ignore it. It was from the producer of *The Big Scary Movie Show*, which was on the Sci-Fi Network in 1996. Maila was offered one thousand dollars to appear on the program with host Dana Gould. She decided she'd give herself one more chance.

The meeting between the two turned out to be providential. At 73, Maila could have been Dana's grandmother, yet inexplicably, the two hit it off so well, they became dear friends for the rest of her life. Dana explained it this way: "My mother always told me that in this life, you take care of yourself and one other person. To me, that person was Maila."

Maila had many acquaintances at that point in her life, but few people did she call friends. There was Audrey and, of course, Hilda, from her days on East Melrose. But as she aged, Maila gravitated toward men more than ever. Young men in their 30s. Perhaps she was still missing the son she gave away at birth. Besides Dana Gould, her small cadre of friends included documentary filmmakers Ray Greene, Tomata du Plenty, her young dog-walking pal Rick, and a man named Mark Carducci. Mark wrote episodic television horror shows, and he created, wrote, and produced the documentary *The Ed Wood Story: The Plan 9 Companion* as well as the horror classic *Pumpkinhead* and the film *Vampirella*. In 1997, Mark was Maila's business manager, brokering sales of her artwork.

The continued popularity of the *Ed Wood* film still compromised Maila's privacy, prompting her to tape a stern admonition to her front door:

NO AUTOGRAPHS! PERMANENTLY BANISHED!

In April of 1997, Greg Herger was planning to write a biography of his cousin, film actor Steve Cochran. To that end, he'd made a list of performers who had worked with the prolific actor and were still alive. Maila Nurmi was on the contact sheet; it listed her address but no phone number. So, when Herger arrived at her North Hudson Avenue apartment, Maila's posted sign left no doubt that she didn't want to be disturbed. He taped a note to her doorknob with his address and phone number, fully expecting never to hear from her.

He was stunned when shortly thereafter, a message was left on his answering machine:

> *"Hello, Greg. This is Maila Nurmi. I remember Steve Cochran very well. I absolutely adored him. I'd love to get together with you and tell you all about him."*

Maila was lonely. She'd obviously not had anyone contact her for an outing for quite some time, and here at last was a new generation with artistic family roots who wanted to interview her. A date was set, and Herger picked up Maila at the curb to take her to lunch at Musso & Frank Grill.

Their lunch stretched into six hours. Maila not only spoke of her time working with Cochran but wanted to know about Greg's life as well. According to him, "What occurred was a strong and undeniable connection between the two of us." They decided on having a lunch date the next Tuesday and every Tuesday thereafter.

When Greg dropped Maila off curbside after their first lunch, she asked that he wait while she ran inside for a moment. She returned with a recently painted self-portrait and asked him what he thought of it. He said he loved it and offered to buy it from her.

Maila posing with her art, 1995. Photo courtesy of Tomi Hinkkanen.

"Not for sale," she said, "because it is a gift. A gift for you."

Two months later, Mark Carducci was dead. Suicide by gunshot. The recent loss of his mother and first child had been too painful. Maila was shattered.

Greg was determined to ease his new friend's anxiety and pain and told her of an auction site on the internet called "eBay" where she could sell her paintings and autographs. Although he'd never sold anything on it, he'd purchased a few things and figured it wouldn't be that hard to learn how to maneuver the site. The advent and popularity of the home computer and the internet came at an opportune time for Maila, and Greg became Maila's new online business manager.

Maila couldn't expect Greg to do all he did without payment and insisted he take 20 percent of what she made from her artwork. He declined, saying he couldn't possibly take cash for his efforts. They went back and forth, until Maila then stubbornly refused to sell any of her artwork until he agreed.

Finally, a consensus was reached when Herger suggested that, for every four paintings, drawings or autographs, Herger would keep the fifth.

"Why would you want all this worthless Vampira stuff?" she asked.

"Because," Greg replied, "all this, what you call 'worthless' stuff, is helping you financially in your old age, and when I'm old, it will be worth even more."

Maila loved the rationale behind the idea and she agreed.

The world still considered her a celebrity, and her artwork sold well. She was earning far more than she did selling locally through Mark Carducci.

Maila and Herger had lunch every Tuesday at 2 p.m. to discuss that week's business. She called it their "Tu-Tu Tuesday meetings." He would pay her the proceeds from the week's eBay sales, and she would give him her new artwork to sell. But it wasn't only artwork anymore. Greg also secured appearances at film festivals and horror conventions as well as interviews with independent filmmakers and TV documentarians. Maila and her alter ego Vampira were in demand yet again. And this time, she could handle it.

She certainly didn't get rich, but for a while, Maila's financial situation improved enough that she hired artist Thomas Bowen to create Vampira statuettes. She commissioned 1,000 of the 14-inch figurines and required they be manufactured to her exact specifications, then sold them at edgy boutiques and Hollywood gift shops. Now, they're valued at north of one thousand dollars, but then they sold for 25 bucks. She also had the cash to hire someone to design a Myspace profile for her and later a Facebook page, which she called Vampira's Attic.

In the meantime, Maila seemed to be losing all her local men friends. Jack Simmons had passed away in 1995. Dana Gould's career took off—he was hired to write and produce for *The Simpsons* and also got married, meaning he had less time to devote to Maila's well-being. While Maila was happy for him, she secretly regretted that another woman had won his heart and that she could expect to spend far less time with him—and when they had children, it'd be even less. (Dana did stay in touch, continuing to invite Maila to various functions and sending her cash in the mail.) Tomata moved to Florida and then Texas. Ray Greene was also busy with his own life. She was down to Rick, the dog-walking trust fund baby, and Greg Herger, her longtime manager.

Then suddenly, in 2000, Maila received an eviction notice. Los Angeles County had a law on their books that if a landlord evicted a tenant through no fault of the tenant's, the landlord must reimburse the tenant five thousand dollars to relocate. That was of little consolation to Maila, who suddenly was forced to pack up all her possessions and find a new place to live. Her tiny reconverted garage on Hudson, her home for over 14 years, was being razed to make room for an apartment complex.

Maila was in a panic and frantically enlisted Greg to find her a new place to live. Her list of criteria was detailed, and in the end, Maila had to give up some of what she wanted. But Greg found her an apartment in a fourplex in the Silver Lake area that she found acceptable. Unfortunately, it was a second-story walk-up, and the only nearby coffee shop was at a McDonald's.

She stayed there for five years, before receiving another eviction notice—the landlord was evicting everyone in the building to remodel. So, once again, Maila was the recipient of a five-thousand-dollar payout. However, she was even more panicked about the move than she had been five years earlier. She called on Dana Gould to help find her a place, and this time, her list of wants and needs was even more daunting. Maila wanted to be back in Hollywood proper—she felt isolated in Silver Lake.

Dana got to work trying to find a place Maila would be happy with, but it wasn't easy. Eventually, she agreed to move into a unit on North Serrano Avenue, only a few blocks from the Carlton Street address she shared with her mother years before. One bedroom for storage. That meant she would need a lot of extra storage space for her memorabilia.

She'd already retrieved her things from Hilda's basement and her new digs could not hold it all. Dana rented storage for her in Glendale. The space was huge, 15 feet by 15 feet with ten-foot ceilings, but Dana needed help for the move. He went to Halloween Town to see if he could find someone there who would like to help Vampira move, and it was there he found employee Matt Montgomery, a.k.a. Piggy D, who was happy to help out. Piggy has since launched a successful musical career and is the current bass player for Rob Zombie's band at the time of this writing.

Maila's treasures were carefully stacked into the storage space. She had more than a hundred boxes, and when they were loaded inside, all the way up to the ceiling, there was not room enough to fit a clothes hanger.

The last five years of Maila's life were peaceful. She was only a block away from a Food 4 Less supermarket and an El Pollo Loco chain. She had a shopping cart of her own to carry her groceries home and a small private outdoor area with a gate to keep Houdini corralled. There were only two steps to get inside her apartment. It was ideal.

Dana often paid Maila's rent, and he had a phone installed, bought her a sofa, and painted a wall for her. When time allowed, he called her or checked in to see that she was comfortable. Greg and Maila continued on with their Tu-Tu Tuesdays. Hilda called and visited often as well. She and Maila had a secret way of communicating—if the phone rang before seven in the morning, it was Hilda.

Maila didn't have caller ID and she wanted to know who was calling before she decided whether or not to answer.

Although she was no longer painting or drawing, she still maintained a small presence on eBay with older art pieces, and they continued to sell well. Sometimes an offer to go out for a meal with a friend came in, and like always, Maila would be waiting for her ride at curbside. But sadly, some weeks went by when there were no visitors at all.

Around that time, Piggy D had a goth girlfriend named Gabrielle who was connected to the Hollywood Museum and was obsessed with Vampira. She figured out that Maila was close with Dana and managed to wheedle her way into Dana's good graces so she could hang out with Vampira. Soon, Dana was giving Gabrielle money to check on Maila as his career dominated more and more of his time. Maila barely tolerated her, while Houdini outright despised her and ripped a hole in her right side. Maila was worried the woman would file charges and have Houdini quarantined or worse, although to her credit, she did not. But after a few months, Maila reached a breaking point and couldn't endure the woman a moment longer, and she finally ordered her out of her house and life.

In November, Maila learned that her dog-walking pal from Hudson, Rick, had died. It seemed he went on his annual sojourn to New Zealand with his mother and while there, didn't feel well and went to the doctor. He was diagnosed with terminal cancer and died.

Maila was gutted. She'd just lost Tomata du Plenty to AIDS. When Dink died in 2002 and Marlon followed in 2004, they were of an older generation. But both Tomata and Rick were far too young to die.

Maila always said she planned on living to be 112, but it was not to be. On her last birthday, a couple weeks before Christmas of 2007, she was invited out to celebrate with friends. She ordered a margarita but felt ill before she could finish the whole thing.

Greg visited Maila in the third week of December. She'd called him because the latch on her outside gate was broken. He came over and fixed it for her and was horrified when he saw Maila's arm. It was blue and badly swollen, a result of several dog bites. He wanted to take Maila to the doctor, but she adamantly refused, and as he later said, "If Maila didn't want to do something, nothing you said or did could convince her otherwise." Come hell or high water, no one was going to take Houdini away from her.

The last week in December, Maila called Dana, but he wasn't home. She left a brief, witty monologue, reminiscent of comedian Brother Theodore. Dana called it a "typical Maila" kind of thing for her to do, and that she sounded great.

Just before Christmas, Hilda came over to take Maila to a health food store to buy some supplements. She'd complained of exhaustion and blamed her thyroid. Hilda said she was going to visit her sister in San Diego over Christmas but that when she got back to town, she'd come over to see Maila. But on her trip south, Hilda caught a cold and couldn't get to Maila's when she returned to Los Angeles.

On January 6, 2008, after church, Hilda knocked on Maila's door. There was no answer, no sound except for Houdini's barking. Hilda thought Maila must be out with friends. She returned on Tuesday the 8th and knocked and still got no answer, just Houdini. Hilda became mildly concerned, only to return the next day. When there was still no answer on the 9th, she left a note on the door telling Maila she was returning the next day, and if she didn't hear from her, she would call the police.

Thursday, January 10, 2008, Hilda found her note still attached to Maila's door and called the police. The police arrived but refused to enter or break down the door because of the dog's ferocious barking. Hilda had told them the dog was dangerous.

Hilda ran down to the Food 4 Less and bought some deli turkey. Even with the turkey to distract the dog, the police refused to enter, so Hilda climbed into a window and threw the turkey into the bathroom. The starving dog ran into the bathroom as Hilda slammed the door shut, to sequester Houdini. She could let the police in through the front door.

Maila was sitting on the sofa with her feet propped on a white plastic patio chair. Her tiny television was on, sitting on the floor opposite her. It looked as if she sat down to watch it and dozed off. She'd been wearing black pants, which she'd taken off and washed in the kitchen sink before hanging them to dry in the kitchen. Her oven was turned on for heat to dry the pants. She was dressed in a brown T-shirt, black underpants, and white socks.

But now, she was gone. Like the mortician later said, "She caught the dream."

Violet, Maila's cat, was dead beside her. Houdini was full of mange and fleas, and he was found to be too violent to be adopted. He was euthanized, cremated, and buried with Maila.

We will never know when Maila passed. I talked to Conrad, her mail carrier, who recalled seeing her the Friday before she was found, waiting on her porch for her Social Security check. But sadly, she died alone with only Violet and Houdini as comfort. As much as she loved them, perhaps that was enough.

The exhaustion she felt was from a failing heart, as it turned out, and not her thyroid. Her injured arm may have hastened her demise, but no one will ever know.

A year and a half before she died, Maila asked Dana to hire a lawyer to send cease-and-desist letters to a person who'd abused her trademark. I guess she wasn't dying fast enough.

When she did pass on, it was intestate, without a will. I remember Maila saying, "The hyenas and vultures are always ready to jump on your bones in this town." Sure enough, while I was still grieving over her death and cleaning out her apartment and storage unit well into March, her cherished Vampira intellectual property was snapped up by someone else. I often wonder if that person understands how fiercely, for 54 years, she protected the rights to her character, even when it would have been easier and far more lucrative for her to cave in. Today, her family doesn't make a penny from any Vampira items for sale.

Maila and Houdini were buried together at Hollywood Forever Cemetery. The employees there have said Maila's grave is one of the most popular ones in the park. Thanks to Dana Gould, Maila is at precisely the spot she herself selected to rest in eternal repose. We know that because in December of 1997, she and Greg Herger, on one of their Tu-Tu Tuesdays, decided they would pay a visit to that particular cemetery. It seems that when Greg was a teenager in the early '80s, he and his friends would scale the walls and light the candles at gravesites until cops in helicopters noticed the blaze and installed barbed wire to keep them out. And Maila was frequently persuaded by the European media to accompany journalists to the cemetery and talk about Vampira. In her youth, Maila learned from silent movie actress Mary MacLane the history of the Hollywood Forever Cemetery, which was established in 1899. At that time, Mary was dating one of the founders. So Maila had a deep affinity for the place. In the midst of the pulsating din of Hollywood, the cemetery was an oasis that offered serenity and beauty.

On that clear December afternoon in 1997, Maila and Greg were seated on the grass almost exactly where Maila would ten years later be interred. A man with a microphone and tape recorder approached them and asked if he could briefly interview them for a PBS segment, and they agreed.

The following is copyrighted material from Greg Herger's archives. It is not allowed to be broadcasted, reproduced, or duplicated without permission. I have received his permission to print it in this book.

Maila is asked to describe what she sees.

We're here by the pond. It has swans and a bunch of ducks but there's a mama and a papa swan and seven babies. The mausoleums are on the one side. It's a clear day, and we have a visual scape which is of beautiful, tall palm trees reaching into a blue sky, and there in the background is like a picture postcard of the Hollywood sign. The sun is turning the letters very white. It's extremely beautiful and still here, and the grass, of course, is very green. We have a lot of obelisks here and crosses but not many angel figures. And lots of flowers. The

Armenians put lots of fresh flowers on their graves. Oh, and you can
also see the Observatory from here. It's like heaven here.

Maila Nurmi was recognized for her contribution to the entertainment industry during the 81st Academy Awards presentation in 2009. Queen Latifah sang "I'll Be Seeing You" for the In Memoriam segment, as Maila's picture flashed upon the television screen.

Epilogue

I came home from the grocery store one day in late November of 2019. My daughter approached me with a big smile on her face and said, "I know who Maila's son is."

"Yeah, ha-ha," I said to myself, waiting for the punchline.

"Not a joke," she said. "I even know his name."

For a moment, I was dumbstruck, unable to speak. Then, the words tumbled out.

"What do you mean, you know who he is? What's his name? How did you find him? Do you have a phone number? An email address? Where does he live? Did you talk to him? Give me his name!"

In 2017, I'd gifted my daughter a DNA kit from Ancestry.com for Christmas. She didn't get around to sending it in until early 2019. I told her I didn't need to send one in because I was 100% percent Finnish and whatever wasn't Finnish in her results was from her father. When her results came in, we laughed because it said she was 55 percent Finnish. Her father was Latino, but apparently either she inherited some extra DNA from my side, or else he was also a little bit Finnish.

And then we put the results out of our minds.

Unknown to both myself and my daughter, on the other side of the country, my first cousin had sent his DNA in to 23andMe and was disappointed when he

David Putter and his partner, Judi Fisher

didn't get any matches. Judi, his significant other, convinced him to try Ancestry instead, and when he did, he learned that my daughter was a close cousin. He left a phone number in the event she wanted to communicate. That was in September of 2019, but my daughter never checked back until November.

Within three minutes of finding out his name, I was dialing his number. And the angels sang. I couldn't believe the voice I was hearing was that of my cousin, David Putter.

Of course, he wanted to know if I knew who his birth parents were, but not right then. He didn't want me to tell him until Judi was with him and he could share the news with her. But I couldn't keep my mouth shut. I had to tell him that, at that moment, I was just finishing up a book on his mother's life. Adopted at birth, and 75 years later, you find yourself talking to the only living person who can give you your birth mother's life story?

And not only that, if he wanted to see pictures of her, all he had to do was type in her name in a search bar. I imagine David was stunned. Who could she be?

And so it was over the phone that David and Judi both learned who his birth parents were. Now, Maila would want you to know about her son.

David and Judi live in a tiny town in Vermont, which overlooks beautiful Lake Champlain. Both are passionate animal lovers, like Maila and myself. He graduated from Syracuse Law School in 1968, with Vice President Joe Biden; they played football on the same team and remain friends to this day.

In 1973, David became the first full-time public defender for Bennington County, Vermont. During his tenure there, he and another attorney defended a client being charged with first-degree murder. David felt his client met the legal definition of insanity, but the judge denied bail because he felt the man was a danger to the public.

This judgment took David and his colleague to the Vermont Supreme Court to argue that the Constitution of Vermont prohibited denial of bail, even to a murder defendant. In a very rare occurrence, the judgment against David's client was overturned by the Vermont Supreme Court. As well, the jury submitted a not-guilty judgment by reasons of insanity.

Three years later, David became the law clerk for all of Vermont's superior judges, shortly before becoming an assistant attorney general in the criminal division, prosecuting homicides and participating in a major investigation into the internal affairs of the Vermont State Police.

The '90s found David in Zambia. The U.S. government sent him to the young African nation to assist in rewriting portions of their constitution. David participated in about one hundred jury trials during his storied career that spanned over 50 years.

There is a tragic irony to this story. In Chapter Twenty-Three, you read these words from Maila. It was 1982.

> *Now as I still count pennies for each can of tomato soup, the world has come to believe that the word "Vampira" is in the dictionary. That it is the female word for the male "Vampire." They believe that Vampira herself is in public domain & lift my product. This is America! Where, then, is this pauper's attorney?*

Life can be cruel. But she didn't know, and more importantly, David didn't know. If he had, he would have rushed to his mother's side and done everything possible to help her. That's the kind of man David is.

Now that he knows, he couldn't be more proud of his mother's accomplishments. And I believe somehow, in this great mystery we call life, Maila knows, too.

It took me 12 years to write my aunt's life story. I'd finished much of the book by the end of 2009, but then everything came to a crashing halt. I was plagued by indecision, writer's block, and self-doubt. I was left without her counsel and had only hundreds of scraps of her writings to guide me. I piddled around with the book for years before I remembered that, in 1955, after she was fired from KABC, she wrote that she wasn't allowed to be Vampira for six months, which was long enough for people to forget about her. Was it now too late for her biography as well?

But I also remembered that *The Vampira Show* was only broadcast in the Los Angeles area and that most people remember her from her appearance in *Plan 9 from Outer Space*, in fact, not from television. If they forgot her, they were to be reminded of her many times after 1955.

I believed that, even without the cloak of celebrity, Maila was still an incredible woman. Her story was unique. Beautiful, yes, but crippled by pernicious anemia at age 46, and then she lost her teeth. She had no husband, no family to support her. She was alone, didn't drive, and lived in abject poverty. Yet she survived for another 40 years this way, on her own.

Finally I understood Maila's plan, and all those empty years of writer's block were explained. It hadn't been the right time. It wasn't time because David and I had not yet found each other. Because without David, Maila's life story would have been unfinished. And now, David and I, the only grandchildren of Onni and Sophie, have found each other, and the story is complete.

David and Judi have graciously invited my daughter and myself to Vermont to meet them and their pets, and we plan to take them up as soon as this COVID-19 pandemic allows us to travel again. We cannot wait.

Less than one month after the phone call with David, Feral House decided to publish this book. I don't know how she did it, but Maila arranged the timing. I am only the vessel she used to relay her story because I was the only one who could.

This book is about Maila but written for David. He's waited over 70 years to know who his mother is, and Maila wanted the world to know her son and learn of his great accomplishments. Now you know both of their stories. Both mother's and son's. A mother's love never dies.

Acknowledgements

I want to thank the many who helped me with their interminable encouragement and love, in big and small ways, to write this book. Thank you to Greg Herger, Dana Gould, Sid Terror, Audrey Antley, Hilda Ruiz, Fabrizio Mioni, Ray Greene and Steve Hayes for the stories you told me and for loving Maila. Audrey, the stories you told me, in Maila's own voice, were spot-on.

Thank you also to Brad "The Bone Jangler" and Halloween Jack for inviting me onto their Saturday night radio show. You are true fans. To my Finnish friend and established author, Ari Vantanen, who helped me immeasurably when I was ready to give up. He tirelessly edited the book, gave me excellent advice, and managed to make this book into a cohesive form electronically. Soon he will be translating a Finnish edition. A huge thank you.

Thank you to my dear friend, Jove de Renzy, an intelligent, highly talented photographer and artist who contributed to this story in many ways with his insight and love of Maila. He's an awesome human being.

And lastly, thank you to my longtime friend, Dawn Holbrook, who accompanied me to Los Angeles four times and without her, this book would never have been written. I can never repay you.

And to those vultures who picked through Maila's memorabilia without permission and continue to profit from her intellectual property... you know who you are. Enough said.

ALSO FROM FERAL HOUSE

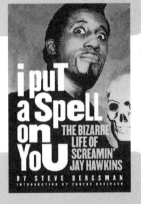

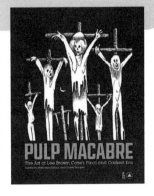